Myth, Scandal,
and History

Schliemann describes his excavations at Mycenae to the Society of Antiquaries, Burlington House, London, 22 March 1877. (Illustrated London News.)

Myth, Scandal, and History

THE HEINRICH SCHLIEMANN CONTROVERSY

AND A FIRST EDITION

OF THE MYCENAEAN DIARY

.

Edited by William M. Calder III
and David A. Traill

WAYNE STATE UNIVERSITY PRESS

DETROIT 1986

Library of Congress Cataloging-in-Publication Data
Myth, scandal, and history.
  Bibliography: p.
  Includes index.
  1. Schliemann, Heinrich, 1822–1890. 2. Archaeology—
Greece. 3. Archaeology—Germany. I. Schliemann,
Heinrich, 1822–1890. II. Calder, William M. (William
Musgrave), 1932–   III. Traill, David A.,
1942–
DF212.S4M97   1986   930.1′092′4   86-1589
ISBN 0-8143-1795-2

D.M.
L.R. Palmer

Contents

7

Preface

ARCHAEOLOGY IS THE ONLY DISCIPLINE in ancient studies which to attain its ends is required to destroy its evidence. Once excavated, a site must be reconstructed from literary evidence, letters, notebooks, diaries, and published reports, aided, if available, by drawings and photographs. From this fact derives the importance of the history of archaeology. To vary a famous epigram of Seneca: *quae archaeologia fuit, philologia facta est.*

Since 1972 Heinrich Schliemann's reports about himself and what he did have increasingly been queried. The advance of the "new skepticism" and the disagreements it introduced convinced me in 1982 that the time had come for an international conference where historians of scholarship and archaeologists could meet to exchange ideas. Mr. George K. Klumb, an energetic undergraduate at the time, procured the necessary funds from the Cultural Events Board of the University of Colorado Student Union and a generous grant from the Colorado Humanities Program. Without his initiative and the support of the donors, the conference could never have taken place.

The conference was held at the campus of the University of Colorado at Boulder on 25–26 February 1983 with the title: "Heinrich Schliemann: Myth or Scandal?" The conference papers of Wolfgang Schindler, Hartmut Döhl, and myself, improved by lively discussion, revised, expanded, and annotated, are published here. Since the substance of David A. Traill's paper on Schliemann's discovery of Priam's treasure has since been published in *Antiquity* (1983) and the *Journal*

9

of Hellenic Studies (1984), he contributes in its place studies on Schliemann's correspondence with Frank Calvert concerning the Helios metope and with P. Beaurain over the projected manufacture of duplicates of gold and silver artifacts. Upon my submission of the papers to him, Dr. Bernard M. Goldman, former director of the Wayne State University Press, kindly invited me to add to them, preferably hitherto unpublished source material. I asked David A. Traill whether he would consider including his planned *editio princeps* of Schliemann's Mycenaean diary, a document of great value for one of the most famous sites in Greece and largely unused by scholars. The edition of this document is entirely his, and I immediately asked him to become co-editor of the volume. His informed attention has improved all the contributions. Our editorial work, however, has inevitably been concerned more with matters of style than substance. Naturally, each contribution should be regarded as reflecting the views of its author rather than the editors. Professor Morton Smith (Columbia University) read the whole manuscript critically. We have all benefited from his suggestions, and the final title of the book is owed him. Only those who knew earlier versions of the manuscript know how much readers owe the professional attention of Wayne's editor-in-chief, Mrs. Jean Owen, and book editor, Mrs. Anne Adamus. Finally, I would like to express the gratitude of the editors and contributors to the University of Colorado and the University of California, Davis, for generously contributing to the cost of producing this volume.

WILLIAM M. CALDER III

The Villa Mowitz
6 January 1985

Abbreviations

ABSA	*Annual of the British School at Athens*
AJA	*American Journal of Archaeology*
AnatSt	*Anatolian Studies*
ArchEph	*Archaiologike Ephemeris*
Briefe	Ernst Meyer, ed. *Briefe von Heinrich Schliemann gesammelt und mit einer Einleitung in Auswahl herausgegeben.* Preface by Wilhelm Dörpfeld. Berlin and Lepzig 1936.
Briefwechsel I	Ernst Meyer, ed. *Heinrich Schliemann Briefwechsel aus dem Nachlass in Auswahl herausgegeben: Band von 1842 bis 1875.* Berlin 1953.
Briefwechsel II	Ernst Meyer, ed. *Heinrich Schliemann Briefwechsel aus dem Nachlass in Auswahl herausgegeben: Band von 1876 bis 1890.* Berlin 1958.
CJ	*Classical Journal*
CR	*Classical Review*
CW	*Classical World*
DLZ	*Deutsche Literatur-Zeitung*
DNB	*Dictionary of National Biography*

EA	P. Arndt and W. Amelung, *Photographische Einzelaufnahmen antiker Skulpturen*
EAZ	*Ethnographisch-Archäologische Zeitschrift*
FAZ	*Frankfurter Allgemeine Zeitung*
G&R	*Greece and Rome*
GRBS	*Greek, Roman and Byzantine Studies*
Ilios	Heinrich Schliemann. *Ilios: The City and Country of the Trojans.* London 1881. Repr. New York 1976.
Ithaka	Heinrich Schliemann. *Ithaka, der Peloponnes und Troja.* Leipzig 1869. Repr. Darmstadt 1963.
Ithaque	Heinrich Schliemann. *Ithaque, le Péloponnèse et Troie.* Paris 1869.
JdI	*Jahrbuch des k. deutschen archäologischen Insitituts*
JHS	*Journal of Hellenic Studies*
Karo	G. Karo. *Die Schachtgräber von Mykenai.* Munich 1930. (Unless otherwise specified, references are always to inventory numbers.)
Meyer, *Schliemann*	Ernst Meyer. *Heinrich Schliemann: Kaufmann und Forscher.* Göttingen 1969.
MG	R. Hope-Simpson, *Mycenaean Greece.* Park Ridge 1981.
Myc.	Heinrich Schliemann. *Mycenae.* London 1878.
Mylonas, *Kyklos B*	G. Mylonas. *Ho Taphikos Kyklos B ton Mykenon.* Athens 1973.
Mylonas, *MMA*	G. Mylonas. *Mycenae and the Mycenaean Age.* Princeton, N.J. 1966.
Mylonas, *MRIG*	G. Mylonas, *Mycenae Rich in Gold.* Athens 1983.
ProcBritAc	*Proceedings of the British Academy*
RA	*Revue archéologique*
Times I–XIV	Schliemann's periodic reports to the *Times* (London), 1876–1877. See Appendix B.

TroyR	Heinrich Schliemann. *Troy and Its Remains.* London 1874.
Wace, *Mycenae*	A.J.B. Wace. *Mycenae.* Princeton, N.J. 1949.
ZfE	*Zeitschrift für Ethnologie*

Part One

FIVE STUDIES
ON HEINRICH SCHLIEMANN

A New Picture of Heinrich Schliemann

William M. Calder III

THE CONTROVERSY

LET ME BEGIN with a not-so-old picture of Heinrich Schliemann: "Unter den Taten deutscher Männer steht das Lebenswerk Heinrich Schliemanns stauenswert und einzigartig da." ["Amidst the deeds of German men the lifework of Heinrich Schliemann stands out as amazing and unique."] With this trumpet blast, the archaeologist Carl Schuchhardt (1859–1943) begins his biography of Schliemann (1822–1890) in volume three of *Die Grossen Deutschen,* last published in West Berlin in 1956.[1] In 1981 the distinguished archaeologist and historian of archaeology Professor Hartmut Döhl published what I have called "the most intelligent book ever written on Heinrich Schliemann." He titled his book *Heinrich Schliemann: Mythos und Ärgernis,* that is, *Heinrich Schliemann: Myth and Scandal.* From this book I have derived in part the title of this volume.[2]

The title epitomizes the situation of Schliemann research today. All is in Heraclitan flux. All is highly controversial. Roy Davies's BBC documentary, *The Man behind the Mask,* aired in the United Kingdom on 20 January 1982 and reviewed in the world press, removed the controversy from the pages of learned journals and set it before a wide and critical audience. An international group of experts, devoted to

I am grateful to H. Döhl, W. Schindler, and especially D.A. Traill for many improvements and suggestions. U.K. Goldsmith has kindly read my manuscript.

learning about the man Heinrich Schliemann and his work, met for the first time at Boulder, Colorado, 25–26 February 1983. Four other congresses are already in the planning stage for the Schliemann Year 1990. Two commemorative museum exhibitions, one in East and one in West Berlin, both with published catalogues,[3] have been held in 1981–1982. Schliemann died alone in Naples ninety-five years ago. Why this present interest? What has happened? Can not the dead bury their dead? The crux, as often, is simple. There are two Schliemanns. There is the myth. There is the scandal. The papers in this volume address the question: Which shall prevail? Or is there room still for both? Let us first look at the myth.

Latet aurum in collibus istis: SCHLIEMANN OF THE BIOGRAPHERS

Heinrich Schliemann by any count is among the five best known Germans of the nineteenth century in this country. Freud, Marx, Nietzsche, and Wagner are his rivals. Unlike them, he took American citizenship. He traveled and sometimes lived in the United States. He published in English. Since 1900 some forty book-length biographies of Schliemann have appeared, not to speak of countless short lives in encyclopedias, dictionaries of biography, or as part of works largely archaeological or historical. A complete and invaluable bibliography of works by or about Heinrich Schliemann, appearing between 1867 and 1975, was published in Athens in 1974 by the indefatigable Professor George Korres.[4] It contains some 2,250 entries. Over one hundred titles have appeared since then. Schliemann, himself not a scholar, early fell into the hands of popular writers and journalists, both dilettantes: Emil Ludwig, the Pooles, Robert Payne, Heinrich Alexander Stoll, recently Irving Stone, and Paul Faure.[5] Because Ludwig, the Pooles, and Stoll used original documents, many of which are now lost, their books cannot be ignored. The last two, to their credit, call their books novels. Millions of copies in hardcover and paperback, in over a dozen languages, have been sold. In 1981, at enormous cost, the Norddeutsche Rundfunk produced a popular and well-received film on Schliemann called *Der Schatz des Priamos: Leben und Werk Heinrich Schliemanns.* Again, it is uncritical hagiolatry. An American film is now under consideration. Thousands and thousands of American students learn the German language annually by reading selections from Schliemann's life. An Englishwoman writing an umpteenth Schliemann biography is in correspondence with me. A new French biography has just appeared. The reason for all this commotion is that Schliemann, unlike numerous scholars far more deserving than he, is an unfailing best-seller. Why? What is there about standard lives of Schliemann that makes them so popular? There are three obvious attractions.

1. Heinrich Schliemann is the poor boy who became rich and famous through hard work and good luck. He has almost become a Jungian archetype for this beloved folk figure.

2. Schliemann traveled in the most exotic places of the world of his time: China and Japan, India, Java, Czarist Russia, the Turkish empire, the jungles of Panama, and the American West, where he participated in the California gold rush.[6] But, with this, he had a beautiful, faithful, intelligent wife, Sophia, a companion and colleague, a fellow archaeologist. Irving Stone called her "the Greek Treasure," and the Pooles' book, *One Passion: Two Loves,* stressed their beautiful love affair. Schliemann had his odyssey and Penelope.

3. Heinrich Schliemann, the uneducated businessman, who left school at age fourteen, proved all the professors wrong by a stubborn, simple faith worth more than their books, their advanced degrees, and hard-earned expertise.

He was the quintessential nineteenth-century hero, the *Held der Gründerzeit,* the self-made man par excellence,[7] millionaire and scholar, friend and correspondent of the great, presidents, emperors, prime ministers, kings and queens. If a poor, uneducated, country pastor's son from Mecklenburg (Bismarck once said that when the world ends it will end three months later in Mecklenburg) did all this, so can you and I. He is the dream figure, the *Ich-Ideal* of every petit bourgeois. Some part of us all hopes to be a Schliemann. Five women have written lives of Schliemann for children: it is a childish tale.

THE *Grundproblem*

I have shown that Schliemann is an unfailing best-seller and tried to explain why. There is another remarkable fact about all these Schliemann biographies. Some are better than others, but not one of them is really good. With words that might equally well be applied to Heinrich Schliemann, Friedrich Nietzsche once coldly remarked of Richard Wagner: "What up to now has circulated as "Wagner-Biography" is *fable convenue,* if not worse. I confess my mistrust of every point that is attested only by Wagner himself. He lacked sufficient pride for any truth at all about himself. No one was less proud. He remained, quite like Victor Hugo, consistent in biographical matters as well. He remained an actor."[8] Nietzsche indicts biographer and source. I shall do the same with Schliemann. His biographers are not Schliemann scholars; they are Schliemann worshipers. This is by no means unique with Schliemann. One thinks only of biographers of Alexander the Great, Julius Caesar, Jesus Christ, Napoleon, Friedrich Nietzsche himself, Abraham Lincoln. Schliemann's worldly success won his male biographers. Women approved his adoration of his mother and, because of the "Dream of Troy," saw in him dramatic confirmation of Wordsworth's "the Child is father of the Man." Schliemann's biographers were prepared to believe. This leads to my second reason, one more peculiar to Schliemann.

Any biography is only the tip of the iceberg. It is based on original documents, usually letters, diaries, memoirs, interviews with survivors, that is, primary sources.[9] With Schliemann the situation is especially unfortunate. Well over 85 percent of the documents upon which all these Schliemann biographies are based were written by Heinrich Schliemann himself.[10] Today, except for a few small private collections, they are housed in the Gennadius Library, part of the American School of Classical Studies at Athens. Until recently these papers were stored casually and scholars had only a vague notion of what was there. Now in a careful, long-needed, and utterly commendable report, D.F. Easton has published a history of the collection and the first systematic, authoritative guide to its contents.[11] Until a detailed catalogue, identifying every document and, when possible, providing its date, appears (on the order of catalogues to the papers of Delbrück, Erman, G. Murray, or Wilamowitz), Easton's article will remain indispensable. Much of what follows derives from it. For a biographer, these documents may conveniently be divided into four classes.

1. Schliemann's autobiographies survive written in various languages and extant in various and often contradictory versions, dating from 1852 until 1891.[12] Most often cited is *Selbstbiographie bis zu seinem Tode vervöllständigt.* This is a version of the autobiography prefixed to *Ilios* (1880–81) and brought up to date by Dr. Alfred Brückner under the guidance of Sophia Schliemann, whose preface to the first edition is dated 23 September 1891. The standard ninth and tenth editions were edited

and revised by Ernst Meyer.[13] I should like to see all these lives arranged chronologically and published critically with the citation of contemporary epistolary evidence in a single volume.

2. Eighteen diaries, three mutilated, exist at the Gennadeion. One has been published adequately, part of another has been published; and a third has been summarized in a volume so remote that a copy cannot be found in this country. The contents of two diaries have been published in "revised" form by Schliemann himself.[14] Easton's remarks on the diaries deserve citation: "The contents are written in ink (usually black) or in pencil. Schliemann's entries are in a variety of languages, but the most common are Greek, German, French, and English. While travelling it was his practice to write his journal in the language of the country he was visiting. There are no 'personal' diaries; they cover only the periods when he was engaged in foreign travel or archaeological fieldwork."[15] These diaries are fundamental for any informed appraisal of Schliemann and his work. Their accurate, uncensored publication with critical commentary may be the first need of Schliemann research at the moment.

3. There exist some sixty thousand letters to and from Schliemann, either originals or blotted copies preserved in old-fashioned copybooks. Of these, some nine hundred letters, dating from 1842 to 1890, have been published in three sizeable volumes with an introduction, selected commentary, and indexes.[16] The editor of these letters, who is as well the author of a biography of Schliemann called by J.M. Cook "authoritative," is Ernst Meyer (1888–1970?).[17] Andromache and Agamemnon Schliemann in 1937 granted to Meyer alone the right to publish their father's letters.[18] A schoolteacher at the Gymnasium Carolinum in Neustrelitz, where Schliemann had once been a pupil, Meyer adored Schliemann, who made the otherwise unknown school world famous. Meyer had a naive, uncritical preconception of what Schliemann ought to have been and into that Procrustes' bed he is determined to fit his subject at whatever the cost. Like Schliemann, he was largely an autodidact and, although a university graduate, never a scholar. His knowledge of English, for example, is so feeble that one can never be certain that the errors in Schliemann's English letters are Schliemann's and not Meyer's.[19] He lacked the passion for detail that a scholar must have; and German texts which I have been able to control against the originals yield frequent errors of transcription within a single letter.[20] Most perniciously Meyer exerts censorship on two levels. First, there is the censor-

ship implicit in choice. He never publishes, for example, all the letters from 1873. The most captious would not complain that Meyer did not publish every letter. My complaint would rather be that he lacks the judgment needed consistently to omit the trivial and to publish the revealing. He censors also the letters that he does publish. Sometimes he indicates omissions. Sometimes he does not. This means that we not only have Meyer's Schliemann in the biography but also in his three volumes of published letters, which should be the sources against which we prove the biography. Worse, occasionally Meyer silently changes a date to allow epistolary evidence to agree with Schliemann's later published accounts.[21] Because we now know that Schliemann deliberately tampered with dates and facts to adorn a public tale, Meyer's practice is methodologically upsidedown. A Schliemann scholar resorts to the epistolary evidence or the diaries to demolish the published version. I suspect that on occasion Meyer, without telling us, may even have added passages to some of the Schliemann letters. Lamentably, the only remedy is the complete reediting of Meyer's letters by a trained, unimpassioned, accurate scholar. One cannot avoid in this context recalling the execrable Elisabeth Förster-Nietzsche, who inflicted incalculable damage on later Nietzsche research.[22] To end on a note of hope, I add that several sets of letters between Schliemann and some correspondents have been edited after the death of Meyer. These editions are of a different order.[23]

4. Finally, Schliemann published in his lifetime what we may euphemistically call twelve "scholarly books." Many scholarly books, not least those written by nineteenth-century German scholars, yield a greater affection for the first person than some modern scholars would approve. Schliemann's scholarly books often read like memoirs. Sometimes they are little more than archaeological reports in the form of edited diaries, filled with anecdotes and personal observations, praise of his wife, Sophia, condemnation of Turkish perfidy, approval of a friend, and excoriation of someone, like Frank Calvert, who dared to disagree. In one case he introduced his book with an extended autobiography. All this makes the twelve books delightful reading and important biographical source material.[24]

To sum up, roughly 85 percent of the materials for a Schliemann biography are written by Schliemann himself. Any undergraduate history major knows the cardinal rule: Never trust only one source! My work on Schliemann during the last eleven years has taught me to read Schliemann's own works as Nietzsche advises us to read Wagner's: with merciless criticism and, wherever possible and at whatever the cost, to seek an external source that one may use as a control over whatever Schliemann himself wrote before accepting it as historical fact.

PROVEN FABRICATIONS IN SCHLIEMANN'S PERSONAL LIFE

In autumn 1971, when preparing my Neubukow address in commemoration of the 150th birthday of Heinrich Schliemann (6 January 1972), I for the first time had occasion to look critically at a life I had "believed" since as a child I had first read C.W. Ceram's *Gods, Graves and Scholars*. In a word, things seemed too good to be true. For what may have been the first time since Schliemann's death, I began to check the accuracy of what he wrote about himself. Here are two examples of what I found then, familiar now to a wide audience because of the BBC documentary "The Man behind the Mask."

Schliemann in his autobiography of 1881 writes: "I at once decided to commence excavations here, and announced this intention in the work *Ithaque, le Péloponnèse et Troie*, which I published at the end of 1868. Having sent a copy of this work, together with a dissertation in ancient Greek, to the University of Rostock, that learned body honoured me with the diploma of Doctor of Philosophy. With unremitting zeal I have ever since endeavoured to show myself worthy of the dignity conferred on me."[25] This "dissertation in ancient Greek" adorns the narratives of Schliemann's biographers down to the present day, a decade after its exposure.[26] I wondered that Schliemann had accomplished what the best Greek scholars of the day would not have dared. I soon discovered that no "dissertation in ancient Greek" existed at Rostock, only a wretched translation into that language of the autobiographical preface to *Ithaque* on which the Greek professor at Rostock, G.L.E. Bachmann, reported to the dean that "the translation into Greek were better entirely omitted; for the ignorance of Greek endings and sentence construction shows that the author has never passed a course in Greek syntax and therefore is incapable of forming a complete, independent sentence in the ancient manner."[27] Twelve years after the incident, Schliemann lied in print in order to create the public impression that he had mastered a learned language which he scarcely knew.[28]

I next adduce a revealing example understandable immediately to the nonspecialist and of importance beyond the matter it concerns because it exemplifies a pattern of prevarication that we shall meet in later contexts of far greater import.[29] Schliemann made the following entry in his American diary for 21 February 1851:

> In Baltimore I enjoyed a good oyster supper, and the following morning a good oyster-breakfast, and on the 21st Febry. at 9 a.m. I started by rail for Washington, together with Mr. Klaener, who had seen my name in the book at Barnum's Hotel, and called at my room in the morning at 4. On my arrival at Washington, I went immediately to the sessions of the House of Representatives and the House of Congress in the Capitol, a magnificent building on the top of a hill. With the most vivid interest and the sincerest delight, I heard the powerful speeches of Henry Clay, Senator of Kentucky, Hale of New Hampshire, Mason of Virginia, Douglas of Illinois, Davis of Massachusetts, etc. The chief topic of discussion was the late negro-riot at Boston. I left the Capitol at 4 o'clock, took then my dinner (together with Mr. Dean, whom I had previously met with on the railroad) at the ladies' table at the National-Hôtel, and in the evening at 7 o'clock I drove to the President of the United States, to whom I made my introduction by stating that the great desire to see this beautiful country of the West, and to make the acquaintance of the great men who govern it had induced me to come over from Russia, and that I now deemed it my first and most agreeable duty to pay my respects to the President. He received me most kindly, presented me to his wife, daughter, and father, and I had 1 1/2 hours conversation with them.
>
> The President is a very plain and friendly looking man of about 50; his name is Fillmore. His wife is about 46, a very noble and friendly looking lady; his daughter may be 17 years and is looking rather green. At 8 1/2 opened the "levee" with the President, and there assembled more than 800 persons, from all parts of the Union, all eager to see and speak to the President. This latter introduced me to Mr. Webster, Secretary of State; to Mr. Clay, Senator of Kentucky, and to several others. The President's palace is a most magnificént mansion; there are no sentinels to watch and bar the doors; there exist no ceremonies to which the stranger has to submit to be presented to the first Magistrate. I staid {sic} there till 11 o'clock.[30]

The entry remains a masterpiece of its genre, the narration of outrageous untruth within the setting of accurate details. We have the precision of train times, traveling companions, hotels, oysters. Famous names adorn the tale: Webster, Clay, Douglas, and, of course, the Fillmores. There is the eyewitness appraisal: the noble site of the Capitol, the pale Miss Fillmore. For any doubter there is what Sir

Ronald Syme has called "the corroborative detail." Unlike Potsdam, the primitive and friendly Americans have no guards before their palaces.[31]

Internal evidence dissuades an attentive reader. Did a twenty-eight-year-old Mecklenburgian boy require no introduction? Would Mrs. Fillmore spend one and a half hours chatting casually with a chance visitor when at the end of this time she was to entertain "more than 800" prominent guests? My suspicions were confirmed when I consulted contemporary newspapers which carried not a word of any such magnificent reception, although papers, such as the *Boston Evening Transcript,* in a Washington column regularly noticed far more modest social occasions. Schliemann's precise dating allowed me to refute him. I drew attention to similar fabrications, a conference with the Governor of Panama on the principles of colonial rule, and a conference with President Andrew Johnson, during which the thirty-five-year-old Schliemann urged upon our president the annexation of Cuba. These never happened.[32]

I add a further example not my own. In 1979 a California Latinist, one David Traill, published an article entitled "Schliemann's Mendacity: Fire and Fever in California."[33] Professor Traill drew attention to a colorful first-person account in Schliemann's published American diary of the burning of San Francisco. The whole entry deserves citation:

> San Francisco, June 4th, 1851. A most horrible disaster has befallen this City! a conflagration greater than any of the preceding fires has reduced nearly the whole city to ashes.
>
> I arrived here last night at 10 1/2 o'clock and put up at the Union Hôtel on the Plaza. I may have slept a quarter of an hour, when I was awoke by loud cries in the street: "fire, fire" and by the awful sounds of the alarm-bell. I sprung up in all haste and looking out the window I saw that a frame building only 20 or 30 paces from the Union Hotel was on fire. I dressed in all haste and run out of the house, but scarcely had I reached the end of Clay street when I saw already the Hôtel on fire from which I had just run out. Pushed on by a complete gale the fire spread with an appaling rapidity, sweeping away in a few minutes whole streets of frame buildings. Neither the iron houses nor the brickhouses (which were hitherto considered as quite fireproof) could resist the fury of the element; the latter crumbled together with incredible rapidity, whilst the former got red-hot, then white-hot and fell together like card-houses. Particularly in the iron-houses people considered themselves perfectly safe and they remained in them to the last extremity. As soon as the walls of the iron houses getting red-hot the goods inside began to smoke,

the inhabitants wanted to get out, but usually it was already too late, for the locks and hinges of the doors having extended or partly melted by the heat, the doors were no more to be opened. Sometimes by burning their hands and arms people succeeded to open the doors and to get out, but finding themselves then surrounded by an ocean of flames they made but a few paces, staggered and fell, rose again and fell again in order not to rise any more. It was tried in vain to arrest the progress of the fire by the blowing up of houses with gunpowder. Wishing to avoid dangers I went up Montgommery street and ascended "Telegraph hill" which is a mountain abt. 300 feet high close to the city. It was a frightful but sublime view, in fact the grandest spectacle I ever enjoyed. The fire continued to spread in all directions sweeping away the whole of Washington street, Kearny street, Montgommery street, California street, Sansome street and many others, and, except a few houses on Battery street, Bush street, and on the Hillside, the whole beautiful city was burned down. The roaring of the storm, the cracking of the gunpowder, the cracking of the falling stone-walls, the cries of the people and the wonderful spectacle of an immense city burning in a dark night all joined to make this catastrophe awful in the extreme. A report having spread out among the people that the fire had been caused by french incendiaries, the scorn of the enraged populace fell upon the french and many a poor french chap was thrown headlong in the flames and consumed. I remained for the night in the restaurant on Telegraph hill and went at 6 in the morning down to the city. It was a horrible sight to see the smouldering ashes and ruins of this a day before so flourishing city. Whilst I saw a great many germans, frenchmen, englishmen and other foreigners half in despair sitting and weeping on the ashes of their destroyed property, the americans never daunted, laughing and joking among themselves just as if nothing had happened, went boldly a-head to construct new houses and I saw them in many places at 6 o'clock in the morning busy to lay on the still hot ashes of their former buildings the foundations for new ones. In the morning from 6 till 10 it is very hot in San Francisco; then all at once a strong gale springs up and from 10 a.m. off the cold increases till 3 o'clock in the morning, so that it is impossible to walk here during the day after 10 or during the night without a very thick overcoat.[34]

There is the familiar high drama, built about the hero Schliemann and buttressed by those details that make for verisimilitude. Traill proved beyond reasonable doubt that Schliemann misdated the fire by one month, that at the time of the fire (3–4 May 1851) Schliemann was in Sacramento not San Francisco, that the source for his entry was the account in the Sacramento *Daily Union* of 6 May 1851, which he transformed into a vivid, first-person narrative with himself at its center, and finally that the leaf, on which the account of the fire was written, Schliemann had skillfully pasted into his diary in the midst of an entry in the Spanish language.

Professor Traill has further shown that Schliemann's sudden closure of his Sacramento bank on 6 April 1852 and subsequent flight from California on the next day were not due to illness as Schliemann stated in his diary (and his obedient biographers repeat[35]) but probably because his partner, B. Davidson of San Francisco, had uncovered fraud in Schliemann's financial transactions.[36] In a subsequent study of equal cogency, Traill presented evidence that proved (in his words) that "there can be no doubt that Schliemann obtained his American citizenship by fraud" and that "there can be no doubt that Schliemann obtained his divorce, like his citizenship, by fraudulent means."[37] The detailed evidence is easily available. I shall not repeat it here. At the end of his second study, Traill wrote an ominous sentence: "It would be remarkable indeed if an individual so inclined to fraud and deceit proved consistently truthful in his archeological reporting."[38]

ON THE WAY TO ARCHAEOLOGY

Every child who has heard the name of Schliemann knows of the remarkable "Dream of Troy." The small boy Schliemann grew up in the beautiful Mecklenburgian village of Ankershagen amidst ruined castles and legends of ghosts and evil tyrants who cooked men alive. He early read Jerrer's *History of the World for Children,* a picture in which determined him some day to lay bare the walls of Troy.[39] At age ten he wrote a Latin essay (not a word of which has survived) for his father on the Trojan War. In his village dwelt a lame tailor, Peter Hoppert, who after hearing Pastor Schliemann's sermon on Sunday, could repeat it word for word on Monday. He was the blind Homer, who had memorized the *Iliad.*[40] Schliemann's Helen was there too, a neighboring farmer's daughter, Minna Meincke, who inspired in Schliemann the dream of greatness.[41]

A scholar must pose a prosaic and indelicate question. Out of the sixty to eighty thousand letters, eighteen diaries, and the clutch of autobiographies, what is the earliest *dated* source attesting the Dream of Troy? A letter to his former schoolteacher, Carl Andress, whom he supported, requests information on local Ankershagen saga in 1866, when Schliemann had already begun his study of antiquity in Paris.[42]

The first mention in print of the Dream of Troy appears in the autobiography introducing *Ithaka, der Peloponnes und Troja* (1869) and is found as well in the Greek and Latin lives of that year. It is highly significant that the American life of 1852 has not a word about it.[43] We have no external confirmation of the dream, even by so old a friend as Wilhelm Rust. We are dependent only on the testimony of a proven perjurer. Until I see uncontrovertible evidence to the contrary, I shall continue to think the Dream of Troy a sentimental elaboration after the fact.[44] It is romantic enhancement of a successful excavation. This romantic enhancement is often found in Schliemann and has infected those Bronze Age archaeologists who followed Schliemann, men like Sir Arthur Evans, Marinatos, and G. Mylonas. In Ithaca in 1868 he finds the ashes of Odysseus—in a Roman glass tomb. In 1873 he finds at Troy the Scaean Gate and a treasure that belonged to Priam. In 1876 he uncovers the body of Agamemnon. How does he know that he has found Agamemnon? From Mycenae he cables the minister at Athens of "the dead man with the round face. This one is very like the picture which my imagination formed of Agamemnon long ago."[45] All this is naive. It is not dishonest. Some think it charming; it has certainly been inspiring. With everything so far those scholars who have defended Schliemann, Hartmut Döhl of Göttingen and D.F. Easton of Clare Hall, Cambridge, so far as I can tell, go along.

Of course, they must obviate difficulties. Easton writes an exemplary formulation of a view opposite to my own: "I do not even follow the initial assumption: that if a man was a fantasist in his private life, and employed devious means to achieve his ends, the same tendencies are likely to have manifested themselves in his archaeology. However, I accept that this is a debateable point." He has further written that prolonged attention to Schliemann's excavation notes has not dissuaded him from reading them with "a presumption of veracity."[46]

Professor Döhl independently adopts the same line of defense: "All these fantasies, conscious or unconscious deformations of reality, concern first of all the area of biography and need not, therefore, *ipso facto* be applied to his archaeological activity."[47] This I call "the Dr. Jekyll and Mr. Hyde theory," that is: beyond reproach in one's professional life, or better in a part of one's professional life (is there anyone who defends Schliemann's business practices?), but without scruple in describing his personal life. I should suggest that a more reasonable hypothesis—other than diagnosing a welcome schizophrenia—is that one cannot compartmentalize morality in a personality. A man scrupulously honest with his income tax is apt to be honest elsewhere, while an adulterer will cheat in other ways as well. Professor Döhl advances two further defenses.

1. "It would be difficult to find autobiographies in which one could not prove retouching, restyling, attempts at self-justification."[48] In principle I agree: *Dichtung und Wahrheit.* Or even with Pilate: *quid est veritas?* But surely the matter is not *either . . . or* but rather *how far?* The distortion of truth and the sheer fabrication of the past that we find in Schliemann's autobiographical writings exceed the natural embroidery of events that the weakness of the flesh prepares us to expect in a genre that too easily becomes self-laudation. Further, with Schliemann we have reason to apply a severer standard. Schliemann wanted to be treated as a scholar. Again and again, in letters and publications, he declared himself to be a man devoted wholly to the pursuit of truth. We have the right to ask how many scholars (I do not speak of poets, musicians, politicians, soldiers, or movie actresses) have provably distorted their memoirs in the way that Schliemann repeatedly did. Test after test on the memoirs of the scholar I know best, Schliemann's younger Prussian contemporary, Ulrich von Wilamowitz-Moellendorff (1848–1931), has revealed the most admirable honesty and accuracy throughout, down to the most trivial details.[49]

2. "As far as the historically false reports in the English diary of the first visit to America go, one ought to remember that they were not intended for publication. Perhaps Schliemann also used his diaries for language training. He has very often described his method for learning languages. An important element in it was to write out 'versions of matters that interest us.' The visit to the President and the burning of San Francisco in the American diary recall such 'exercises.' "[50] I do not find the distinction between not-to-be-published diary and published book convincing in Schliemann's case. Schliemann often published his diaries. His books on China and Japan (1867) and on Ithaca, the Peloponnesus, and Troy (1869) are little more than edited diaries, often edited *ad maiorem gloriam Schliemanni.* In the midst of busy travel, Schliemann scrupulously kept his diaries up. He preserved them all, as did his widow after his death, until, finally, his grandchildren sold them to the Gennadeion. Even admitting the element of language drill, are we to assume that Schliemann never expected people to read and believe what he had written there? Professor Traill has remarked

that "it is almost as if Schliemann knew from the beginning that he would be famous and carefully concocted his diaries with future biographers in mind."[51] Schliemann composed his diaries as Pliny did his letters.

Döhl documents at some length Schliemann's friendships with two great scholars, Rudolf Virchow (1821–1902) and Wilhelm Dörpfeld (1853–1940).[52] The implication is "by their friends shall ye know them." These men would have seen through Schliemann immediately if he were as bad as some of us would have him. One must pause to look carefully at Virchow and Dörpfeld. Rudolf Virchow, a polymath, a seminal figure in the history of nineteenth-century medicine, an eminent pathologist, the discoverer of the cell, an anthropologist, and a prehistorian, in several respects was remarkably similar to Schliemann.[53] He was the self-made man, a poor country butcher's son, who through innate intelligence, hard work, and some luck made his remarkable career. On graduating from school, he wrote a paper on the theme "A life full of work and toil is no burden but a blessing."[54] He worked his way through medical school and suffered often from extreme poverty and the humiliation that it exacts. In the revolution of 1848 he sided with workers which, temporarily at least, cost him his hospital post. There was the idealist in him. He always felt himself an outsider, cut off from the academic establishment. One sees immediately what made him Schliemann's champion. He shared Schliemann's uncritical enthusiasm for what he did not understand. In 1892 he published in the papers of the Prussian Academy of Sciences, the skull of Sophocles.[55] Any man who did that would have little difficulty believing in the ashes of Odysseus, the Treasure of Priam, or the body of Agamemnon. Since his student days he had been interested in archaeology. Meyer reports that Virchow arrived at Troy on 4 April 1879 carrying his schoolboy's Homer and inspired by the greatness of epic poetry.[56] Virchow and Schliemann quickly became friends, but Virchow was in no position to judge Schliemann's Trojan work professionally. They were both enthusiastic amateurs.

Wilhelm Dörpfeld, again, is problematic. Regrettably, a critical biography does not exist.[57] Schliemann discovered the young architect, who was neither a classical scholar nor a professional archaeologist, at Olympia on 16 March 1881. More than thirty years younger than Schliemann, Dörpfeld owed his career and, for a number of years, his livelihood to his older friend. Schliemann introduced him to Bismarck and to Wilhelm II. The Serbian diplomat Georgevice in 1893 called Dörpfeld "Schliemann's most beautiful find."[58] Georgevice was a diplomat and not a scholar. In 1909, although supported by Alexander Conze, Reinhard Kekulé von Stradonitz, and Heinrich Dressel, Dörpfeld was denied a corresponding membership in the Berlin Academy because of his "notorious position in scholarly questions."[59] Wilamowitz on 24 June 1900, with the frankness a private letter permits, wrote to Ferdinand Noack: "I hope that you will not be compromised by the infantilities [*Kindereien*] of Dörpfeld. Now it goes too far and I do not intend to allow that the Institute be associated with this rubbish [*Blödsinn*]. In comparison spiritualism is harmless. He is going to hear what I think." That Dörpfeld, himself an autodidact and an outsider, remained loyal to Schliemann is no surprise. It was the loyalty of the *cliens,* not proof that Schliemann was honest and a scholar. It is revealing that Dörpfeld was always reluctant to speak of Schliemann.[60] After Schliemann's death, Dörpfeld's work grew more and more eccentric. Döhl noted that "highly esteemed, but written off and forgotten by his professional colleagues, Dörpfeld died in 1940 in his Homeric Ithaca."[61]

ARCHAEOLOGICAL INTEGRITY

So far, I have discussed only what I call Schliemann's romantic enhancement of his finds. In 1972 I wrote of Schliemann: "How did his psychopathy affect his archaeology? The disinterested recording of finds, their description, the drawings need not be universally doubted. Much can be controlled by the extant objects themselves."[62] The brilliant work of Professor David A. Traill has proven these words to be wildly optimistic.

One must understand the origin of Traill's methodology in order to evaluate the present crisis. Professor Traill is not an archaeologist. He has never said that he was. He began life as a Latin paleographer and philologist. That means that he was taught to decipher scribbles illegible to most people and that he was taught to elucidate historically, critically, and with the utmost accuracy difficult passages of ancient prose and poetry. This is not the training one requires if one is to devote one's life to reassembling and dating prehistoric pots and pans. It is precisely the training one wants if one is to deal with unpublished nineteenth-century letters and diaries, carelessly written in a foreign language, which must first be transcribed, sometimes dated, then understood and finally reconciled with conflicting sources in order to reconstruct the past accurately. This is traditional historical-philological method. Professor Traill owes his unsettling discoveries to his expertise, bolstered by a sharp eye and keen intelligence. He reads Schliemann's published accounts critically. He goes to the Gennadius Library in Athens and compares them with unpublished letters and diaries. Then he starts to ask questions, usually about discrepancies in the accounts, and soon he is supplying answers. The method is through and through philological and the discipline is not Bronze Age archaeology. It is the history of classical scholarship in the nineteenth century, a specialized but rewarding branch of *Geistesgeschichte,* in which much important work is still to be done.[63] Opposing methodology is responsible for much mutual misunderstanding. Few Bronze Age archaeologists are capable of writing a history of their own discipline in the nineteenth century. Equally, few intellectual historians could plot a trench or date a sherd. The state of archaeology in classical lands is especially vulnerable as the discipline, much like its sister classical philology, risks growing, worse, willing self-isolation, caused only in part by the narrowing education of its practitioners. That the standard history of art history omits the subject of archaeology that a hundred years ago would have been at its center tells us something.[64] With this background, let us recall three discoveries made by Traill in the last three years and two made by European archaeologists.

1. Traill has shown that *Ithaque, le Péloponnèse et Troie* (Paris 1869), the book that gained Schliemann his Rostock doctorate, differs considerably from the documents upon which it is based. Schliemann did not hesitate to omit or change annoying facts, to conceal what he owed others, to glorify his own ability and intuition at the expense of changing dates and alleging excavations that were never made or were made on a far more modest scale than suggested in the published version.[65]

2. At the annual meeting of the Archaeological Institute of America in December 1982, Traill drew attention to the old chronological puzzle posed by two terra-cotta figurines of LH III B type found, according to Schliemann's published account, in a LH 1 burial (Shaft Grave I). Lame explanations have been provided by G. Karo and Mylonas. Traill, on the evidence of the diaries bolstered by his view of Schliemann's honesty, argues convincingly "a darker explanation." Schliemann had good reason to commit fraud. The figurines were

"horned Hera idols" which Schliemann wished to be contemporary with the "owl-headed Athenas" he had found at "Homeric Troy" (Troy II). This would provide the desperately needed link between "Homeric Troy" and "Agamemnon's Mycenae."[66]

3. The most famous single discovery in the history of nineteenth-century classical archaeology was Heinrich Schliemann's discovery of the "Treasure of Priam" at Troy in May 1873. In the popular imagination it ranks with Howard Carter's discovery of King Tut's tomb on 26 November 1922. On 30 December 1981, at the San Francisco meeting of the Archaeological Institute of America, Professor Traill first sought to examine the legend critically. His careful comparison of some four reports, all written by Schliemann, of the discovery of the Treasure of Priam yielded startling and telling contradictions. He discovered also what we always require when dealing with Schliemann: an independent witness. This witness, whose reliability, ironically, is enthusiastically attested by Schliemann himself, damningly contradicts the great man. Traill concluded that " 'Priam's Treasure' appears to be a composite of numerous small finds made over the three years of excavation (1871–73), possibly augmented by purchases."[67] "Priam's Treasure" was "found" at the end of the season and the end of the excavation. Schliemann needed to make a big splash. Priam's treasure made him world famous within a year and gained him the coveted permission to excavate Mycenae.

4. In an article of considerable importance published in 1975 by George S. Korres of the University of Athens, the author proved that a group of Attic inscriptions published by Schliemann in *AthMitt* (1888), and said by him to have been discovered in the garden of his Athenian villa, were in fact purchased by him from private collections.[68]

5. In this volume Wolfgang Schindler, through critical analysis of Schliemann's correspondence on the matter and through expert stylistic analysis of the Berlin head, demolishes the contention that it could be Cleopatra and puts into gravest doubt Schliemann's assertion that the head was excavated in 1888 by him in Alexandria.[69] That he bought it somewhere, as he did his "excavated" inscriptions, agrees with the extant evidence.[70]

The discoveries of these three scholars have placed the reputation of Heinrich Schliemann as archaeologist and scholar in jeopardy. Deliberately to falsify and suppress evidence, to present as truth what one knows is falsehood, and to do so for one's personal aggrandizement are for a scholar the sin against the Holy Ghost. These scholars, Professor Traill and two archaeologists, have drawn up an indictment against Schliemann that is of a wholly different character from the naive but well-intentioned romantic enhancement of finds. They are causing us to revise radically our traditional conception of the father of field archaeology.

WHERE DO WE GO FROM HERE?

"I have yet to find Schliemann wrong," wrote J.M. Cook in December 1970.[71] A new age has dawned. I shall conclude my essay, which is intended to show where we are now, by asking and attempting to answer three questions, which, I think, will be occurring to many readers. I, certainly, am frequently asked them.

1. Why were Schliemann's lies undetected for almost one hundred years? There are several reasons. First, Schliemann wrote what readers wanted to believe. His tales mesmerized his biographers, who copied uncritically from him and then from each other. It is a great deal easier when writing a book to copy what someone else has written than to refute, by independent thought and research, what someone else has written. Any experienced book reviewer knows this.

Next, scholarly contemporaries thought Schliemann a thorough rogue, not deserving refutation. For Ernst Curtius to refute Heinrich Schliemann would be like my refuting Mary Renault. The targets are not worth the powder and shot. How many serious scholarly reviews by Germans did Schliemann's books receive? Here are a few opinions. Certainly there is an element of snobbery in them all. The mandarins detested the self-made man. This does not mean that their criticism is not just. Ernst Curtius (1814–1896), the Berlin ancient historian and the excavator of Olympia, told Prince von Bülow in 1877 that Heinrich Schliemann was a botcher and a con man (*Pfuscher und Schwindler*). Adolf Furtwängler (1853–1907), arguably the greatest archaeologist of Wilamowitz' generation wrote his mother in July 1881 that "Schliemann is and remains a half-crazy and confused human being, who has no idea whatsoever of the meaning of his excavations. . . . In spite of his passion for Homer, he is at heart a speculator and businessman. He can never get rid of that."[72] In 1873 the youthful Ulrich von Wilamowitz-Moellendorff wrote to his parents from Rome:

You ask after the Treasure of Priam and instead of the bilgewater of the journalists it is good that you hear the truth. Because the kingdom of Priam lies in the same land where does the Heavenly Jerusalem, Dante's Hell, Schiller's Bohemian Forests, the Castle of Lear, and that Iceland, where Brunhilde reigns, one can as well find Priam's Treasure as one can the rungs of Jacob's Ladder and the place where, if Romulus did not found Rome, Remus founded Rome (which N.B. has been found).[73]

Sir F. Max Müller (1823–1900), a supporter and correspondent of Schliemann, "used smilingly to say 'He destroyed Troy for the last time.' " His wife also reported:

When Dr Schliemann exhibited his Trojan treasures at the South Kensington Museum, Max Müller spent some time in London helping him to arrange the things—an arduous task, for, as is well known, though he had the scent of a truffle dog for hidden treasures, he had little or no correct archaeological knowledge, and Max Müller found the things from the four different strata which Schliemann considered he had discovered at Troy in wild confusion—though he maintained they were all carefully packed in different cases. One day when Max Müller was busy over a case of the lowest stratum, he found a piece of pottery from the highest. "Que voulez-vous," said Schliemann, "it has tumbled down!" Not long after, in a box of the highest stratum appeared a piece of the rough pottery from the lowest. "Que voulez-vous," said the imperturbable Doctor, "it has tumbled up."[74]

On the other hand, Schliemann amused the Emperor Wilhelm II. And the English were kinder to an amateur.[75]

As time passed, only Schliemann's books remained. Those who had known him departed, their impressions recorded haphazardly in memoirs and unpublished letters. I met an aged Greek at Mycenae in 1960 who alleged that he had seen Schliemann. There is no man alive today who knew Schliemann personally. Even the considerable polemic literature (one recalls especially Bötticher) surrounding Schliemann has been forgotten. Succeeding generations of Bronze Age archaeologists worship a distant patron saint wreathed in legend whom they have never understood. Many will not admit that their saint is a pretender.

Finally, the incriminating sources—I mean the diaries and letters—were, most of them, not published until after World War II. Although, as I have observed, often censored, they provided the first clues. The *Nachlass* is only now in the process of being suitably arranged. Consultation remains difficult. D.F. Easton's catalogue will surely facilitate access. These, then, are reasons why only now are Schliemann's secrets being disclosed.

2. Why was it necessary for Schliemann to lie? He was already rich and famous. Is not this what Pentagon generals call "overkill"? Remember, you cannot expect a rational answer. The M'Naghten rules still provide the best test in litigation for an insanity plea. Was the accused at the moment of the crime able to distinguish between right and wrong? If he was not, he was insane and should be committed to an insane asylum rather than be sent to prison.

I do not think that Schliemann could distinguish between right and wrong. Take, for example, the incident of Queen Sophie of Holland and the ten Tanagra figurines. Schliemann had been guest of the queen at The Hague in early August 1875.[76] He wrote to her from Athens on 2 March 1876 that "only today I have returned to Athens and my first care has been to select from my collection of Greek antiquities the 10 Tanagra-*figurines* for Your Majesty. . . . I have carefully packed the . . . figurines in a box, which I shall forward to Your Majesty by the first opportunity; unfortunately I cannot send it by the direct steamer, the exportation of antiquities being strictly prohibited in Greece."[77] In fact, Schliemann had arrived in Athens eight days before.[78] He tactlessly made the queen an accomplice in smuggling antiquities out of Greece. He also lied to her, because, in an earlier letter to his wife, Sophia, neither published nor cited by Meyer, he "asked that she select the statuettes, but cautioned her to 'find very nice ones at a very low price. I can't pay much because I have to give them away.' "[79] He wrote these letters without the slightest twinge of guilt. L.R.B. Farnell (1856–1934), the Rector of Exeter and Vice-Chancellor of the University of Oxford, visited Schliemann in Athens in 1886 and recorded that "his daughter of twelve was Nausikaa and throve under the name; but his son Agamemnon was a bright boy with a Greek profile that did not look altogether natural; and we were told that it was the result of much twisting and manipulation of his infant-features."[80] Such cruelty is not the act of a doting parent and must have caused equal pain to the mother.

In short, the answer to our question becomes a diagnosis rather than an explanation. Doctors provide diagnoses, not classical scholars. Fortunately, a distinguished New York psychoanalyst, a Freudian theorist, and a specialist in the area of creativity, Dr. William G. Niederland, has published three studies on this problem.[81] Dr. Niederland attributes the compulsive need of Schliemann to prove himself to his disgraced authoritarian father (Schliemann's clerical father was removed from his post because of an affair with a maid) to the predicament of the self-made man and to the attested fact that Schliemann was what Dr. Niederland calls "a replacement child." Schliemann's elder brother had died in his infancy. His parents gave Schliemann the name of the deceased brother, and, Schliemann, in the pscyhoanalytical sense, was never certain that he was not himself the dead brother. Hence the compulsive need to do things and the morbid attraction to the dead, of which his interest in archaeology is only one example.

I am not a psychoanalyst. I am an historian. I can show you that Schliemann lied and deceived, that he altered, suppressed, and forged documents to make falsehood seem truth, that he bought objects and said that he had excavated them, that he fabricated a past that had never been, that he bribed and betrayed to gain his ends. I have never published a moral judgment on Schliemann. I have on his biographers. I consider them lazy and incompetent. But Schliemann was ill, like an alcoholic, a child molester, or a dope-fiend. He did not know the difference between right and wrong. We must be thankful for his illness. It made him great.

3. Where do we go from here? Ironically, we are in the very situation that Schliemann was in one hundred years ago when he sought to convince a stubborn establishment that he was right. Our first task must be to overcome the archaeologists' refusal to judge the new discoveries without prejudice. Reaction to what Konrad Zimmermann has called "die neuere Schliemann-Forschung" is revealing.[82] Patricia Meyer Spacks, in her book on autobiography and novel in eighteenth-century England, has seen what has been gained immediately:

> Every lie tells some truth: knowing that Heinrich Schliemann's autobiography is largely the product of his fantasy, we perhaps know more about him—how he wishes, how he dreams—than we would have learned from a meticulously factual report. His identity as comprehended by his readers, then, derives from his imagination more than his memory, and one suspects that his sense of subjective identity, too, rests largely on the testimony of imagination. The autobiographer's "fiction" is stronger and more telling than his "truth."[83]

Because Spacks is not burdened with Schliemann as the heroic founder of her discipline and has not committed herself regarding his character or his finds, the truth or falsehood of what he writes do not warp her judgment. She deals with autobiography on its own terms. The ancient historian, Moses Finley, views recent work as "an important exposé of the hagiography that is current in the guise of biography of Schliemann."[84] He encourages the pursuit of truth. Archaeologists hedge. Åke Åkerström, much to his credit, has considered the work on Schliemann the autobiographer, and concluding that it might affect his archaeology, resorts to a *petitio principi:* "Scholars involved have asked, what are the implications, when we come to Schliemann's archaeology. There, the situation ought to be different, of course especially, when it comes to controllable finds."[85] The situation is not different and I do not admit that it ought to be. This is the Dr. Jekyll and Mr. Hyde approach, which would later find its most eloquent exponent in Professor Döhl. Åkerström, Döhl, and Zimmermann have recognized that a problem exists and have sought to deal with it.

Worse are the American Bronze Age archaeologists, who refuse to admit a problem exists. They have until now successfully prevented the publication in American journals of the new discoveries.[86] The president of the Archaeological Institute of America, Machteld J. Mellink, has accused Traill in print of waging a "vendetta against Schliemann" that "threatens to obscure his archaeological contributions."[87] The courageous pursuit of truth is not a vendetta.

In a more positive vein, our great need is an honest edition of the letters, competently transcribed with critical commentary. A well-chosen selection with summaries in the notes of less important ones would suffice. Critical and accurate publication of the diaries would also be welcome. Only with such source material available in publications that one can trust can some scholar write the first critical biography of Heinrich Schliemann. He must believe nothing and question everything until a control is available. Assumption of Schliemann's mendacity must be the guiding principle when dealing with any document written by Schliemann himself. Research has advanced sufficiently since 1972 that the burden of proof lies now with those who assume his veracity.

Finally, Wolfgang Schindler has suggested that the answer to how Schliemann behaved lies in the time in which he lived and not in the man.[88] That is, the explanation is not, as Dr. Niederland argues, psychoanalytical but rather historical. We must set Schliemann into the context of the age that created him. We must compare him with men like Sir Edmund Backhouse as he is revealed in Hugh Trevor-Roper's

Hermit of Peking, or with Wolfgang Helbig, a correspondent of Schliemann, a respected and prolific scholar, and now proven to have forged the *fibula Praenestina.* We must compare Schliemann's diaries with Sir Roger Casement's, long thought a libelous forgery by British Intelligence. We must examine the memoirs of contemporary German romantics like Karl May or Richard Wagner and even those of Bismarck, who was not immune to rewriting the past. Or we must consider, as some of us already have, the great literary monument to this type, Ibsen's *Peer Gynt,* the story of a figure whom, were it not impossible chronologically, we should think modeled on Heinrich Schliemann.[89] The subject entrances. Opportunity for new discoveries is endless. Scholars are persistent. I doubt that we shall decide between myth or scandal. Our goal is to make Schliemann more historical.

NOTES

1. See Carl Schuchhardt, "Heinrich Schliemann 1822–1890," *Die Grossen Deutschen: Deutsche Biographie* III[2], edd. Hermann Heimpel, Theodor Heuss, and Benno Reifenberg (Berlin 1956) 540. This life is uncritical hagiography and perpetuates the curious error (551) that Schliemann—not K.O. Müller—is buried at Colonus: see Schuchhardt's autobiography, *Aus Leben und Arbeit* (Berlin 1944) 181. Among German scholars Schuchhardt is a rare, though critical, supporter of Schliemann; see his *Schliemann's Excavations: An Archaeological and Historical Study,* trans. Eugénie Sellers (London and New York 1891) and *Aus Leben und Arbeit* 176–82.

2. Hartmut Döhl, *Heinrich Schliemann: Mythos und Ärgernis* (Munich 1981). The book was reviewed by me in *German Studies Review* 6 (1983) 602–3; by D. Easton in *CR* n.s. 33 (1983) 286–87; W. Schindler in *DLZ* 104 (1983) 898–901; and David A. Traill in *Gnomon* 55 (1983) 149–52. Professor Döhl has kindly approved of my use of this variation on his title.

3. See Gustav Mahr, *Troja: Heinrich Schliemanns Ausgrabungen und Funde, Ausstellung des Museums für Vor- und Frühgeschichte Preussischer Kulturbesitz und der Berliner Gesellschaft für Anthropologie, Ethnologie und Urgeschichte im Schloss Charlottenburg-Langhansbau* (Berlin 1981) and E. Hühns, *Troja und Thrakien: Ausstellung Berlin-Hauptstadt der DDR und Sofia veranstaltet vom Archäologischen Institut und Museum der Bulgarischen Akademie der Wissenschaften und dem Museum für Ur- und Frühgeschichte der Staatlichen Museen zu Berlin, Hauptstadt der DDR, in Verbindung mit dem Zentralinstitut für Alte Geschichte und Archäologie der Akademie der Wissenschaften der DDR* (Berlin 1982). Both volumes contain numerous essays by various scholars. Add now the exemplary summary of the controversy by Harald Steinert, *FAZ* 30 April 1984.

4. George S. Korres, "Bibliographia Errikou Sleman," *Library of the*

Archaeological Society at Athens 78 (Athens 1974); see the remarks of Wolfgang Schindler, *Philologus* 120 (1976) 289.

5. I refer to Emil Ludwig, *Schliemann: The Story of a Gold-Seeker*, trans. D.F. Tait (Boston 1931), on which see John A. Scott, *CJ* 27 (1931–1932) 20–21; Lynn and Gray Poole, *One Passion, Two Loves: The Story of Heinrich and Sophia Schliemann, Discoverers of Troy* (New York 1966), in which (70) George Grote is called a German; Robert Payne, *The Gold of Troy: The Story of Heinrich Schliemann and the Buried Cities of Ancient Greece* {sic} (New York 1959), with the critical review by C.H. Whitman, *CW* 53 (1959–1960) 259–60; Heinrich Alexander Stoll, *Abenteuer meines Lebens Heinrich Schliemann erzählt* (Leipzig 1958) and *Der Traum von Troja: Lebensroman Heinrich Schliemanns*[8] (Leipzig 1965); Irving Stone, *The Greek Treasure: A Biographical Novel of Henry and Sophia Schliemann* (New York 1975); and Paul Faure, *Henri Schliemann: Une vie d'archéologue* (Jean-Cyrille Godefroy 1982).

6. For Schliemann's travels see Meyer, *Schliemann* 165–251.

7. See now Wolfgang Schindler, "Schliemanns Selbstporträt: Die Inszenierung eines Self-made-man," *EAZ* 21 (1980) 655–58 and *Festschrift Irmscher* (forthcoming).

8. Friedrich Nietzsche, "Der Fall Wagner: Nachschrift," *Sämtliche Werke Kritische Studienausgabe* 6, edd. Giorgio Colli and Mazzino Montinari (Munich/Berlin 1980) 41 n. (= II.929n Schlechta). The translation is my own. For the persistence of untruth in Wagner biography see Philip Winters, "Wagner: Writing the Wrongs," *The New Criterion* 1.6 (1983) 41–50.

9. For the method of compiling a biography see my "*Doceat mortuus vivos:* In Quest of Ulrich von Wilamowitz-Moellendorff," *Emerita* 48 (1980) 209–19 = Ulrich von Wilamowitz-Moellendorff, *Selected Correspondence 1869–1931*, ed. William M. Calder III, *Antiqua* 23 (1983) 1–19.

10. Homeric and New Testament scholars are familiar with this problem, lack of a control and the need to determine historicity on internal grounds.

11. D.F. Easton, "The Schliemann Papers," *ABSA* 77 (1982) 93–110. To Easton's list of published letters (94) one must add the following: Karl J.R. Arndt, "Schliemann's Excavation of Troy and American Politics, or Why the Smithsonian Institution Lost Schliemann's Great Troy Collection to Berlin," *Yearbook of German-American Studies* 16 (1981) 1–8 (letters to Kate Field, 1878–1881); J.V. Luce, "Five New Schliemann Letters in Belfast," *Hermathena* 132 (1982) 8–14 (five letters to Lord Dufferin, 1882); and Heinrich Alexander Stoll, *Abenteuer meines Lebens: Heinrich Schliemann erzählt* (Leipzig 1958) 223–377 (sixty-nine letters to Wilhelm Rust, 1868–1890).

12. For an example see my "Heinrich Schliemann: An Unpublished Latin *Vita*," *CW* 67 (1973–1974) 272–82 = *Antiqua* 27 (1984) 109–119.

13. Heinrich Schliemann, *Selbstbiographie bis zu seinem Tode vervöllständigt*, ed. Sophie Schliemann; tenth edition, ed. Ernst Meyer (Wiesbaden 1968). *Ilios* 1–66. A.H. Sayce, *Reminiscences* (London 1923) 181, attests that due to the insistence of the publisher, John Murray, the version in *Ilios* is considerably abridged. Meyer writes in the tenth edition of *Selbstbiog-*

raphie (12): "Der Text des Buches, der seit der ersten Auflage (1892) festliegt, blieb unverändert." H.A. Stoll, *Das Altertum* 4 (1958) 52 n. 1, reports that, in fact, Meyer had made sufficient deletions so as to make the book unsuitable for scholarly citation.

14. For the three mutilated diaries see Easton (supra n. 12) 100, 102. In the case of Diaries No. 10 and No. 11, the first six and eight pages respectively have been cut out. I wonder whether they did not, as did the published American diary, contain autobiographies that were removed and sold by Schliemann's grandsons Alex or Leon Mélas. The loss of the manuscript drafts "for practically all of Schliemann's major works" (Easton, 99) suggests that they were sold to dealers. That I have discovered one page of *Troja* in a West German private collection confirms my suspicions. There is a still unexplained paradox in the great wealth of Schliemann and the comparative poverty of his children. For the fully published diary see Shirley H. Weber, "Schliemann's First Visit to America 1850–1851," *Gennadeion Monographs* 2 (Cambridge 1942). In fact, Schliemann was in America between 15 February 1851 and 19 May 1852; see W.B. Dinsmoor, "Early American Studies of Mediterranean Archaeology," *The Early History of Science and Learning in America* (Philadelphia 1943) 103 n. 59. See also the critical review by Carl Blegen, *CW* 36 (1942–1943) 135–36. Pages 1 through 20 (26 March–18 July 1869) of Diary No. 13, covering Schliemann's infamous visit to Indianapolis, are published by Eli Lilly, *Schliemann in Indianapolis* (Indianapolis 1961) 11–23. These pages were cut out of the diary and placed on extended loan at the Lilly Library in Bloomington in July 1967: see Easton, 105. Diary No. 17 "Travels in Egypt, November 1886–March 1887" for which see Ernst Meyer, "Schliemanns ägyptisches Reisetagebuch (1886–1887)," *Charisteria Gymnasium* (Giessen 1955) 153–69, after Easton, 104. Large parts of Diary No. 6, "Travels in China and Japan, April–June 1865," formed the basis of Henry Schliemann, *La Chine et le Japon au Temps présent* (Paris 1867) 3–202, a fact not noticed by Easton, 101. I have not yet compared the published version with the diary, but I should expect revisions. Did Schliemann in fact leave Yokohama on the Fourth of July as noted in *La Chine* 205? Diary No. 12, "Study-Trip to Italy, Ithaca, the Peloponnese, and the Troad, May–August 1868," "forms the basis of Schliemann's book *Ithaka, der Peloponnes und Troja* (Leipzig 1869)" (Easton, 103). David A. Traill has exposed the damning revisions in the published version: see *Boreas* 7 (1984) 295–316.

15. Easton (supra n. 11) 100.

16. The often cited figure of sixty thousand letters (see most recently Easton [supra n. 11] 95) derives from *Briefwechsel* II 406 (see infra). It serves its purpose, that of a large round number. David Traill now thinks eighty thousand is closer. I have estimated that in his lifetime Wilamowitz wrote ca. 67,000 letters and postcards: see *Selected Correspondence* 7. For the authoritative description of the copybooks see Easton, 104–106. The three volumes of letters are *Briefe, Briefwechsel* I, and *Briefwechsel* II.

17. Meyer, *Schliemann;* see J.M. Cook, *CR* n.s. 20 (1970) 391: "An authoritative book like this has been badly needed."

18. See *Briefwechsel* I, 7 and II, 406.

19. One does not expect Ludwig Schliemann, Heinrich's brother, to write: (*Briefwechsel* I, 45) "a nudden {sudden} lightening"; "prospecting for the beglumps {big-lumps}"; (46) "I keep a small stove {store} on Front street"; (47) "Colds {Colts} Revolvery Pistols." One certainly does not expect Heinrich Schliemann to write: (*Briefwechsel* I, 237) "I take the liberty of trembling {troubling} Y Exc"; (282) "a more {mere} trifle"; (*Briefwechsel* II, 110) "Mere and Taylors {Merchant Taylors} College in London"; (245) "an undepend outchampion" {independent champion}; (275) "a[n] unless {a useless} waste of time"; (327) "both equably {equally} poor and ambitious." My conviction that Meyer did not know English well enough to edit Schliemann's English letters is confirmed by the ignorant misspellings and omissions in *Briefwechsel* II, 231 (No. 214), in a letter written by a highly educated native speaker of English, the Harvard Hellenist and grammarian W.W. Goodwin. A scholar would have checked his transcriptions with a native speaker. Meyer did not.

20. See Calder, *CW* 67 (1973–1974) 280–81.

21. David Traill queries the date of No. 6 in *Briefwechsel* II, 31. I suspect that the date "22 Febr." has been inserted at *Briefwechsel* II, 281. Traill, however, cautions *per litt.*: "I know of no instance where Meyer has *changed* a date. I now think that the date at *BW* II. 31 is correct. Schliemann with deliberate deception has used a *Julian* date to a correspondent with whom he regularly uses *Gregorian* dates. I have found a parallel for this."

22. See Curt Paul Janz, *Die Briefe Friedrich Nietzsches: Textprobleme und ihre Bedeutung für Biographie und Doxographie* (Zürich 1972) and H.F. Peters, *Zarathustra's Sister: The Case of Elisabeth and Friedrich Nietzsche* (New York 1977). Madame Hensler plays a similar role in Niebuhr studies.

23. See supra n. 11.

24. Schliemann's twelve scholarly books are conveniently listed in Meyer, *Schliemann*, 444–45. See Schliemann, "Introduction: Autobiography of the Author, and Narrative of His Work at Troy," in *Ilios* 1–66. An autobiographical foreword began *Ithaka, der Peloponnes und Troja* (Leipzig 1869; repr. Darmstadt 1963) xix–xxviii. I cite the Darmstadt reprint, my copy of which I owe to the generosity of Erich Schliemann of Hamburg. Even so great a scholar as Wilamowitz introduced autobiographical elements into his work, but in a far more complex way than did Schliemann: see "*Ecce homo:* The Autobiographical in Wilamowitz' Scholarly Writings," *Wilamowitz nach 50 Jahren,* edd. William M. Calder III, Hellmut Flashar, and Theodor Lindken (Darmstadt 1985), 80–110.

25. *Ilios* 20.

26. See *GRBS* 13 (1972) 336 n. 9 and especially the careful discussion of the Rostock *Dozent* Wolfgang Richter, "*Ithaque, le Péloponnèse et Troie* und das Promotionsverfahren Heinrich Schliemanns," *EAZ* 21 (1980) 667–78; see for the preservation of error Wolfgang Schiering, "Heinrich Schliemann und die Archäologie," *Meyers Grosses Universallexikon* (Mannheim, Wien, and Zürich 1982) 542. Schiering further errs in writing that Schliemann submitted

Ithaka, der Peloponnes und Troja for the degree. Schliemann submitted the French original and not the German translation of Carl Andress, his former teacher.

27. I cite the German in *GRBS* 13 (1972) 337.

28. Schliemann wrote to his cousin, Adolph Schliemann, from Paris on 12 March 1869 (*Briefe* 112): "Ich sende Dir nun einliegend im gelben Couvert die Vorrede auf Altgriechisch und Lateinisch, auch einen Brief an den Dekan." ["I am sending you herewith in a yellow envelope the foreword in ancient Greek and Latin, also a letter to the dean."]

29. I think of Cleopatra and the Treasure of Priam.

30. See Weber (supra n. 14) 25–26, and my discussion in *GRBS* 13 (1972) 338–41, with the remarks of Wolfgang Schindler, *Philologus* 120 (1976) 278–79.

31. I have rephrased what I wrote in *GRBS* 13 (1972) 339 in this paragraph.

32. See *GRBS* 13 (1972) 341–43 for details and Schindler, *Philologus* 120 (1976) 278–79.

33. *CJ* 74 (1978–1979) 348–55.

34. The text is in Weber (supra n. 14) 53–54, and is reprinted by Traill in *CJ* 74 (1978–1979) 348–50. Traill's exposé is well known because of its inclusion in the BBC program.

35. See Ludwig (supra n. 5) 58 and Meyer, *Schliemann,* 120. Leo Deuel, *Memoirs of Heinrich Schliemann: A Documentary Portrait Drawn from His Autobiographical Writings, Letters, and Excavation Reports* (New York 1977) 79, reprints Schliemann's account without a trace of skepticism.

36. Traill, *CJ* 74 (1978–1979) 351–55.

37. David A. Traill, "Schliemann's American Citizenship and Divorce," *CJ* 77 (1981–1982) 336, 337.

38. *CJ* 77 (1981–1982) 341. These words have proven prophetic.

39. For Georg Ludwig Jerrer, a nom de plume for the prolific writer of children's books, Johann Heinrich Meynier, see Johannes Irmscher, "Über Heinrich Schliemanns erstes Trojaerlebnis," *EAZ* 21 (1980) 659–65. Irmscher, like all scholars who have treated the matter, assumes that the child Schliemann signed the flyleaf of his Jerrer. Traill now argues that the signature is that of the adult, and, hence, the volume ceases to be evidence for the Dream of Troy: see David A. Traill, *CJ* 81 (1985) 23.

40. This implies the view of F.A. Wolf that the Homeric poems were composed without the aid of writing and handed down orally: see R.C. Jebb, *Homer: An Introduction to the Iliad and the Odyssey* 3 (Glasgow 1888) 108.

41. For the authorized version of all this material see Schliemann, *Ilios* 1–7, repeated ad infinitum by the biographers.

42. See the Latin letter of Andress (No. 95) with the date, 27 March 1866, added by Meyer in *Briefwechsel* I, 125–26. Traill notes: "I suspect the Andress letter should be dated much later. Andress himself put no date on it. Schliemann marked the date on the back of all the letters he received. This one is dated only by Schliemann."

43. See *Ithaka*² xix–xxi. For a discussion on the lives, see Calder, *CW* 67 (1973–1974) 275–76. See Schliemann's published American diary in Weber (supra n. 14) 3–12.

44. See my analysis of the evidence in *GRBS* 13 (1972) 350–52 and the important remarks of Schindler, *Philologus* 120 (1976) 273–75, which were accepted by Traill in *CJ* 74 (1978–1979) 348. I detect skepticism in Deuel (supra n. 35) 274.

45. I cite the version in Ludwig (supra n. 5) 173: see *GRBS* 13 (1972) 350 with n. 73 and O.T.P.K. Dickinson, "Schliemann and the Shaft Graves," *G&R* n.s. 23 (1976) 164. I do not know that the Greek (?) original of the famous telegram has been published.

46. Letters to the author, 17 May 1982 and 18 Februrary 1982. Subsequent accumulation of evidence has caused him to modify his view.

47. Döhl (supra n. 2) 77.

48. Döhl (supra n. 2) 76.

49. See my assessment in *Selected Correspondence* (supra n. 9) 4–5.

50. Döhl (supra n. 2) 76–77. One might add Dr. W.G. Niederland's clinical observation that Schliemann could say things in a foreign language that he would not in German: see *GRBS* 13 (1972) 340–41 and "An Analytic Inquiry into the Life and Work of Heinrich Schliemann," *Drives, Affects, Behavior* 2 (1965) 374. I may add that my need to refute Döhl in no way indicates lack of esteem for his book. The contrary is true. For those deprived of revelation, truth is reached through dialectic.

51. Traill, *CJ* 77 (1981–1982) 341.

52. Döhl (supra n. 2) 49–61.

53. For a brief and readable biography see Arnold Bauer, *Rudolf Virchow: Der politische Arzt* (West Berlin 1982); for detailed documentation and selected letters see Christian Andree, *Rudolf Virchow als Prähistoriker*, 2 vols. (Köln and Wien 1976). I have been unable to obtain Ernst Meyer, "Virchows Anteil an Schliemanns Werk," *Nachr. der Giess. Hochschulgesellschaft* 24 (1955) 150–64.

54. Bauer (supra n. 53) 14.

55. See Ulrich von Wilamowitz-Moellendorff, *Erinnerungen 1848–1914*² (Leipzig 1929) 302.

56. Meyer, *Schliemann*, 26.

57. We have only hagiography: see Peter Goessler, *Wilhelm Dörpfeld: Ein Leben im Dienst der Antike* (Stuttgart 1951) with the review of A. von Gerkan, *Gnomon* 24 (1952) 166–68.

58. See Goessler (supra n. 57) 69: "Dörpfeld Schliemanns schönster Fund"; cf. Andreas Rumpf, *Archäologie I: Einleitung Historischer Überblick* (Berlin 1953) 95, who does not know the source.

59. For details see *Philologus* 124 (1980) 148–49.

60. Goessler (supra n. 57) 65. One recalls Sophia's silence on certain matters.

61. Döhl (supra n. 2) 61.

62. *GRBS* 13 (1972) 349–50.

63. See my "Research Opportunities in the Modern History of Classical Scholarship," *CW* 74 (1980–1981) 241–51 = *Antiqua* 27 (1984) 3–13.

64. See my remarks at *CW* 75 (1981–1982) 362–66 and Udo Kultermann, *Geschichte der Kunstgeschichte: Der Weg einer Wissenschaft* (Frankfurt, Berlin, and Wien 1981).

65. See Chapter 2 and Traill, "Further Evidence of Fraudulent Reporting in Schliemann's Archaeological Works," *Boreas* 7 (1984) 295–316.

66. See Schliemann, *Mykenae: Bericht über meine Forschungen und Entdeckungen in Mykenae und Tiryns* (Leipzig 1878; repr. Darmstadt 1969) 185–86; Traill, *AJA* 87 (1983) 265; and, for the detailed argument, Traill, *Boreas* 7 (1984) 295–316.

67. Traill, *AJA* 86 (1982) 288, and "Schliemann's 'Discovery' of 'Priam's Treasure,' " *Antiquity* 57 (1983) 181–86. D.F. Easton, "Schliemann's Mendacity—a False Trail?" *Antiquity* 58 (1984) 197–204, in an attempt to refute Traill's charges if anything provides further evidence for Schliemann's mendacity. For the full-scale attack on the Treasure of Priam see now David A. Traill, "Schliemann's 'Discovery' of 'Priam's Treasure': A Re-examination of the Evidence," *JHS* 104 (1984) 96–115.

68. George S. Korres, "Inscriptions en la possession de Henri Schliemann," *Athena* 75 (1974–1975) 54–67, 492 (French résumé).

69. This is no straw man: see Roland Hampe, *Gnomon* 35 (1963) 417: "Das Urteil, er [Schliemann] habe für die Kunst keinen Sinn gehabt, ist nicht aufrecht zu erhalten. Dies zeigt unter anderem eindringlich sein Verhältnis zu dem von ihm in Alexandrien ausgegrabenen Frauenkopf." ["The opinion that Schliemann had no feeling for art is not tenable. This is clear from his relation to the female head excavated by him in Alexandria."]

70. See Chapter 3.

71. J.M. Cook, *CR* n.s. 20 (1970) 391.

72. For Curtius' view see *Memoirs of Prince von Bülow* IV: *Early Years and Diplomatic Service 1849–1897,* trans. Geoffrey Dunlop and F.A. Voigt (Boston 1932) 429. For Furtwängler's letter, see Adolf Greifenhagen, *Adolf Furtwängler: Briefe aus dem Bonner Privatdozentenjahr 1879/80 und der Zeit seiner Tätigkeit an den Berliner Museen 1880–1894* (Stuttgart, Berlin, Cologne, and Mainz 1965) 77, 88.

73. See my "Wilamowitz on Schliemann," *Philologus* 124 (1980) 149 = *Studies in the Modern History of Classical Scholarship, Antiqua* 27 (1984) 229–34.

74. See E. Meyer, "Schliemann's Letters to Max Müller in Oxford," *JHS* 82 (1962) 75–105; for citations see *The Life and Letters of the Right Honourable Friedrich Max Müller,* edited by his wife, I (New York, London, and Bombay 1902) 474.

75. See Tyler Whittle, *The Last Kaiser: A Biography of Wilhelm II, German Emperor and King of Prussia* (New York 1977) 46: "Schliemann fascinated William." For the English opinions see A.H. Sayce, *Reminiscences*

(London 1923) 150, 166–67, 181, 218–20, 275–76, and Flinders Petrie, *Seventy Years in Archaeology* (New York 1932; repr. New York 1969) 89 (for a description of a meeting with Schliemann, Virchow, and Schweinfurth). Tennyson dined with Schliemann on 28 March 1877: see *Alfred Lord Tennyson: A Memoir by His Son* II (New York and London 1897; repr. New York 1969) 217–18. The irony of the Tennysons is unmistakable.

76. *Briefwechsel* I, 287 (No. 268).

77. *Briefwechsel* II, 36 (No. 8).

78. *Briefwechsel* II, 416 n. 29.

79. Cited by L. and G. Poole (supra n. 5) 223. Meyer's ignoring of this letter is a further example of his tendentious editing. He wished, of course, to include the letter that proved his hero had dined with royalty. I drew brief attention to this matter at *GRBS* 13 (1972) 349 n. 71 = *Antiqua* 27 (1984) 103 n. 71.

80. Lewis R. Farnell, *An Oxonian Looks Back* (London 1934) 183. Farnell erred in calling Schliemann's daughter, Andromache, Nausikaa.

81. Niederland (supra n. 50) 369–96; "Das Schöpferische im Lebenwerk Heinrich Schliemanns im Lichte psychoanalyticher Forschung," *Carolinum* 32 (1966–1967) 9–16; and "Heinrich Schliemann: Leben und Werk in tiefen-psychologischer Sicht," *Carolinum* 37 (1971) 34–41. I provide only the briefest summary of his argument.

82. Konrad Zimmermann, "Heinrich Schliemann—ein Leben zwischen Traum und Wirklichkeit," *Klio* 64 (1982) 521. Zimmermann's article (513–32) is a conservative and conscientious review of recent work with a valuable bibliography.

83. Patricia Meyer Spacks, *Imagining a Self: Autobiography and Novel in Eighteenth-Century England* (Cambridge and London 1976) 18, cf 318 n. 25. I owe this reference to Professor Marshall J. Brown.

84. M.I. Finley, "Schliemann's Troy—One Hundred Years After," *ProcBritAc* 60 (1974) 403 n. 1 = *The World of Odysseus*[2] (Harmondsworth 1979) 167 n.

85. Åke Åkerström, "Mycenaean Problems," *Opuscula Atheniensia* 12.3 (Stockholm 1978) 44. It is untrue (42) that "Schliemann kept diaries throughout his active life." He kept diaries only when traveling or when excavating. I owe this reference to Traill.

86. I do not refer to *biographical* publications about Schliemann. Such articles are not submitted by editors to Bronze Age archaeologists for refereeing.

87. Machteld J. Mellink, *AJA* 86 (1982) 561. That Mellink includes Donald F. Easton in the vendetta against Schliemann can only mean that she has not read his work. He defends Schliemann against Traill: see especially his vigorous letter in the *Manchester Guardian* of 8 February 1982 and his remarks in *Antiquity* 58 (1984) 197–204. See further Mellink, *AJA* 89 (1985) 553.

88. *EAZ* 21 (1980) 655–58.

89. See Hugh Trevor-Roper, *Hermit of Peking: The Hidden Life of Sir Edmund Backhouse* (New York 1977). Backhouse's fictitious memoirs are

often influenced by contemporary romantic novelists (256, 264). They are "constructed within a historical framework which has been carefully studied, and they are illustrated by an elaborate and historically plausible apparatus of circumstantial detail" (260). This is precisely Schliemann's technique. For Wolfgang Helbig see Margherita Guarducci, "La Cosiddetta Fibula Prenestina: Antiquari, Eruditi, e Falsari nella Roma dell'Ottocento," *Atti della Accademia nazionale dei Lincei,* Ser. 8, vol. 24, fasc. 4 (Rome 1980) 486–509, with the important review by Arthur E. Gordon, *CJ* 78 (1982–1983) 64–70. For an attempt by a distinguished legal scholar to defend Helbig see Franz Wieacker, "Die Manios-Inschrift von Präneste: Zu einer exemplarischen Kontroverse," *Nachrichten der Akademie der Wissenschaften in Göttingen I. Philologisch-historische Klasse* (1984) No. 9. For Casement, see B.L. Reid, *The Lives of Roger Casement* (New Haven and London 1976). Trevor-Roper, 267 n. 2, accepts the view of Jeffrey Meyers that much of the "Black Diaries" is sheer fantasy. For comparative memoirs see Karl May, *Mein Leben und Streben,* ed. with commentary by Hainer Paul (Hildesheim/New York 1982); Richard Wagner, *Mein Leben,* ed. Martin Gregor-Dellin (Munich 1983) esp. 771ff.; and Otto von Bismarck, *Gedanken und Erinnerungen* (Munich 1982). For *Peer Gynt* see *GRBS* 13 (1972) 352–53 and Schindler, *Philologus* 120 (1976) 281–82.

Schliemann's Acquisition of the Helios Metope and His Psychopathic Tendencies

David A. Traill

WHAT IS NOW KNOWN

AS HAS BEEN AMPLY DEMONSTRATED by W.M. Calder III and others, Schliemann's autobiographical writings are filled with fictitious episodes, distortions, and what most of us would regard as lies.[1] His archaeological works, however, while colored by hasty judgment and naive romanticism, are generally held to be free from deliberate falsification. Thus, when H. Döhl writes in his recent, stimulating book that "Schliemanns wissenschaftliche Berichte sind wörtlich zu nehmen" ["Schliemann's scholarly reports should be taken literally"], he merely reflects the opinion prevailing among archaeologists today.[2] Yet, as early as 1969 E. Meyer pointed out that in *Trojanische Altherthümer* many of Schliemann's references to Sophia as present at Troy, assisting him, were last-minute additions to the manuscript, which are belied by his own correspondence.[3] More recently, G. Korres has shown, in an important article, that Schliemann "contre toute conscience scientifique" claimed to have excavated in the garden of his house in Athens a number of inscriptions which he had in fact acquired from existing private collections.[4] Thus it can no longer be argued that Schliemann's scholarly writings are free from misrepresentation and deceit. It remains to determine the extent of the damage. The unreliability of Schliemann's testimony in archaeological matters has been the theme of some of my own recent studies of the 1868, 1873, and 1876 diaries. The claims in his published works which initially aroused my suspicion are: 1) that Schliemann conducted three days of excavations at Bunar-bashi in 1868 after his survey work had convinced him that it could not be the site of Troy; 2) that Schliemann, witnessed only by his wife, discovered and excavated the Treasure of Priam towards the end of his 1871–1873 campaign at Troy; and 3) that in 1876 Schliemann discovered two figurines, now known to be of LH III B date, in Shaft Grave I at Mycenae.

Knowing Schliemann's proclivities, I suspected that he was not telling the unvarnished truth in these particular instances. The methodology I used in each case was the same: I carefully sifted through the primary evidence of Schliemann's diaries and letters in an attempt to find out whether the claims in his published works were confirmed or refuted by the appropriate diary entries or his contemporary correspondence. The results were both predictable and surprising. It was no surprise to find Schliemann displaying the same disregard for truth in the archaeological sphere as he did in his other writings. On the other hand, it was surprising to find that an incident as famous in the history of archaeology as the discovery of the Treasure of Priam should, on closer examination, turn out to be a mere figment of Schliemann's fertile imagination. Summaries of these studies follow. Those seeking the argumentation and documentation are referred to the articles themselves.[5]

1. Comparison of *Ithaque, le Péloponnèse et Troie* with the diary which Schliemann kept of his 1868 trip to Greece and Turkey reveals that the published work describes a trip that differs substantially from that recorded in his diary. The following findings are among the most significant: a) Schliemann went to the Troad convinced, like most travelers before him, that Bunarbashi was the site of Troy. His claim that his excavations at Bunarbashi were carried out "á la poursuite du but désintéressé d'extirper le dogme absurde et erroné que Troie a été située sur les hauteurs de Bounarbaschi" is quite untrue.[6] b) He visited Hissarlik and other sites in the Troad before he excavated at Bunarba-shi, not after, as he reports in *Ithaque*. He clearly did not recognize Hissarlik as Troy on his first visit there, as he claims in *Ithaque*. c) His archaeological work (survey and excavations) at Bunarbashi lasted for one and a half days and not for four days and an evening, as he reports in *Ithaque*. d) He was assisted by one workman for half a day and by two workmen for one day and not, as reported in *Ithaque*, by five workmen for three days. e) Though a letter to his father dated 12

August 1868 (*Briefwechsel* II, 31) and a diary entry dated 14 August would appear to date Schliemann's conversion to Hissarlik to 12 August, when his excavations at Bunarbashi had proved disappointing, there are grounds for believing that both the letter and the diary entry were written after Schliemann's meeting with Frank Calvert at the Dardanelles on 15 August and that Schliemann never seriously considered Hissarlik before this encounter. Schliemann's claim in 1875 that he had determined that Hissarlik was the site of Troy years before he went to the Troad in 1868 is quite untrue.

In *Ithaque* Schliemann seems to have altered the facts of his visit in 1868 to cast himself in the role of the perceptive, conscientious, and well-informed scholar. It should be remembered that Schliemann submitted *Ithaque* to the University of Rostock for his doctorate.[7] It would not have done to record his failure to recognize Hissarlik as the site of Troy on the occasion of his visit there. On the other hand, he could hardly report that he recognized Hissarlik as Troy on that occasion and then spent the next two days excavating at Bunarbashi. Accordingly, in *Ithaque* his visit to Hissarlik is postponed until after his excavations at Bunarbashi. His desultory and unsuccessful quest for Troy on the slopes of that hill becomes transformed in *Ithaque* into a diligent search for negative evidence, for Schliemann claims that before he excavated, he had already determined from the number and temperature of the springs, from the impossibility of running around the site, and from other evidence that Bunarbashi could not be the site of Troy. There is no mention in the diary of Schliemann's examination of the springs or of his attempt to run around the hill. These arguments against Bunarbashi, which are presented in *Ithaque* as vivid personal experiences, probably derive from his conversations with Calvert on 15 August or from his subsequent study in Paris. The same can be said of the learned arguments adduced in *Ithaque* in favor of Hissarlik and against Bunarbashi, for no trace of them is to be found in the diary. The few signs in the diary of any familarity with the debate over the site of Troy can be attributed to his conversation with the architect Ernst Ziller, whom he records having met in Athens on 25 July 1868 shortly before his departure for the Troad. Ziller had assisted Johann G. von Hahn in 1864 in his excavations on the Balli Dağ, a lofty ridge on the mountain south of Bunarbashi, on which the acropolis of Troy was generally thought to be situated. It may well be that Schliemann's interest in finding the site of Troy dates from this meeting. I am not aware of any earlier evidence documenting this interest. Schliemann's claim in *Ilios* to have dreamed of excavating Troy from his earliest childhood has now been thoroughly discredited.[8]

2. Schliemann's discovery of the Treasure of Priam at the end of May 1873 is familiar to most classicists and archaeologists from his description in *Troy and Its Remains.*[9] Less familiar are the earlier 31 May accounts in his diary and in a letter to his publisher, Brockhaus, the 17 June diary version, and the testimony of his most trusted workman Nicolaos Yannakis. Comparison of this evidence with the text and plans of *Troy and Its Remains* and with other entries in Schliemann's own diary and correspondence points to the following conclusions: a) Though she is cited in the published version as the sole witness of the discovery, Sophia was not present when the discovery allegedly took place. She left Troy on 7 May 1873 and did not return before the excavations closed in mid-June. b) Schliemann's earliest plans indicate, and Yannakis's testimony confirms, that the treasure Schliemann identified as Priam's was found outside the wall and not on the wall, as Schliemann reports in *Troy and Its Remains,* or inside "Priam's Palace," as he claims in his earliest reports. c) The treasure was apparently found in a tomb. Yannakis flatly contradicted Schliemann's statement that the treasure showed signs of having been compacted into a chest, maintaining "that it was contained in a little place built over with stones and having flat stones to cover it."[10] d) Some part of the treasure appears to have been discovered on 31 May. e) Schliemann appears to have supplemented the 31 May discovery with earlier, undisclosed finds in order to fabricate one strikingly large treasure which he could pass off as Priam's. f) Among these earlier finds were the thirty-seven copper weapons and all the gold pieces, including the jewelry, which is not mentioned in his earliest accounts and was only added as an afterthought to the 17 June diary entry, and the gold sauceboat, which is quite inaccurately described in the earliest accounts. g) The compatibility of all the finds in Priam's treasure with Early Bronze Age Troy appears to rule out the possibility that some of the pieces were purchased.

3. The two figurines which Schliemann claims to have found at Mycenae in Shaft Grave I have been firmly dated to LH III B by Arne Furumark. Mylonas's suggestion that they may have worked their way down into the LH I tomb through an opening in the cave between Graves I and IV is unconvincing. It seems more likely that Schliemann

simply reported finding in the tomb pieces which he had in fact found elsewhere. There is clear evidence in the 1876 diary that pottery fragments, which in *Mycenae* Schliemann reports having found in Shaft Grave I (i.e., Schliemann's Shaft Grave II), were in fact found elsewhere in the grave circle. Schliemann wanted to find these fragments in the shaft graves because he considered them analogous to pottery from Troy II, the level he considered Homeric. Obviously, if the shaft graves were to be the tombs of Agamemnon, Cassandra, etc., they would have to be contemporary with the Homeric level of Troy. Schliemann very probably added the figurines to Shaft Grave I for a similar reason. Just as he had found at Troy idols which he identified with Athena Glaucôpis, so at Mycenae he wanted to find idols of Hera Boôpis. Unfortunately, he was not finding the idols at early enough levels. The addition of the two figurines to Shaft Grave I appears to have been his solution to the problem.

Among the many questions which these studies raise, the one that is perhaps the most fundamental is, "What kind of individual would behave in this manner?" Certainly not the Schliemann of the biographies. Nor is this the Schliemann of Carl Blegen, A.J.B. Wace, and G. Mylonas. Piety has stultified the prevailing view of his achievements. Clearly, Schliemann's life needs to be critically reexamined. The following excerpted correspondence reveals facets of his character about which the biographers have little or nothing to say but which are of fundamental importance for our understanding of the man and his work.[11] The personality that emerges from this correspondence fits well with the behavior outlined above. The subject matter is Schliemann's protracted negotiations with Calvert over the Helios metope. The letters published by E. Meyer on this topic give little idea of the real nature of these negotiations, presumably because they reveal Schliemann in an unsympathetic light.[12] The correspondence on the Helios metope is followed by an attempt to account for Schliemann's extraordinary behavior in this and similar episodes.

THE HELIOS METOPE

Early in June 1872 Schliemann started excavating on the eastern segment of Hissarlik. The owner of this part of the mound was Frank Calvert.[13] Calvert was the most distinguished of a family of British expatriates that was prominent in the Dardanelles and the Troad throughout the nineteenth century. Besides varied commercial interests, he had a good knowledge of geology and paleontology. He acted as host and cicerone for large numbers of European visitors to the Troad. He had an unrivaled knowledge of the sites and monuments of the region. He excavated Hanay Tepe (1856 and 1878–1879) and numerous tombs and built up a fine collection of antiquities. After excavating the "Tumulus of Priam" on the Balli Dağ (1863) and reading Charles Maclaren's *A Dissertation on the Topography of the Plain of Troy* (Edinburgh 1822), he decided that Hissarlik must be the site of Troy. He purchased part of the mound and started to excavate in 1865, but lack of funds and the pressure of other commitments caused him to abandon the task, though he had uncovered the Hellenistic temple of Athena and pottery dating back to the archaic period.

After Schliemann's unsuccessful diggings at Bunarbashi in 1868, Calvert persuaded him, as previously noted, that Hissarlik, not Bunarbashi, was the true site of Troy. Schliemann later downplayed both the significance of Calvert's excavations and his role in awakening Schliemann's interest in Hissarlik and successfully appropriated all the glory for himself. Calvert, however, was much the better scholar. His perspicacity and objective approach are evident in all his writings. His article, "Excavations in the Troad," in the *Levant Herald* of 4 February 1873, in which he reviewed Schliemann's excavations at Hissarlik, deserves particular mention. He pointed out that while the site was clearly occupied from a very early date, evidence of occupation for the period 1800–700 B.C.,was wanting. To appreciate the full significance of this observation it should be recalled that Troy VI and VII levels (1800–1100 B.C., according to Blegen) were not discovered till much later and that no sign of occupation for the period 1100–700 has been found to this day. Thus Calvert's dating of the remains at Hissarlik anticipated the main lines of Dörpfeld's chronology by some twenty years. Calvert's achievement is all the more remarkable in that he reached his conclusions before the excavation of Mycenae and the discovery of Mycenaean material at Troy made the task much simpler.

Schliemann had agreed to share with Calvert half the finds made in his field. On 13 June he hit upon the finest piece of sculptured marble ever found at Troy—the Helios metope, now in the Pergamon Museum in Berlin.[14] Since the piece was unique, it posed a special problem. It obviously could not be divided between Schliemann and Calvert. Either the piece had to be sold to a third party or Schliemann or Calvert had to purchase the other's half interest. Initially, however, the problems were of a more academic nature. On 18 June Schliemann wrote to Calvert: "I cannot think that the sculpture represents Eos, for it is a man's face in female attire; of the Char nothing is visible; in fact there is none. Besides Eos cannot have the Sun on her head." In his letter of 29 June, however, Schliemann suggests sawing up the piece to facilitate its transportation: "I would by all means advise to saw off from the marble of the Sungod a long piece to the right and left, so that on either side only one column remains, for it can lose *nothing* by that operation and it will gain that much that it can thus be loaded on one cart and transported to your house. If there is a man at the Dardanelles capable of sawing marbles pray send him here at once." On 3 July Calvert wrote asking Schliemann to lay the marble on its face. Schliemann's letter of 4 July, which is published by Meyer (*Briefe,* 120f.), indicates that he complied but that he still wanted to saw off the end pieces of the marble. Calvert responded the next day, urging him not to do this, as it would destroy the object's value as a work of art.

About 8 or 9 July Schliemann must have offered to buy Calvert's half interest in the marble, for on 10 July Calvert writes that "you ask me what I would take for my half of the sculptured marble. It is rather difficult for me to say, not knowing its value—and I must ascertain something about it, before giving a definite reply." In his letter of 13 July, part of which is published at *Briefe,* 121f., Schliemann again asks Calvert to quote a figure for his share in the marble:

> Could you not ascertain now at once the value of the marble and tell me whether and for how much you would let me have your half, for, if I take it I must needs forward it whilst I am still here and write for a marble sawyer to Athens, for I would reduce the weight to one half otherwise the piece cannot be transported by any vehicle I ever saw in this country. Or do you think it more advisable to build a tremendous cart which would carry the block as it is to the Dardanelles and ship it to London leaving it at the discretion of Mr. Newton[15] of the British Museum to fix himself the price he would give for it? If you think this wise I consent to it at once.

The proposal to have Newton evaluate the piece in London is disingenuous. As Schliemann well knew, Calvert considered the British

Museum to make unreasonably low evaluations.[16] Calvert responded on 16 July:

> For the marble slab or sculpture, I have talked over the matter with my brother Frederick. As to Newton, he is renowned as being one of the greatest screws—and always offers a tenth of the real price of a thing and then will ask for something to be deducted, or other object to be thrown into the bargain. We think £500 would be given by an amateur for this beautiful marble. And we do not take our standard from what you write in the newspaper respecting it, but on its own merits. You will have expenses to move it, say £20, to London—therefore £480 would be its value here or £240 for my share; however if you give me £125 stg. I shall let you have it—that is for my part of the same.

Calvert sent a second letter later that day: "Perhaps you may think the price of £125 I put on the marble for my share as too much. I assure you it is under the mark. However, let us hope, if you do not accept it, that another marble may turn up, and thus solve the matter." Schliemann responded on 18 July by offering Calvert less than a third of his asking price:

> I assure it by God and on my honor, the sculptured marble is not worth more than frs. 2000 and thus 1000 frs. for your share and that this is even the highest figure. I told it immediately to Mrs. Schliemann when it was brought to light. I assure you on my honor of my firm belief that *no* man will ever offer you even this. If you accept it, then please take £40 from the group you are going to get for me from Constantinople. . . . I assure you I would never make the offer of £40 for the marble had I *not* found it myself.

Calvert's answer of 19 July noted that "You have very different ideas of the value of this marble to what I entertain. I think the *lowest* offer you ought to have made is not less than *£50* at which price I shall alone be disposed to accept. If this suits you make your arrangements accordingly."

Astute businessman that he was, Schliemann then rejoined on 21 July: "I cannot give you a penny more than £40 for the marble, but I will pay you £50 FOB the french steamer of 27/8 August, that is to say, you transport the block, *so as it is,* at your expense, to the steamer in the Dardanelles." A considerable number of letters were then exchanged between Schliemann and the Calverts as to the logistics of transporting the massive block. It was finally loaded on the Greek ship

Taxiarches five kilometers north of Hissarlik. Later a hitch developed. Schliemann wrote to Calvert on 3 August, "I hasten to inform you that the Koumkale authorities having got notice of the vessel having taken in the marble refuse to give her her pass and have today telegraphed twice to the Pasha at the Dardanelles for orders what they have to do. For heaven's sake settle the matter forthwith through the medium of Mr. Dokos[17] and Mr. Didymos the Pasha's secretary."

Evidently, Calvert's intervention was successful, for on 6 August Schliemann writes: "Many thanks for your two kind letters. Nicolas will have telegraphed to you that the vessel with the marble is off and all right. Of the fifty pounds I owe you for your part Nicolaos has disposed of one pound saying that he had your authority to do so and thus I hold the remaining 49 at your disposal." The piece was safely conveyed to Athens, where Schliemann had it set up in the garden of his house.

One might have thought that this was the end of this transaction, but the issue came up again the following year. First, however, there were similar negotiations over three inscriptions, which Schliemann found in March 1873 on Calvert's property among the ruins of the Temple of Athena. On 18 March he writes to Calvert:

> The Greek vessel has come in which took last year the Apollo and she is anchoring near Karanlik. I want to ship by her what trifles I have got *before* she proceeds to the Dardanelles and if possible tomorrow night, for on her return from the Dardanelles she will be closely watched by the authorities. I also want to ship by her the inscriptions if you agree to let me have your share of them at a small price. You know that an inscription once published has *no* value whatever and has only an interest to him who found it. If you offer the inscriptions to Mr. Newton he would *certainly* not give you 50 franks for them, but I pay you one hundred franks for your share in them. But please give me your answer at once for there is no time to be lost; the vessel wants to proceed to the Dardanelles. I have offered you a big price such as nobody else would offer.

Calvert notes in his reply of 19 March that "As regards the inscriptions, the price you offer instead of being a big price, is on the contrary, a very low one. I am not a rich man, yet I will willingly give you 150 francs for your half share, for one of the inscriptions is historical and valuable and the others are always worth money. If you added another 0 to the 100 francs you offered, I would have accepted it." Schliemann's letter of 20 March is largely devoted to proving that the inscriptions are of no historical value:

You have not accepted my fair offer for the inscriptions (for only those you saw, *no* fresh one having turned up) because you think one of them to be historical. You remember that I thought so myself at first, for I thought that the inscription in honor of Caius Caesar would prove his visit to Ilium. But I now see he has been governor of Asia of which I was not aware. . . .[18] You see by this that this inscription is neither historical nor has any historical interest. The other inscription, which is half-broken, records the fine to which several unknown persons have been put.[19] The long inscription merely records the donations of lands made by king Antiochus to a certain Aristodikides (a person whose name never occurred in history and is *not* met with in the Corpus inscriptionum graecarum) leaving it at his option to give these lands either to Ilium or to Skepsis. . . .[20] No more mention is made of Skepsis in the inscription and since it merely records donations of land it is of course of no historical value whatever. The other inscription on the immense block of marble is merely to praise a treasurer whose name has never occurred yet and therefore neither this inscription has the slightest historical value. . . . I make you the proposal to avail ourselves at all events of the vessel now at Koumkale to send off the inscriptions by way of Syra to my old friend Messrs. J. Henry Schroder and Co. in London, begging them to sell them as they best can either to the british museum or otherwise. If you like we can limit £40 or more; you will then see what is offered. But I entertain great doubts that one hundred franks may be offered for them and freight to and charges in London are heavy.

You offered me 150 fr. for my share when you still thought the one inscription was historical; to settle the question I will give this amount for your share even now when it is certain that none of the inscriptions has any historical interest. But this is the very outside figure I can afford to give.

Calvert was about to leave for Constantinople and wanted the matter settled quickly. He replied on 21 March: "I accept your offer for the marble fcs 150 but think it very little, but as I cannot discuss the matter, I prefer to settle it at once." The three inscriptions are described at *Troy and Its Remains,* 231f. and 240–47. Schliemann begins his discussion of the long inscription concerning Antiochus as follows (italics added): "This inscription, *the great historical value of which cannot be denied,* seems certainly to belong to the third century B.C."

In Constantinople Calvert learned some disturbing news. He wrote to Schliemann on 7 April:

At the capital, I made the acquaintance of many antiquarian and professional people. Amongst others, some who have seen the bas relief found in my field, I mean that representing Apollo, now in your collection at Athens. They informed me the value you fixed on it was francs 150,000 but that was too high a figure, as francs 25,000 to 30,000 was its market value. This latter estimate however is 10 to 12 times the amount you *swore* to me was the value, and I cannot believe you could have been aware at the time of its great worth.

Schliemann's reply is not preserved. On 14 April Calvert wrote again:

Having consulted with my friends regarding the differences existing between us on the subject of the Apollo bas-relief found by you in my field at Hissarlik last year, they are of opinion that you are in no ways *morally* released to give me half the value of this marble—the assertion on your oath as per letter of 18th July last being sufficient between gentlemen to decide the value of an object, notwithstanding previous ideas on the subject entertained on either side—the marble being worth some 10 to 12 times greater than that sworn by you points clearly to the fact that you are not morally released, and I trust on considering the matter you will see it in its proper light—and consent to a valuation to be made by competent persons—for otherwise you leave yourself open to the accusation that you have taken undue advantage of me and I would be sorry to be obliged by my friends to publish your letters and show how you obtained the bas relief in question for £49 stg. With kind regards to Mrs. Schliemann and yourself.

Schliemann's reply is dated 17 April. In it he reviews the various steps in the transaction, concluding: "Vous avez rejeté mon offre d'envoyer le bloc à Londres et vous m'avez demandé £50 pour votre moitié en ajoutant que vous ne prendriez pas un sou de moins. Je vous ai payé cette somme mais, par Dieu, j'ai cru que je payais beaucoup trop."[21] We may note in passing that in his attempts later in 1873 to sell his Trojan collection to the Louvre, Schliemann valued the Helios metope at 100,000 francs (£4000).[22] The most revealing section of the letter of 17 April is published in *Briefwechsel* I, 227, where Schliemann holds to the position that there is no going back on a bargain once it has been struck: "L'affaire faite est *sacrée;* on n'y revient plus et l'on n'y peut plus, tel est l'usage du monde." Schliemann then holds out the hope that the companion or "brother" metope may be found. Towards the end he adds: "Voulez-vous, oui ou non, que si je découvre le frère, il soit envoyé pour notre compte commun à Londres ou à Paris pour y être vendu aux enchères après avoir été mis en vente dans les journaux? Si vous y consentez, veuillez m'informer de suite, car autrement je ne remettrai plus la pioche dans votre champ."[23]

Calvert's reply is also dated 17 April:[24]

You are mistaken, I think, in making the affair of the marble, a *commercial* transaction, for it is not one, the basis of our agreement being founded on mutual confidence as gentlemen. We both mistook the worth of the relic, in undervaluing it, I, in estimating it at £450, and you at £80, but when you gave me your word of honour, that it was not worth more than the latter sum, as a gentleman, I accepted your statement, and closed for £50 (£40 for the marble and £10 for the damage done to the field)—or rather £49, which was the sum I received. On finding out your error, it was for you to have come forward, and made up the difference to me, whether you had paid me £225, £50, £40 or any other amount—that is, the half of its *real* value (less expenses of transport).

I did not consider London the best place for disposing of this marble, which was the reason of my refusal. This, however does not in any way bear on the question, nor your idea of its being confiscated by the Turkish Govt., which could not be done, antiquities discovereed on private property, appertaining by law, to the proprietor—nor whether you leave either the whole of your antiquities and fortune, or not a lepta, to the Greek Govt.

I regret accordingly the misunderstanding which has arisen between us, and would suggest some method by which it may be removed. Suppose we each ask a friend to meet the other and discuss the matter—and abide by the decision (that is, if they agree) they may come to.

Schliemann responded to Calvert on 20 April:

Je m'empresse à répondre à votre estimée lettre du 17 inst., que, d'après les lois de tous les peuples et de tous les temps, un échange fait entre homme et homme et soldé en monnaie sonnante est consideré comme une transaction à jamais terminée sur laquelle il est impossible de revenir.

Quant aux excavations que je vous ai proposées à faire dans votre champ pour retrouver la contre-pièce de la métope d'Apollon, votre offre de tirer au sort est tout-à-fait inacceptable. Je ne vois pas d'autre alternatif que d'envoyer à Londres ou à Paris le résultat de mes fouilles en fait de marbres sculptés. Si vous y consentez veuillez m'en informer par Nicolas, car le temps presse. Les difficultés que vous prévoyez pour l'exportation des marbres ne semblent pas exister, car il n'y a que deux jours j'ai expédié trente immenses collis. Je crois vraiment que j'ai à présent plus de facilité pour l'exportation que jamais.[25]

Calvert's reply is also dated 20 April:

Your letter of this day has just been received. You are mistaken in considering a bargain cannot by law be rescinded under any circumstances—for there are several exceptions to this general rule, and which are applicable in the present instance—and moreover the sale of the Apollo marble was made to you on an assurance on your solemn oath and word of honour as a gentleman—and I therefore hold you both legally and morally responsible for the difference in value of the marble and of the amount paid to me by you.

I am sorry not to be able to come to any immediate decision as to the best mode of disposal of any future marbles that may be discovered—for I wish to consider the matter, as your mode of dealing, makes me take all due precaution.

This letter of Calvert's, with its implied threat of a lawsuit, led Schliemann to seek the assistance of the American consul at the Dardanelles, who was none other than Frank Calvert's brother James.[26] He complained that he was being threatened with a lawsuit. The opening of the letter, including the date, is illegible. However, from its position in the copybook it appears to have been written on 24 April. Schliemann writes (208):

de m'intenter un procès impossible au lieu de me prouver sa gratitude pour l'immense bien que j'ai fait à son champ. Mais veuillez bien m'informer par le porteur de la présente si vous consentez à le faire, car autrement je me vois forcé à recourir à mon ambassadeur à Constantinople pour qu'il me protège contre les tracasseries de Mr. Fr. Calvert. Veuillez lui dire, au lieu de perdre son temps inutilement en tracasseries odieuses qui ne peuvent que retomber sur lui-meme, de venir ici pour excaver ensemble avec 120 ouvriers et à mes ouvriers {sic; presumably for "frais"} son théâtre à la partie nord de son champ car je suis parfaitement sûr, non seulement d'y trouver le frère (la contre-pièce de l'Apollo) mais encore une masse d'autres statues et de consigner le tout, à notre risque commun, à Sir John Lubbock[27] pour qu'il en soigne la vente.[28]

Frank Calvert wrote to Schliemann 25 April:

Your letter to my brother James being addressed as U.S. Consul, I, as gérant in his absence, opened it—but finding it did not relate to official matters, will forward it to him at Constantinople on Sunday.

With regard to future excavations in my field, in the interest of science, I shall not in any way stop them on account of the misunderstanding between us. I accept your offer to send to England (that is, if possible to be got out of the country) such of the marbles discovered, that may be worth the expense of transport, to be sold there—but with the condition that you make all the necessary shipping and other expenses in England, such amounts to be deducted when value is realised. I do not think Sir John Lubbock as a banker, and with his multifarious occupations in the House of Commons, would consent to charge himself with our mutual interests. I place entire confidence in your friend Mr. Schröeder {sic} however, if you prefer him. Pray let me know if you accept these modifications.

I feel much hurt by the expressions you make use of in your letter to my brother—if I give you "tracasseries," you must remember that it is in upholding what I consider to be my right, and that I have done all in my power to assist you in your works, since your first arrived—and always sacrificed my time when your interests were concerned—if now, you consider you have no further need of me, it is very ungracious of you to use that word, in recompense for all that I have done for you. And remember *if it was not for me,* and the excavations made previously in my field (purchased *expressly* for that purpose) you would never have undertaken the work, and reaped the benefit of my experience.

Do not suppose that I shall write to you further, on the subject of the Apollo marble. I had hoped for an amicable agreement, but am disappointed. At the same time, for the sake of science, I assure you, I will not distract you in your work, nor bring an action against you before consulting a lawyer, and if he sees that justice is on my side, not until you have finished your labours, and returned to Athens—I would prefer infinitely to leave the affair to Mr. Boker's decision.[29]

I shall go to my brother's farm in a few days,[30] and pay you a visit from thence, when all your visitors have left—it is impossible for me to be long absent from here, to look after the excavations, but although our views differ as to the Apollo marble, I place this confidence in you, that, if I am present or not, at the excavations, the result will be the same.

With kind regards to Mrs. Schliemann and yourself.

P.S. I would write to you in French, were I a sufficient master of the language.

James Calvert answered Schliemann from Constantinople on 30 April: "I need scarcely say how much I regret that between you and my brother Frank, an unfortunate misunderstanding has arisen. I must, however, decline to interfere in a matter which is of a specially delicate nature as this is; besides which, even looking at the case in the light of an ordinary transaction, as you represent it, I could not but think you adopt an erroneous method for appraisements of objects distant from a market."

Schliemann replied to Frank Calvert's letter on 4 May:

En réponse à vos estimées lettres du 25 passé et d'hier j'ai l'honneur de vous dire que par suite de la première j'avais donné ordre de recommencer les fouilles sur le versant Nord de votre champ et dans votre théâtre, mais que Mme. Schliemann s'y est opposée, en disant que nous ne pouvons pas aborder cette entreprise gigantesque en vue du procès dont vous nous menacez à la fin de nos fouilles. Ayant mûrement réfléchi sur ce sujet je trouve qu'elle a parfaitement raison, car, seulement sur le versant Nord il y a à déblayer non pas 8500 comme j'avais cru mais bien 17000 metres cubes de débris et si, avec des peines inouies, je réussis à arracher des objets d'art du fond de ces ruines, je n'en aurais rien que des désagréments.

Je regrette beaucoup que vous n'êtes pas venu voir mes excavations car depuis votre dernière visite nous avons mis à jour des monuments qui sont du plus haut interêt pour la science et entre autres la Porte de Scées et j'ai aussi constaté des faits curieux quant à la topographie d'Ilion. Mme S. vous presénte tout à vous l'estime des hommages respectueux.[31]

The primary interest in this correspondence lies not so much in the documentary evidence for the transaction as in the light it throws on Schliemann's character. On 1 November 1868 Calvert had written to Schliemann: "I trust that you will not give up your intended excavation as it will afford me much pleasure and satisfaction in giving you all the assistance I can in carrying out your excavations at Ilium Novum." Throughout his three seasons of excavations (1871–1873), Schliemann took Calvert up on his generous offer, calling constantly on him for assistance in a wide variety of tasks, such as having more shovels sent, wheelbarrows repaired, or his mail picked up or dispatched. Calvert also helped him in his financial transactions and in his representations to the diplomatic corps at the Dardanelles and in Constantinople. In almost all of the letters from which the above excerpts are taken, Schliemann asks some favor of Calvert. Typically, he asks for two or three favors in one letter. Calvert appears to have performed these services willingly and gratis. Schliemann's treatment of his benefactor in the matter of the Helios metope points to a serious defect in his personality. His failure to recognize that his relationship with Calvert obligated him to treat him fairly, even generously, over the matter of the metope betrays a moral blindness. It has been suggested elsewhere that Schliemann's personality was tinged with psychopathy.[32] His behavior over the Helios metope provides striking evidence of this disorder.

WHY DID SCHLIEMANN BEHAVE AS HE DID?

In the *The Encyclopedia of Human Behavior* the psychopathic personality is described as follows:

62

The antisocial, or psychopathic, individual acts as if he has no conscience, no sense of responsibility, and no concern for the welfare of other people. He lives for the moment, fails to profit from experience, feels no genuine loyalty to any person, group, or code of behavior. He is clearly abnormal, yet he cannot be classified as neurotic, psychotic or mentally retarded.

This type of personality occupies a twilight zone between the ordinary individual and the hardened criminal. The category includes a varied assortment of unscrupulous businessmen, confidence men, shyster lawyers, quack doctors, crooked politicians, prostitutes, and imposters. They are rarely committed to mental institutions but sometimes serve jail sentences for their offenses. Most of them, however, manage to keep out of the hands of the law and talk their way out of conviction.[33]

In his classic study of the psychopath, *The Mask of Sanity,* H. Cleckley sets forth a list of symptoms, which forms the most widely recognized basis for diagnosing the type.[34] Not all of these traits are found in every case, but collectively they form a useful profile.

Superficial Charm and Good Intelligence

"More often than not, the typical psychopath will seem particularly agreeable and make a distinctively positive impression when he is first encountered. Alert and friendly in his attitude, he is easy to talk with and seems to have a good many interests. . . . Very often indications of good sense and sound reasoning will emerge, and one is likely to feel soon after meeting him that this normal and pleasant person is also one with high abilities."[35] Yet, the intelligence, though impressive, is often somewhat superficial. In the case history of Max, Cleckley observes: "Here was a man of exceptional acumen. His versatile devices of fraud . . . his shrewd practical reasoning in the many difficulties of his career demonstrate beyond question the quickness and accuracy of his practical thinking. His memory is unusually sound; his cleverness at manipulating bits of information so as to appear learned is exceptional. He is not a man to be taken in by the scheming of others, though he himself takes in many. One can truthfully say about him that he is 'bright as a dollar,' 'smart as a whip,' that 'his mind is like a steel trap.' "[36] Yet Cleckley was able to show that though Max professed to have studied philosophy and Shakespeare at Heidelberg and could bandy about the names of Kant, Schopenhauer, and several Greek philosophers and the titles of Shakespeare's plays, he knew nothing of these writers or their works.

Schliemann appears to have had no difficulty in making new acquaintances. He was outgoing, affable, and ready to talk on and listen to a wide variety of topics. His lively enthusiasm, which still exudes from his writings, gained him ardent supporters in his own day, among them Gladstone, Virchow, Max Müller and, at least initially, Frank Calvert, and has won him millions of admirers since.

No one would deny Schliemann's remarkable intelligence. He had an uncanny ability to absorb and manipulate information, particularly when it came to learning foreign languages. He quickly picked up a smattering of archaeology and eventually developed an impressive knowledge of the subject. Yet, as late as September 1876, we find him expressing surprise at coming across pottery in tombs.[37] Small wonder that most of the academic establishment initially had as little regard for his "discoveries" as Cleckley had for Max's knowledge of philosophy and Shakespeare. A more important shortcoming in Schliemann's case is his inability to form a synthesis of his work.[38] Even his most highly regarded work, *Ilios,* is often little more than a list of finds with explanatory comment. One misses too a sense of perspective, a realization of the continuum of which his work formed a part, even an interest in the lives of the people whose cities and artifacts he had unearthed. In the more synthetic and humane aspects of intelligence, Schliemann is sadly lacking. It is to these defects, I believe, Furtwängler was referring when he said of Schliemann: "he is and remains a half-crazy human being, who has no idea whatsoever of the meaning of his excavations."[39]

Absence of Delusions

Schliemann was preeminently a man of practical common sense. He did not suffer from delusions. He did not hear voices.[40]

Absence of Nervousness or Psychoneurotic Manifestations

This trait can hardly be determined from written records. His contemporaries, while testifying to his enthusiasm and cheerful disposition, say nothing about signs of nervousness or anxiety.

Unreliability

Cleckley points out that "at the crest of success in his work [the psychopath] may forge a small check, indulge in petty thievery, or simply not come to the office."[41] Like many psychopaths Schliemann seems to have performed reliably most of the time. However, there are indications that in 1852 his successful business relationship with the San Francisco banker B. Davidson came to an abrupt end because Schliemann's consignments of gold dust were of short weight.[42] This was by no means the only occasion in which Schliemann's business practices came under suspicion. In 1858 he was sued for fraud and for forging bills of exchange.[43] Given Schliemann's methods of acquiring his American citizenship and divorce in 1869, the charges seem plausible enough despite his acquittal. His treatment of Sophia discussed below also demonstrates his unreliability.

Untruthfulness and Insincerity

"The psychopath shows a remarkable disregard for truth," Cleckley notes further. "He gives the impression that he is incapable of ever attaining realistic comprehension of an attitude in other people that causes them to value truth and cherish truthfulness in themselves. . . . He will lie about any matter, under any circumstances, and often for no good reason. . . . After being caught in shameful and gross falsehoods, after repeatedly violating his most earnest pledges, he finds it easy, when another occasion arises, to speak of his word of *honor,* his *honor as a gentleman.*"[44] Schliemann's disregard for truth has by now been thoroughly documented.[45] Frank Calvert ends his article in the *Athenaeum* of 14 November 1874 with a bemused observation on Schliemann's failure to understand the value of the truth (644): "Dr. Schliemann has taken occasion to express surprise that, as proprietor of part of Hissarlik, I should, against my material interest, have published my doubts as to the age and origin of the antiquities discovered by him. He seems unable to understand that in a question of this kind no personal considerations whatsoever ought to have any weight, and that it is simply childish to hope that they can prevail against scientific truth."

The interviews with Presidents Johnson and Fillmore and the governor of Panama and the "eyewitness" account of the 1851 fire of San Francisco are examples of Schliemann's gratuitous lies.[46] The only motive appears to have been to build himself up by adding colorful incidents to his life. In 1878 the testimony of Yannakis, as revealed in W. Borlase's article, exposed Schliemann's false account of the discovery of the Treasure of Priam.[47] Yannakis pointed out that Sophia had been in Athens at the time of the discovery and that the "key" had been found about two hundred yards from the rest of the treasure. In his letter of 22 August 1878 to Max Müller Schliemann did not hesitate to swear "on the bones of my father" that the key had been found with the treasure and to insist that Sophia had been present and had never left him.[48] In his letter of 18 July 1872 to Frank Calvert, quoted above, we read Schliemann swearing "by God and on my honor" that the Helios metope was worth no more than 2,000 francs. Shortly afterwards, as we have seen, he was assuring others that it was worth 150,000 francs.

Lack of Remorse or Shame

When caught in his dishonest dealing over the metope, Schliemann shows no sign of remorse or even of comprehension that he has acted badly.

Inadequately Motivated Antisocial Behavior

"Not only is the psychopath undependable, but also in more active ways he cheats, deserts, annoys, brawls, fails and lies without any apparent compunction," explains Cleckley. "He will commit theft, forgery, adultery, fraud, and other deeds for astonishingly small stakes and under greater risks of being discovered than will the ordinary scoundrel."[49] An example of this type of behavior can be seen in Schliemann's repeated attempts to cheat Davidson even after his suspicions had been aroused, thereby endangering their profitable relationship.[50] Also, Schliemann's decision to cast Sophia as the sole witness to his discovery of Priam's treasure was particularly foolhardy, for her absence from Troy in late May and early June of 1873 must have been known not only to Yannakis, his other workmen, and the Calvert family but also to a good many others at the Dardanelles and in Athens.

Poor Judgment and Failure to Learn by Experience

According to Cleckley, "despite his excellent rational powers, the psychopath continues to show the most execrable judgment about what one might presume to be his ends."[51] Conforming to this description, Schliemann, while waiting in 1870 for permission to excavate from the Turkish authorities, proceeded to excavate at Hissarlik illegally. This needlessly complicated the business of obtaining the *firman* and enraged the proprietors from whom he hoped to purchase the western portion of the mound. He appears to have learned nothing from this experience, for, in 1874, while waiting for permission from the Greek authorities to excavate at Mycenae, he went to the site and illegally dug some thirty-four trial trenches.[52] He thereby once again infuriated the authorities whose permission he was seeking.

Pathologic Egocentricity and Incapacity for Love

"The psychopath is always distinguished by egocentricity. This is usually of a degree not seen in ordinary people and often is little short of astonishing." Schliemann's biographers have been struck by his egocentricity. E. Ludwig calls him "a complete egoist." R. Payne speaks of Schliemann's "ruthless egoism," and L. Deuel describes him as "extraordinarily . . . self-centered."[53]

Cleckley further describes the psychopath as "plainly capable of casual fondness, of likes and dislikes, and of reactions that, one might say, cause others to matter to him. These affective reactions are, however, always strictly limited in degree. In durability they also vary greatly from what is normal in mankind."[54] Schliemann perhaps comes closest to love in his relationship with his second wife, Sophia. True, he was often solicitous about her health and welfare, but his concern gives the impression of being self-centered—like a hermit's careful tending of the fire on a cold winter's night. For all his flowery protestations of affection he spent remarkably little time with Sophia. In his relationship with her he could sometimes be quite remiss and even callous. Consider his behavior during Sophia's second pregnancy from June 1877 to March 1878. He left her and their daughter, Andromache, alone in Paris without sufficient funds for their support. Even Lynn and Gray Poole, who go out of their way to romanticize and idealize the marriage, are forced by the evidence to observe "she could not count on him. He frequently went through Paris without stopping off to see Sophia and Andromache and sent money grudgingly and sporadically."[55] Schliemann promised faithfully to join her in Paris for Christmas 1877 but failed to do so. Sophia was left to endure her pregnancy in a foreign city without the support of her husband, though she repeatedly begged him to join her. Schliemann finally came to see her after the birth of Agamemnon in March 1878. Sophia's plaintive letters make it clear that such inconsiderate behavior was by no means exceptional.[56]

General Poverty in Major Affective Reactions

About this trait, Cleckley explains that

> the psychopath always shows general poverty of affect. Although it is true that he sometimes becomes excited and shouts as if in rage or seems to exult in enthusiasm and again weeps in what appear to be bitter tears or speaks eloquent and mournful words about his misfortunes or his follies, the conviction dawns on those who observe him carefully that here we deal with a readiness of expression rather than a strength of feeling. Vexation, spite, quick and labile flashes of quasi affection, peevish resentment, shallow moods of self-pity, puerile attitudes of vanity, and absurd and showy poses of indignation are all within his emotional scale and are freely sounded as the circumstances of life play upon him. But mature, wholehearted anger, true or consistent indignation, honest, solid grief, sustaining pride, deep joy, and genuine despair are reactions not likely to be found within this scale.[57]

A careful study of Schliemann's writings leads to the conclusion that the emotions expressed in them are always of the showy, shallow type indicated by Cleckley.[58] On the other hand, the death of his eleven-year-old daughter Natalie might reasonably be supposed to have been one of the most traumatic events in Schliemann's life. When he learned the news in December 1869, he wrote to his son that it "was God's punishment for your mother's misdeeds towards your father." Even Ernst Meyer, who finds little to fault in Schliemann, comments on the superficiality of this reaction.[59]

Cleckley also reports that psychopaths always lack a sense of humor: "Psychopaths are often witty and sometimes have a superficial impression of that far different and very serious thing, humor. Humor, however, in what may be its full, true sense, they never have."[60] Carl Schuchhardt recalled an incident at Troy in 1890 in which he was taken aback by Schliemann's lack of a sense of humor. A poem had been published in *Kladderadatsch* satirizing the dispute between Schliemann and Bötticher. A typical stanza ran:

> Hier sieht man stehn die Lithoi,
> Die Priamus einst gebaut,
> Und dort stehn die Pithoi
> Gefüllt mit Erbsen und Sauerkraut.

Schliemann read the poem and handed it back to one of Schuchhardt's companions with the simple observation: "Er nimmt also nicht Partei." Schuchhardt's comment reveals his astonishment at this reaction: "Der Humor der Verse hatte ihm gar keinen Eindruck gemacht."[61] In my own reading of thousands of Schliemann's letters and many of his diaries, I have encountered no sign of a sense of humor and only a few instances of a rather superficial form of wit, usually sarcastic.

Specific Loss of Insight

The psychopath "has absolutely no capacity to see himself as others see him," discloses Cleckley. "It is perhaps more accurate to say that he has no ability to know how others feel when they see him or to experience subjectively anything comparable about the situation. . . . Usually, instead of facing facts that would ordinarily lead to insight, he projects, blaming his troubles on others with the flimsiest of pretexts but with elaborate and subtle rationalization."[62] The Pooles related an incident which illustrates this defect in Schliemann. In the fall of 1877 Sophia complained that she was not receiving sufficient funds for Andromache and herself. She understandably

resented a letter in which Heinrich criticized her for not properly managing her affairs, and in answer wrote:

Dear Henry:
    Is it not enough that I remain here in poverty by your request? Do not complain that I cannot manage what I do not have. Were it not for friends like the Rallis, I could not make all things come together. They know you do not provide. So, it is your responsibility that all know.
                                                                Your wife (?)

That letter elicited from Heinrich the assurance, "All I do is for you alone. Do you think that I consider myself? Not for a moment." Unconvinced, Sophia pointed out how selfish he was, and wondered to him,

"How the human mind and soul can delude itself and find in every action a justification."[63]

Cleckley notes that the psychopath appears to assume that "the legal penalties for a crime he has committed do not or should not apply to him."[64] In this connection Schliemann's behavior after his illegal removal of Priam's treasure from Turkey is significant. Incredibly, within two weeks of his public revelation of his discovery of the treasure, Schliemann wrote a letter to the Turkish authorities asking permission to resume excavations at Troy.[65] Ludwig writes: "He was morally convinced that he owed the Turks nothing, for, as he wrote to Brockhaus, his publisher, 'all firmans always contain a clause that half must be given up, but Turkey has never yet received the smallest thing from any one, and it must be so now too, for if the Turks had got the treasure, they would have melted it down and not made 12,000 francs out of it, whereas in my hands, it is of incalculable value for scholarship.' "[66]

Unresponsiveness in General Interpersonal Relations

"The psychopath cannot be depended upon to show the ordinary responsiveness to special consideration or kindness or trust," remarks Cleckley. "No matter how well he is treated . . . he shows no consistent reaction of appreciation except superficial and transparent protestations." This trait is spectacularly illustrated by Schliemann's treatment of Frank Calvert over the Helios metope. Some may point to Schliemann's financial support of his father and other relatives and argue that Schliemann was generous and considerate. However, it needs to be recalled that Schliemann was an extremely wealthy man and that these remittances were no great sacrifice. Cleckley also observes: "In relatively small matters psychopaths sometimes behave so as to appear very considerate, responsive, and obliging. . . . The psychopath who causes his parents hardship and humiliation by repeatedly forging checks . . . may gain a considerable reputation in the community by occasionally volunteering to cut the grass for the frail old lady across the street."[67] The motivation behind the generous act is clearly what is important. Ludwig appears to me to catch the essence of it in Schliemann's case when he remarks: "Throughout his life Schliemann took pleasure in bestowing gifts liberally in the manner of the *grand*

70

seigneur."[68] A letter announcing a remittance to his father in 1855 is particularly revealing: "By today's post I have forwarded instructions for 500 Prussian thalers to be credited to your account, which sum I expect you to use in establishing yourself in the neighbourhood of Danzig in a manner befitting the father of Heinrich Schliemann."[69]

Fantastic and Uninviting Behavior

Cleckley writes that "a peculiar sort of vulgarity, domineering rudeness, petty bickering or buffoonish quasi maulings of wife, mistress, or children, and quick shifts between maudlin and vainglorious moods, although sometimes found in ordinary alcoholics with other serious patterns of disorder, are particularly typical of the psychopath and in him alone reach full and precocious flower."[70] Evidence for this behavior in Schliemann is scanty but nonetheless telling, J.M. Radowitz records that at a formal dinner given to celebrate the completion of Schliemann's house in March 1881, to which a number of foreign ambassadors and Greek dignitaries had been invited, "Schliemann got up and held a speech, in which he took each of the diplomats to task. He discussed the various countries they represented in an odd kind of French, spiced with even odder comments, which frequently, though most likely unintentionally, verged on insults and which produced varying degrees of embarrassment on the stunned faces of my colleagues. Schliemann, nevertheless, sat down fully satisfied with his performance."[71] It is significant that Radowitz does not attribute this peculiar behavior to the influence of alcohol, though it is likely that Schliemann had had at least one or two drinks. Cleckley observes: "Most of this asocial, unacceptable, and self-defeating behavior associated with the psychopath's drinking seems to occur without the benefit of extreme inebriation."[72]

Suicide Rarely Carried Out

Had Schliemann committed suicide this would have argued against the hypothesis that his personality was psychopathic, but he did not.

Sex Life Impersonal, Trivial, and Poorly Integrated

Cleckley's observations suggest that psychopaths generally have an underdeveloped sex drive and an unusually casual attitude to sex, which for them has none of the strong emotional concomitants experienced by most people.[73] Evidence on Schliemann's sex life is, not surprisingly, sparse and inconclusive. The disproportionate amount of time he spent away from each of his wives suggests that his sex drive was not particularly strong. Nothing in his writings indicates otherwise. He reports having been troubled with impotence.[74] Largely on the basis of Schliemann's own letters, his first wife has been regarded as frigid.[75] This seems a rash conclusion and may be quite erroneous. She may have had good cause for refusing sexual relations with her husband. She apparently considered him a "libertine."[76] The term suggests casual adultery on Schliemann's part.

Failure to Follow Any Life Plan

Cleckley states that "the psychopath shows a striking inability to follow any sort of life plan consistently, whether it be regarded as good or evil. He does not maintain an effort toward any far goal at all."[77] Of all the traits typical of the psychopath this seems the least applicable to Schliemann. For the last twenty years of his life he pursued a career in archaeology with stunning success.[78]

The foregoing attempt to compare Schliemann's behavior with the standard profile of a psychopath should not be misunderstood. Clearly, many of these traits are shared by perfectly normal people. It is the constellation of most or all of these traits in a single personality rather than the presence of any one or two that points to psychopathy. Thus I am certainly not suggesting that Schliemann was a psychopath because he indulged in sharp business practices and may have had an affair with a maid. Moreover, the above evidence, often tenuous and unsatisfactory, does not seem to me sufficient to prove that Schliemann was a psychopath. However, I do believe that Schliemann's extraordinary behavior needs some kind of explanation. The present study constitutes a modest contribution toward that goal. The evidence adduced suggests, I hope, that the hypothesis that Schliemann's character was tinged with psychopathy is a reasonable one. I trust that others more competent than myself in these matters will give Schliemann's personality a more detailed study. I conclude with the observations of Dr. Cleckley, written in a letter to me dated 25 January 1984:

Thank you for sending me several of your articles, including "Schliemann's 'discovery' of 'Priam's Treasure' " and "Schliemann's Acquisition of the Helios Metope and His Psychopathic Tendencies." While I feel one should hesitate to make psychiatric diagnoses or tentative estimates without personally examining patients, it is true that the psychopath's diagnosis does rely on the history of the patient's behavior over a long period of time and can not be made merely by direct examination. From your study of the diaries, facts, reactions of others clearly documented, it seems highly likely that he did indeed have many characteristics of the classic psychopath.[79]

NOTES

1. See especially Calder, "Schliemann on Schliemann: A Study in the Use of Sources," *GRBS* 13 (1972) 335–53; W. Schindler, "Heinrich Schliemann: Leben und Werk im Spiegel der neueren biographischen Forschungen," *Philologus* 120 (1976) 271–89; and D. Traill, "Schliemann's Mendacity: Fire and Fever in California," *CJ* 74 (1979) 348–55, and "Schliemann's American Citizenship and Divorce," *CJ* 77 (1982) 336–42.

2. H. Döhl, *Heinrich Schliemann: Mythos und Ärgernis* (Munich 1981) 7; see reviews by me at *Gnomon* 55 (1983) 149–52 and by D. Easton in *CR* (1983) 286f., where he remarks: "But he [Döhl] is right, I believe, to insist that there is no evidence of fraud in Schliemann's archaeology, whatever the situation in the rest of his writings." In two more recent articles, in *Antiquity* 58 (1984) 197–204 and *AnatSt* 34 (1984) 141–69, Easton now concedes that there are lies and misrepresentations of fact in Schliemann's archaeological publications.

3. Meyer, *Schliemann* 429 n. 148.

4. G. Korres, "Epigraphai ex Attikes eis Katochen Herrikou Sleman," *Athena* 75 (1974–1975) 54–67 and 492 (French résumé).

5. See Traill, "Schliemann's 'Discovery' of 'Priam's Treasure,' " *Antiquity* 57 (1983) 181–86; and a fuller version at *JHS* 104 (1984) 96–115; also "Further Evidence of Fraudulent Reporting in Schliemann's Archaeological Works," *Boreas* 7 (1984) 295–316.

6. *Ithaque* 161f. (151f. in the German edition). The translation of the French is "in pursuit of the disinterested goal of eradicating the absurd and erroneous dogma that Troy was situated on the heights of Bunarbashi."

7. For further discussion see Calder (supra n. 1) 336f. and "Heinrich Schliemann: An Unpublished Latin Vita," *CW* 67 (1974) 272–82; also W. Richter, *"Ithaque, le Péloponnèse et Troie* und das Promotionsverfahren Heinrich Schliemanns," *EAZ* 21 (1980) 667–78.

8. See Calder (supra n. 1) 350–52; Schindler (supra n. 1) 273–75; J. Herrmann, *Heinrich Schliemann: Wegbereiter einer neuen Wissenschaft* (East Berlin 1974) 13; K. Zimmermann, "Heinrich Schliemann—ein Leben zwischen Traum

und Wirklichkeit," *Klio* 64 (1982) 521f., n. 10; and Traill, "Schliemann's Dream of Troy: The Making of a Legend," *CJ* 81 (1985) 13–24.

9. *TroyR* 323–40 and *Ilios* 40f. and 453–85.

10. W. Borlase, "A Visit to Dr. Schliemann's Troy," *Fraser's Magazine* 17 (1878) 236.

11. All these letters are housed in the Gennadius Library, American School of Classical Studies, Athens. I am indebted to the Librarian, Mrs. Sophia Papageorgiou, for permission to publish extracts from them. All of the letters written by Frank Calvert, with the exception of that of 14 April 1873, are to be found in the appropriate boxes of correspondence received by Schliemann. The letter of 14 April survives only in the draft preserved by Calvert and now kept in the Calvert file. The originals of most of the letters written by Schliemann are preserved in the Calvert file. However, his letters of 13, 18, and 21 July 1872 and 17 and 20 April 1873 to Frank Calvert and his letter of 23(?) April 1873 to James Calvert are preserved only in the copybooks. For a systematic account of the Schliemann papers see D. Easton, "The Schliemann Papers," *ABSA* 77 (1982) 94–110.

12. Meyer states with refreshing candor his intention to present an idealized picture of Schliemann at *Briefe* 22: "galt es auszuschneiden, was allzu transitorisch ist und dem Wesen des Schreibers widerspricht" ["it seemed appropriate to omit what is all too transitory and opposed to the essential nature of the writer"]. The published letters which deal with some aspects of the Helios metope transactions are at *Briefwechsel* I, 212f., 215, 227 and *Briefe* 120–23. He provides no clarification of his observation at *Briefe* 132 n. 1: "Mit Frank C. z. Zt. gespanntes Verhältnis wegen des Ankaufs des auf seinem Gebiet gefundenen 'Triglyphenblocks' " ["Relations with Frank C. were strained at this time over the purchase of a metope found on his property"].

13. History, following the lead of Schliemann, has been unkind to Frank Calvert. Though admired by a few Anatolian specialists, most classicists and classical archaeologists have never heard of him. Biographical references to him are sparse; see *Briefe* 86–90; J.M. Cook, *The Troad* (Oxford 1973) 35f. and passim; A.C. Lascarides, *The Search for Troy 1553–1874* (Bloomington 1977) 63–65; and Michael Wood, *In Search of the Trojan War* (London 1985) 42–46 and passim. An article on him will appear in the forthcoming *Historical Dictionary of Classical Archaeology,* ed. Nancy T. de Grummond.

14. The find date is given in the 1873 diary entry of 13 June; see also Meyer (supra n. 3) 266. On the Helios metope see F. Goethert and H. Schleif, *Der Athenatempel von Ilion* (Berlin 1962) 24f. and B. Holden, *The Metopes of the Temple of Athena at Ilion* (Northampton, Massachusetts, 1964) 6–18.

15. C.T. Newton was Keeper of Greek and Roman Antiquities at the British Museum from 1861 to 1885. See further *DNB* (to 1900) XXII (supp.) 1096f. (A.W. Ward).

16. In an unpublished letter of 1 November 1868, Calvert had written to Schliemann: "I would feel very much obliged to you by your giving me, if

possible, any information as to the best place for disposing of marble statues, bas-reliefs and other antiques. Both Paris and London do not give good prices. I mean the Louvre and the British Museum."

17. Dokos was the Greek consul at the Dardanelles.

18. At this point in the letter Schliemann gives an account of Gaius' career similar to that found in *TroyR* 231f. C. Julius Caesar, the eldest son of Julia and Agrippa and the adopted son of Augustus, visited the province of Asia in 1 B.C.; see D. Magie, *Roman Rule in Asia Minor* (Princeton 1960) 482 and 1343 n. 41. For a modern, annotated edition of the inscription see Peter Frisch, *Die Inschriften von Ilion, Inschriften griechischer Städte aus Kleinasiens,* III (Bonn 1975) 187f.

19. Frisch (supra n. 18) 166–68.

20. For the text of this inscription see Frisch (supra n. 18) 92–100. At this point Schliemann digresses on the question of a reading on the inscription.

21. "You rejected my offer to send the block to London and you asked me for £50 for your half, adding that you would not take a sou less. I paid you this sum, but, by heaven, I thought that I was paying far too much."

22. In an unpublished letter to Emile Burnouf, the director of the French School in Athens, dated 18 October 1873, Schliemann asks him to convey the following to the French government: "j'accepterai pour toute ma collection troyenne, y compris le trésor de Priam, la belle Métope d'Apollon (métope qui est à elle seule 100,000 fcs), toutes mes inscriptions grecques d'Ilion etc. la somme d'un million" ["I will accept for the entire Trojan collection, including the Treasure of Priam, the fine Apollo metope (which alone is worth 100,000 francs), all my Greek inscriptions from Ilium etc., the sum of one million"] (Copybook 32, 185).

23. "Do you wish, yes or no, that if I discover its brother, it should be sent at our joint expense to London or Paris to be sold at auction after being put up for sale in the newspapers? If you agree, please tell me right away, for otherwise I will not resume digging in your field."

24. Since the letters of this correspondence were hand delivered by servants or acquaintances, replies written on the same day are not uncommon. In this case, however, it appears from a remark Calvert makes elsewhere in this letter that Schliemann's was actually sent on the sixteenth and simply misdated.

25. Translated, the French reads:

I hasten to reply to your esteemed letter of the 17th inst., that according to the laws of all nations and of all periods, an exchange made between individuals and paid for in cash is considered a transaction settled once and for all, on which there is no going back.

As for the excavations which I proposed to make in your field to find the counterpiece to the Apollo metope, your offer to draw lots is quite unacceptable. I see no alternative than to send to London or to Paris any sculptured marbles resulting from my excavations. If you agree, please inform me through Nicholas, for time is pressing. The difficulties that you foresee over the exportation of the marbles do not seem to exist, for just two days ago I sent off thirty huge packages. I truly believe that at the moment I can export with greater ease than at any other time.

26. Schliemann's American citizenship had been acquired by fraud; see Traill, *CJ* 77 (1982) 336–42. It proved useful to him in dealing with the Turkish government. He also made use of it to obtain numerous favors from James Calvert in his capacity as U.S. consul.

27. Sir John Lubbock, who from 1900 was known as Lord Avebury, was a distinguished banker, a reforming statesman and an entomologist of some note. Today he is best known for his contributions to archaeology. In *The Origin of Civilization and the Primitive History of Man* (London 1871), he coined the terms "paleolithic" and "neolithic." His *Prehistoric Times* (London 1865) was long and widely read as an introduction to archaeology; see further *DNB* (1912–1921) 345–47 (A. Smithells).

28. The translation of this passage reads:

to lodge an impossible suit against me instead of showing his gratitude for the immense good I have done for his field. But please inform me by the bearer if you agree to do it, for otherwise I see myself forced to resort to my ambassador in Constantinople to protect me from the harassment of Mr. Fr. Calvert. Instead of wasting his time uselessly in odious harassment, which can only hurt himself, please tell him to come here to excavate together with 120 workmen and at my expense his theatre on the north part of his field, for I am perfectly sure not only of finding the "brother" there (the counterpiece to the Apollo) but also a mass of other statues and to consign everything, at our joint risk, to Sir John Lubbock, so that he can take care of the sale.

29. After achieving little success as a playwright and poet, George H. Boker served as American ambassador to Turkey from 1871–1875. See further Edward S. Bradley, *Geo. Henry Boker—Poet and Patriot* (Philadelphia 1927) and *Dictionary of American Biography* II (1929) 415–18 (A.H. Quinn).

30. Calvert's brother Frederick owned a farm at Thymbra, about four miles from Hissarlik.

31. Translated, this reads:

In reply to your esteemed letters of 25th last and of yesterday I have the honor to tell you that as of the first, I had given orders to resume excavations on the north slope of your field and in your theater, but that Mme Schliemann was opposed, saying that we cannot undertake this gigantic enterprise in view of the suit with which you are threatening us at the end of our excavations. Having carefully reflected on this matter, I find that she is quite right, for on the north slope alone there are not 8,500 cubic meters of debris to remove, as I had thought, but 17,000, and if, after enormous trouble, I succeed in retrieving art objects from the depths of these ruins, I would only meet with unpleasantness.

I regret very much that you did not come to see my excavations, for since your last visit we have brought to light monuments which are of the highest interest for science and, among other things, the Scaean Gate, and I have also discovered some remarkable facts regarding the topography of Ilium. Mme S. respectfully sends you her regards.

32. Calder (supra n. 1) 348f. and Traill, *CJ* 74 (1979) 354f. For a Freudian view see W.G. Niederland, "An Inquiry into the Life and Work of Heinrich Schliemann," *Drives, Affects, Behavior,* ed. Max Schur (New York 1965) II 369–96.

33. Robert M. Goldenson, *The Encyclopedia of Human Behavior* (Garden City, New York, 1970) 86.

34. H. Cleckley, *The Mask of Sanity* (St. Louis, Missouri, 1982) 204–25. I am much indebted to the C.V. Mosby Company for granting permission to quote from this book.

35. Cleckley (supra n. 34) 205.

36. Cleckley (supra n. 34) 26.

37. See Mycenae diary entry of 6 September.

38. It is interesting to compare the extraordinary case of the noted orientalist, Sir Edmund Backhouse, whose forgeries, lies, and other fraudulent activities have recently been exposed by Hugh Trevor-Roper in *A Hidden Life* (London 1976). He appears to have been an almost textbook case of a psychopath, though Trevor-Roper does not identify him as such. His talents and shortcomings were remarkably similar to Schliemann's. Like Schliemann he rendered his fantasies credible to the reader with his lavish use of circumstantial detail; cf. Trevor-Roper, 277f. and Calder (supra n. 1) 353. He had a "miraculous linguistic flair" and "mastered one language after another" (Trevor-Roper, 283), had "great personal charm and the appearance of transparent honesty" and an impressive business acumen (276). There are even invented episodes in which Backhouse, like Schliemann, mingled on equal terms with the great (279). Of his intelligence Trevor-Roper writes: "He was indeed a marvellous linguist and even those who disliked him in China admitted that he was a first-class sinologue and scholar of Japanese. He was tolerably well read in the conventional classics. But his writings show no power of thought, no familiarity with philosophy, with science, with other than fashionable current literature . . . there is no depth in him, even of literary sensibility" (279). Despite Backhouse's undoubted flair for anecdotal writing, Trevor-Roper finds in him the same inability to synthesize that characterizes Schliemann's works: "he lacked the architectonic gift, and in the end would use his documents only to create another document like them: a pastiche, a tour de force" (286).

39. See Adolf Greifenhagen, *Adolf Furtwängler: Briefe 1879–80 und 1880–1894* (Stuttgart 1965) 77. Quoted at Calder (supra n. 1) 347.

40. The "vision" of Pallas Athena described in his letter to Conze of 9 December 1890 (*Briefwechsel* II, 389) is almost certainly a mere elaboration of the notion "Pallas Athena was kind to me"; cf. his letter to Schöne of 9 October 1890 (*Briefwechsel* II, 382).

41. Cleckley (supra n. 34) 207.

42. Cf. Traill, *CJ* 74 (1979) 353f.

43. See *Ilios* 17 and Emil Ludwig, *Schliemann* (Boston 1931) 84.

44. Cleckley (supra n. 34) 207f.

45. See the first section of this article, the literature cited in note 1, and my introduction to the Mycenaean diary.

46. On the interviews see Calder (supra n. 1) 338–43. On the fire see Traill, *CJ* 74 (1979) 348–51.

47. W. Borlase, "A Visit to Dr. Schliemann's Troy," *Fraser's Magazine* 17 (February 1878) 228–39, esp. 235f.

48. E. Meyer, "Schliemann's Letters to Max Müller in Oxford," *JHS* 82 (1962) 98.

49. Cleckley (supra n. 34) 209.

50. Traill, *CJ* 74 (1979) 353f.

51. Cleckley (supra n. 34) 210.

52. Meyer (supra n. 3) 252, 280.

53. Cleckley (supra n. 34) 280; Ludwig (supra n. 43) 123; Robert Payne, *The Gold of Troy* (London 1959) 176; and Leo Deuel, *Memoirs of Heinrich Schliemann* (New York 1977) 8.

54. Cleckley (supra n. 34) 211.

55. Lynn and Gray Poole, *One Passion, Two Loves* (New York 1966) 203.

56. Cf. the letter in Poole (supra n. 55) 204, from which the following is excerpted: "Why do you demand, yet ignore? I thanks {sic} god for you, yet wonder what manner of man you are. No, my friend, I do not wonder because I know. I understand you and know the fate of every woman who is joined to a genius. How do I know? Because I have lived with you, been your partner, friend, lover, and slave since our marriage. Also I know because I have asked for books about men whose fame has lasted through centuries, as will yours, my Henry. These books tell me that their wives have suffered as I do."

57. Cleckley (supra n. 34) 212.

58. Consider, for example, the incident at Memel in October 1854. Schliemann's large shipment of indigo was spared the fire which destroyed most of the warehouse. At first, however, he thought that all was lost: "The blow was tremendous. . . . But no sooner had I acquired the certainty that I was ruined, than I recovered my presence of mind." Later: "The transition from profound grief to great joy is difficult to bear without tears; I was for some moments speechless." See also the glib letter of commiseration to Max Müller on the death of his daughter in *JHS* 82 (1962) 95f.

59. Meyer (supra n. 3) 149.

60. Cleckley (supra n. 34) 213.

61. The poem translates as:

> Here one sees the Lithoi [stones]
> Which Priam once set out [built]
> And there stand the Pithoi [pitchers]
> Filled with peas and sauerkraut.

Schliemann observed: "So he doesn't take sides." Schuchhardt commented: "The humor of the verses made no impression on him." See Carl Schuchhardt, *Aus Leben und Arbeit* (Berlin 1944) 179f.

62. Cleckley (supra n. 34) 214.

63. Poole (supra n. 55) 202f. I have not seen the original of this letter and reproduce it here exactly as it appears in Poole. Presumably, the question mark at the end following "Your wife" is Sophia's, indicating that in her view Heinrich is not behaving as a man ought towards his wife.

64. Cleckley (supra n. 34) 215.

65. *Briefwechsel* I, 238.

66. Ludwig (supra n. 43) 150. Borlase (supra n. 47) 229 questioned Turkish authorities about Schliemann's allegation that European archaeologists habitually broke their contracts with the Turkish government. He was assured, rightly or wrongly, that this was not the case.

67. Cleckley (supra n. 34) 217.

68. Ludwig (supra n. 43) 49. Cf. Theodor Wiegand's recollection of how after entertaining guests in a hotel Schliemann would ostentatiously pay for the meal in front of everyone. See Carl Watzinger, *Theodor Wiegand: Ein deutscher Archäologe 1864–1936* (Munich 1944); cited at Calder (supra n. 1) 348.

69. Ludwig (supra n. 43) 63f. As a dutiful son, Schliemann, when a successful businessman in St. Petersburg, set up a monumental cross over his mother's grave in Ankershagen, but, as Calder (supra n. 1) 348f. points out, the egotistical details of the inscription "make the cross rather a monument for Schliemann himself than for his mother."

70. Cleckley (supra n. 34) 218.

71. Joseph M. von Radowitz, *Aufzeichnungen und Erinnerungen aus dem Leben des Botshafters J.M.v.R.*, ed. Hajo Holborn (Stuttgart 1925) II 168f., as translated by Deuel (supra n. 53) 350f.

72. Cleckley (supra n. 34) 219.

73. Cleckley (supra n. 34) 221–24.

74. Eli Lilly, *Schliemann in Indianapolis* (Indianapolis 1961) 33, and H.A. Stoll, *Abenteuer meines Lebens* (Leipzig 1965) 257f.

75. See Poole (supra n. 55) 53.

76. In a letter to a friend of his first wife Schliemann wrote that: "she represents me everywhere as a tyrant, as a despot and a libertine"; see Ludwig (supra n. 43) 90. Unfortunately, Ludwig chose to suppress further details: "Anything of an intimate nature contained in the innumerable letters exchanged between the husband and wife and close friends on the subject of the preservation of their union has been omitted from this study, since it cannot be checked, and only in rare instances throws any light on Schliemann's character. In these letters his wife's family saw fit to criticize on moral grounds certain cosmopolitan usages of the husband" (86). As to these "cosmopolitan usages," a reasonable guess is that Schliemann followed his father's example and had an affair with the maid. In 1869 in Indianapolis Schliemann had a series of black female housekeepers in rapid succession. His inability to retain their services

for more than a day or two may well have been due to his making improper advances; see Lilly (supra n. 74) 18–20. Also significant in this connection is the dream which Schliemann claims to have had on the night of his shipwreck off the Dutch coast in December 1841. He dreamed that he had reached South America, found employment on a plantation, poisoned the plantation owner, and married his widow: "I dreamt further that besides my wife I also enjoyed—had relations with my black female slaves." This version of the shipwreck was written between 1858 and 1862; see further Niederland (supra n. 32) 382–83. Cleckley (supra n. 34) 223f. remarks that psychopaths tend to seek sexual partners of "low intellectual or social status." I have seen nothing, on the other hand, that would indicate that Schliemann frequented brothels or sought the services of prostitutes.

77. Cleckley (supra n. 34) 224.

78. On Schliemann's famous claim, however, to have had a lifelong passion to excavate Troy from early childhood, see the first section of this essay and note 8.

79. I am indebted to Dr. Cleckley for taking the time to read my articles on Schliemann and for granting permission to publish this letter.

Schliemann's Cleopatra

Wolfgang Schindler

1.

TEN YEARS AGO the heroic figure of Heinrich Schliemann, the excavator of Troy, first entered the cross fire of modern criticism. W.M. Calder III began this. On the occasion of Schliemann's 150th birthday, Calder delivered at midnight on 6 January 1972, in the pastor's house in Neubukow (midway between Rostock and Wismar, German Democratic Republic), his lecture "Schliemann on Schliemann." This broke the ice. H.A. Stoll, the epic poet for Schliemann's "Dream of Troy," anticipated him by one day with his memorial address in the same town. In February 1972 the Academy of Sciences of the German Democratic Republic organized a Schliemann colloquium to honor the same occasion. A critical approach to Schliemann could no longer be avoided.[1]

In the years that followed, the voices that demanded a closer scrutiny of our picture of Schliemann grew stronger. At first, Schliemann's assertions in the autobiographical writings were the center of interest. A series of falsehoods were uncovered. The process of demythologizing Schliemann then began to create opponents. They, however, fo-

I am grateful to my friend William M. Calder III, who first drew my attention to Schliemann's Cleopatra and who later helped to translate the German version of this article into English. I thank also Dr. M. Kunze, the director of the antiquities department of the Staatliche Museen in Berlin, German Democratic Republic, who kindly allowed me to study and photograph the original head. The two photographs of the Schliemann head published in this book were generously supplied by Dr. Kunze.

81

cused their criticism for the most part on the exaggerated enthusiasm of the iconoclasts.[2]

Between these extremes—on the one side, a rash exposé of the discoveries about Schliemann, and, on the other, a timid attempt to preserve the traditional view of the great man—many scholars have sought refuge in an uncontroversial dependence on what Schliemann himself has given us in his own writings.[3] Some of the new revelations concerning Schliemann have been taken over, as though common knowledge, with no reference to their discoverers.[4] Several scholars, while profiting from these insights, went on to react with indignation at the lack of piety on the part of those who brought these matters to light.[5]

I consider the present sharpening of the controversy unfortunate. It can only do harm to research. Too much time and trouble are devoted to the unproductive delineation of opinions, to their rhetorical justification, to the uncertain rescue of some questionable, traditional way of thinking. From the spectacular exaggeration of the discoveries and their total condemnation come only profit for the press and no gain for scholarship.[6]

2.

Calder, in his midnight lecture, formulated a remarkable paradox: "The egoistic, incomparable, tortured, romantic, infantile, brilliant Schliemann discovered the historical Agamemnon."[7] In my review of the life and work of Heinrich Schliemann in the light of recent biographical research, I have tried to use this paradox as the key for understanding the lifework and scholarly activity of Schliemann. Schliemann was able to achieve what he did thanks to his excessively productive imagination. The restless energy, the feverish initiative and arrogance of the self-made man, Schliemann owed to his time, the *Gründerzeit,* the 1870s and 1880s. To push aside the role of Zeitgeist, as Döhl does, I consider unwise. It hinders our understanding of Schliemann's personality.[8]

Schliemann's self-dramatizations can be explained as dream-fantasies, which were often forcibly realized. How very convincing they were is best illustrated by the fact that only during the last ten years has scholarly criticism been drawn to them. To these products of Schlie-

82

mann's fertile imagination belong the following: the creation of the "Dream of Troy," the thread which guided his steps from earliest youth until its realization; the romantic glorification of Minna Meincke, the beloved of his childhood with whom he had planned everything; the fictive visit to U.S. President Millard Fillmore in February 1851; the backdating of his American citizenship; and the doctoral dissertation written in ancient Greek with which he supposedly gained a Rostock degree. All these Calder exposed as falsehoods in 1972.[9]

Thanks to D.A. Traill's research, further weak points in Schliemann's autobiographical writings have been brought to light. For example, Traill exposed the fictive account of Schliemann's presence at the fire of San Francisco 3–4 May 1851 and revealed that Schliemann's reason for leaving the Sacramento Valley was apparently financial dishonesty and an angry partner rather than poor health.[10] These corrections have now become a permanent part of modern Schliemann research. In part, they have even been accepted by those opposed to the dethronement of Schliemann.[11]

3.

When scepticism proved to be well-founded in the biographical realm, Schliemann's scholarly work inevitably came under suspicion. Here, Traill has taken the decisive step. He has presented evidence that the "Treasure of Priam" was a composition of its discoverer, or, rather, of its inventor. Unfortunately, this great revelation, about which in my opinion there can be no doubt, has been complicated by the hypothesis (not necessarily untrue) that a number of the objects published by Schliemann as part of the treasure were purchased. This raised astonishment and even anger among colleagues, particularly among those who are specialists in research in the Bronze Age.[12]

As a result of the scepticism concerning this hypothesis, the doubters naturally questioned the main part of this extraordinarily important discovery, namely the irrefutable fact that Schliemann himself assembled, dramatized, and even misrepresented the find. The delay in publishing this addition to our knowledge stands on the negative side of the scholarly ledger.

83

Schliemann's Cleopatra. (Photograph courtesy of Staatliche Museen zu Berlin, German Democratic Republic.)

4.

Now, a new fraud has been posited, one which Calder has announced to the press.[13] It concerns the marble head with melon hairdo that Schliemann claimed to have found in an excavation at Alexandria in Egypt and called a portrait of Cleopatra VII, the famous friend of

84

Schliemann's Cleopatra, profile. (Photograph courtesy of Staatliche Museen zu Berlin, German Democratic Republic.)

Caesar and Antony. For this reason, I shall refer to this head as "Schliemann's Cleopatra."

The head is not lost, as Döhl alleges in his recent book. It can be found in the storage rooms of the antiquities department of the Staatliche Museen in Berlin, registered under the number K 205 given it by C. Blümel in his 1938 catalogue of sculptures in the museum. At that time the head was still kept in the Schliemann Collection at the Museum for Prehistory in Berlin. After the war it became part of the antiquities department of the Pergamon Museum with no record of its acquisition.[14] The director of this department, M. Kunze, generously permitted me to study and photograph the head.

The more or less life-size marble head is partially damaged on the surface of the face. The nose, parts of the mouth, and the chin are restored. The right side of the head is the better preserved. The profile view clearly reveals the melon hairdo without bun. The hair is drawn together by a ribbon, which is tastefully tied over the forehead. From this ribbon comes another, which passes over the center of the skull.

5.

First, a few words on the circumstances of the find, which has been thought to be another fabrication of Schliemann. He wanted badly to find a portrait of one of the most infamous women of antiquity. I shall first cite a letter of Schliemann to his friend, the anthropologist R. Virchow, dated Athens 1 May 1887: "Then the question arises: do you want to make the Nile trip, visit the Fayum with Schweinfurth and me, and make an excavation in Alexandria, where I expect to find Cleopatra's Palace?" In the same letter, in which he later speaks of permission to excavate and the possible acquisition of a find for Berlin, he assures his friend that he is "especially eager to find a few statues of Cleopatra VII (Mark Antony's Cleopatra)." He continues: "According to Plutarch, in the year 30 B.C. Alexandria possessed several thousand portraits of the beautiful woman, but through an irony of fate not one statue or even a gold coin of her has been found."[15]

We learn the results of his efforts from a letter to the general director of the Berlin Museum, R. Schöne, written one year later from Athens on 17 May 1888. Schliemann wrote:

> I could not decide whether to continue the excavations east of the city, where I consider the Palace of the Ptolemies to be located, beyond the date of Virchow's arrival (22nd February). The palace along with the gardens, the museum etc., according to Strabo, took up a quarter or a third of the whole city (of at least 500,000 inhabitants). Because of this any success on the part of my shovel could only be by accident. To my greatest astonishment, this time too Lady Luck was good to me. I found there a female marble head of splendid workmanship, with very charac-

teristic, beautifully preserved hairdo (similar to that of Mark Antony's Cleopatra) and a well-preserved face, except for the nose, which has only partly survived. In spite of the many guards who watched me with Argus-eyes and even followed me wherever I went, I succeeded not only in causing the head to disappear before their eyes but also, even though it weighed some 80 pounds, in getting it through customs at Alexandria in a little box as hand-luggage and bringing it here. On my arrival I left it at the customs in the Piraeus and on the same day on the correct form with stamp submitted a request to the Ministry, in which I sought to record the head as a foreign import so that at any time I could export it again.[16]

From the letter to T. Schreiber, dated Athens 24 July 1888, we learn further that "because I did not want to stay in Alexandria doing nothing, with Nubar Pasha's permission I excavated outside of the city where I assumed the Palace of the Ptolemies to be, near the station where the train goes to Ramle. There I found, at a depth of 12 meters, a marble head of splendid workmanship, apparently of the Ptolemaic period. I am presenting it to Germany and send you a picture of it."[17]

As one can see from these passages I have cited from the letters, we are dealing with a situation that is similar to the removal of the "Treasure of Priam" from Troy.[18] (Traill has succeeded in presenting the circumstances surrounding that archaeological find.) In the case of the Cleopatra head, the excavator again found the object when he was alone—*before* the arrival of Virchow. Originally, Schliemann had written of excavating along with his friend Virchow, but in a letter to F.A. Brockhaus, dated Athens 29 December 1887, he made the following stipulation: "I have planned a scholarly trip to Egypt with Virchow. I intend to start on January 27th. He will meet me there in February and it is possible that I may make an interesting archaeological discovery there, which will be rich enough for a rather large publication for us both. Such a discovery could only be made in Alexandria. I shall carefully search there until the arrival of Virchow."[19]

Let us, for a moment, consider the timing. In his letter to Brockhaus, Schliemann discloses that he intends to arrive in Alexandria on 27 January. In the letter to Schöne (written half a year after his stay in Alexandria), he notes that Virchow arrived 22 February. E. Meyer, Schliemann's biographer and editor of his letters, apparently working from the Egyptian diary, says that Virchow arrived 8 February.[20]

If Meyer is right, Schliemann had only ten days in which to settle into a foreign city, find the spot he wished to excavate, obtain official permission from the corrupt Turkish government, hire workers, and dig a trench twelve meters deep (at the bottom of which is a head of Cleopatra). Schliemann even said that he continued digging to a depth of sixteen meters, only one meter less than that of the huge trench at Troy.[21] Meyer tells us that Schliemann found this head after a week of excavation. The matter is further complicated by Schliemann's statement in his letter of 6 February 1888 to Virchow that he began excavating on that day.[22] If true, Schliemann would have had only two days in which to accomplish the whole adventure.

Independent evidence casts further doubt on Schliemann's veracity. After consulting the Virchow Papers in the archives of the Academy of Sciences in Berlin, German Democratic Republic, I can report that in his calendar ("Preussischer Medicinal Kalender") for the year 1888, Virchow notes his arrival in Alexandria on 22 February. He indicates that he met Schliemann but continued on to Cairo the same day. There is no reference to an excavation by Schliemann or to the marble head. Nor is there any mention of either during Virchow's visit to Greece 20 April to 4 May.

Next, Schliemann hid his find from all possible eyewitnesses. Obviously, if the head were seen by anyone he would risk being forbidden to take it out of the country. He succeeded in smuggling it through customs. One only has to try to lift the head to judge how difficult this escapade must have been—if indeed it ever took place—especially for a small man of sixty-eight.

One may ask if we do not have here a case analogous to the "Treasure of Priam." Have we found a topos? After Traill's discoveries concerning Schliemann's account of the Treasure, our suspicions move in this direction. It is particularly suspicious that Schliemann predicts the find before he actually finds it. Of course, he expresses this as a wish, but such clairvoyance can only be suspect.

One should now ask: Did Schliemann himself connect the Cleopatra head with his excavation in Alexandria? If so, where did he obtain it? In Alexandria? We shall return to this question. Or did he bring the head from somewhere else to Alexandria? Or was the head never even in Alexandria? On this point a remark preserved by E. Schmidt could be important. He says that the inventory of the Schliemann Collection in the 1930s reports that the head "allegedly comes from Alexandria Troas."[23]

On the basis of the Schliemann letters that have so far been published, we can go no farther. Further study of the diaries and the

unpublished letters may some day cast more light on the problem.[24]
Now, I should like to say something about the origin and dating of the
marble head from an art historian's point of view.

6.

It has been generally assumed up to now that the marble head has
nothing to do with Cleopatra VII. In fact, so far as we know, portraits
of the queen are attested only on coins. Among the preserved authentic coin types one finds portraits similar in shape and profile to the
Schliemann head.[25] However, the eye of the queen on the coins is
more deeply recessed than those on the marble head. Nevertheless, in
several particulars the arrangement of the hair on the Berlin head
differs only slightly from that on the coins. This superficial similarity
with the coin types must have played a role in Schliemann's identification. In a letter to Schöne of 17 June 1888, Schliemann reports from
Athens: "In any case the head is the portrait of a Ptolemaic princess
and probably Cleopatra VII, for the head only fits her as she is de-
picted on the medallions." I still cannot determine to which medallions
Schliemann refers in this letter.[26]

At the end of the nineteenth century W. Amelung placed the Berlin
head in a stylistic group with two others: namely, a head in the Vatican
collection (which was earlier in the Museo Chiaramonti) and a head
formerly on the antiquities market, now in the Astor Collection at
Cliveden Hills near London. This head type may be called the Astor-
Vatican-Berlin type.[27]

S. Reinach first associated this type with the so-called Corinna
marble statuette in Compiègne, France. He attributed the lost original
to the sculptor Silanion. Amelung doubted the attribution. He adduced the differences in the shape of the head and the hairdo and drew
attention to the Praxitelean characteristics of the Astor-Vatican-Berlin
type.[28]

Schmidt, in his studies of Silanion in the 1930s, accepted the thesis
of Reinach. He considered the three portraits, including the Schliemann head, to be copies of Silanion's Corinna. The statuette type, he
argued, was an independent invention of the late Hellenistic period.
He also maintained that the earlier motive of Corinna playing the
cithara was later replaced by the poetess reading a scroll.[29]

While C. Blümel, in his catalogue of the Berlin sculptures also accepted Reinach's thesis that the statuette in Compiègne was closely modeled on the lost Corinna of Silanion, he denied any connection between the Berlin head and the Corinna, stressing in particular the differences in the handling of the hairdo.[30] G. Lippold, too, defended Reinach's assertion, although he considered the statuette only an inferior copy. The high position of the belt points, in his opinion, to the time of Alexander, an observation which he defended by parallels from the related types of the Muses on the Mantinea relief.[31]

The Corinna statuette was similarly interpreted by H. von Heintze in her book on Sappho: "I see no reason not to believe S. Reinach, not to consider the head and inscription genuine or to deny that the head belongs to the statuette. Reinach emphasizes that when a cast was made at the Louvre, the statuette was carefully studied."[32]

J. Frel of the Getty Museum in Malibu, however, informs me that he carefully examined the statuette in Compiègne and discovered that the head certainly does not belong to the statuette. The marble is not the same, and the join is modern. He adds that G. Daux does not consider the inscription (Corinna) original either.[33] Heintze does not connect the Corinna portrait with the Astor-Vatican-Berlin type. She prefers a different parallel, a Vatican head in the Galleria dei Candelabri.[34] That is a provocative suggestion but it leads us far away from our Berlin head.

7.

How are we to date the Berlin head? What is the date and provenance of the lost archetype? Blümel suggested a date for Schliemann's head in the first century A.D.[35] Much supports such a dating, not least the careful workmanship of the well-preserved surface on the right side of the head. Such chisel work can be dated at the earliest to the Claudian-Neronian period and at the latest to the Flavian. Now what about the archetype for the head?

The *opinio communis* places it some time in the fourth century B.C. This is clear from scholars' attributions to the masters of this period, Silanion or Praxiteles. Originally, Amelung had thought of a date in the early fourth century.[36] Today, the second half of the century is preferred. The closest parallels to the Berlin head are the Brunn head in Munich[37] or "la petite Herculanienne"[38] for instance, the example in Dresden. Both pieces belong to the last quarter of the fourth century B.C. The Brunn head is now considered an original from this period.

Recently, the Astor-Vatican-Berlin type has been associated with the circle of Lysippus.[39] I do not agree with this suggestion. In the late fourth century, typical characteristics of the various schools are mingled so that the Berlin head might just as easily derive from the school of Praxiteles, as Amelung earlier suggested. As an example of this fusion of styles, we may cite the Muses of the Mantinea relief. A glance at the preserved heads suffices to prove my point. From this stylistic *koine* the Schliemann head probably derives.

8.

An entirely different question is how far beyond Athens was this type influential? This brings us back to the circumstances of the find of Schliemann's Cleopatra. I can adduce no parallel in Hellenistic Alexandrian art that I can without hesitation compare with the Berlin head. The same holds true for the Roman period in Alexandria. Admittedly, a new find there could provide an important parallel.

The hypothesis that Schliemann's Cleopatra derives from a different context than that to which Schliemann ascribes it is by no means impossible. Perhaps he bought the head in Alexandria. The presence of the melon hairdo on Alexandrian coin types of Cleopatra may be adduced as evidence that the Praxitelean-Lysippan type, as exemplified in the Berlin head, was known there.

On the other hand, one must pose the question: has the head anything at all to do with Alexandria? Except for Schliemann's report, we have no solid evidence to support this. During the last ten years, sufficient evidence has accumulated to doubt any assertions made by Schliemann that are not corroborated by an independent source. On the basis of the evidence above, I do not believe that Schliemann ever made excavations twelve or sixteen meters deep at Alexandria and found his head in them. The high water table is also an argument against this fabrication. Whether he purchased the head in Alexandria or elsewhere cannot be proven from the extant evidence.

91

NOTES

1. W.M. Calder III, "Schliemann on Schliemann: A Study in the Use of Sources," *GRBS* 13 (1972) 335–53 = Calder, *Studies in the Modern History of Classical Scholarship, Antiqua* 27 (1984) 87–107. Cf. J. Herrmann, *Heinrich Schliemann: Wegbereiter einer neuen Wissenschaft* (Berlin 1974).

2. See W. Richter, "*Ithaque, le Péloponnèse et Troie* und das Promotionsverfahren Heinrich Schliemanns," *EAZ* 21 (1980) 667–78, esp. 671; W. Richter, "Ein unveröffentlichter Brief Heinrich Schliemanns aus dem Jahre 1869," *Wissenschaftliche Zeitschrift der Universität Rostock, Gesellschafts-u.sprachwissenschaftliche Reihe* 29 (1980) 55–64, esp. 58 and 63; and H. Döhl, *Heinrich Schliemann: Mythos und Ärgernis* (Munich 1981) 15 and 77. I review this book in *DLZ* 104 (1983) 898–901.

3. See as an example L. Deuel, *Memoirs of Heinrich Schliemann: A Documentary Portrait Drawn from His Autobiographical Writings, Letters, and Excavation Reports* (New York 1977).

4. See Deuel (supra n. 3) 17f., 22f., 64; Döhl (supra n. 2) 76, 77; Gustav Mahr, *Troja: Heinrich Schliemanns Ausgrabungen und Funde, Ausstellung des Museums für Vor- und Frühgeschichte* (Berlin 1981) 2; E. Hühns, *Troja und Thrakien: Berlin–Hauptstadt der DDR und Sofia* (Berlin 1981) 10, 17; and K. Zimmermann, "Heinrich Schliemann—ein Leben zwischen Traum und Wirklichkeit," *Klio* 64 (1982) 513–32, esp. 518, 521f.

5. See esp. Richter (supra n. 2) *EAZ* 671; Richter, *Wiss. Zeitschr. Rostock* 58, 63; and Döhl (supra n. 2) 15.

6. "Troy's Treasure," *Observer* (London) 17 January 1982; "Schwere Vorwürfe gegen den Vater der Archäologie—'Heinrich Schliemann ein Lügner und Aufschneider,' " *Berliner Morgenpost* 23 January 1982, 16; "Scholars Discredit Archaeologist's Fantastic Legend," *Rocky Mountain News* 15 February 1982, 6; and S.K. Levin, "CU Prof Seeks to Debunk Legend: Famous Mask May Be Fake, Too," *Colorado Daily* 12 October 1982. See now Harald Steinert, *FAZ* 30 April 1984, a judicious summary of the present state of the question.

7. Calder (supra n. 1) 353.

8. See W. Schindler, "Heinrich Schliemann: Leben und Werk im Spiegel der neueren biographischen Forschungen," *Philologus* 120 (1976) 271–89, esp. 283. See contra Döhl (supra n. 2) 10. Compare Deuel (supra n. 3) 3.

9. Supra n. 1

10. D. Traill, "Schliemann's Mendacity: Fire and Fever in California," *CJ* 74 (1979) 348–55.

11. Supra n. 4.

12. See D. Traill, "Schliemann's 'Discovery' of 'Priam's Treasure,' " *AJA* 86 (1982) 288 and "Schliemann's Discovery of 'Priam's Treasure': A Reexamination of the Evidence," *JHS* 104 (1984) 96–115 and *Antiquity* 57 (1983) 181–86. For such a specialist in Bronze Age archaeology see M.J. Mellink, "Archaeology in Asia Minor," *AJA* 86 (1982) 561; *AJA* 89 (1985) 553.

13. Levin (supra n. 6) 12.

14. Döhl (supra n. 2) 72; C. Blümel. *Römische Kopien griechischer Skulpturen des IV. Jahrhunderts vor Chr.* (Berlin 1938) 8, K 205, Taf. 19. I have to thank Dr. H. Heres, Staatliche Museen of Berlin, for the information concerning storage of the head in the Pergamon Museum.

15. *Briefe* 263, 264.

16. *Briefe* 278.

17. *Briefwechsel,* II, 287.

18. See Herrmann (supra n. 1) 91f. (from the Schliemann autobiography in *Ilios: Stadt und Land der Trojaner* [Leipzig 1881]) and Heinrich Schliemann, *Selbstbiographie bis zu seinem Tode vervöllständigt*[10], ed. Ernst Meyer (Wiesbaden 1968) 66f.

19. *Briefwechsel* II, 279.

20. Meyer, *Schliemann,* 235. To the best of my knowledge, the Egyptian diary is still unpublished.

21. *Briefwechsel* II, 288; Schliemann, *Selbstbiographie* (supra n. 18) 59; Herrmann (supra n. 1) 82.

22. Meyer, *Schliemann,* 235. *Briefe* 275.

23. E. Schmidt, "Silanion, der Meister des Platonbildnisses," *JdI* 47 (1932) 281 n. 2

24. The diary for the excavations at Alexandria and for the journey up the Nile with Virchow is missing from the Schliemann Collection at the Gennadius Library: see D.F. Easton, "The Schliemann Papers," *ABSA* 77 (1982) 99.

25. J.M.C. Toynbee, *Roman Historical Portraits* (London 1978) 86, 87 fig. 138, 88. For the new West Berlin marble portrait, see *JbPreussKulturbesitz* 13 (1976) 245ff.

26. *Briefwechsel* II, 285. The coins in the possession of Schliemann were listed in the catalogue by A. Postolaca, published by G.St. Korres, *Deltion* 29 (1974) 245–71. Among these coins there is one which pictures Antony and Cleopatra.

27. See W. Amelung, *Die Sculpturen des Vatikanischen Museums* I (Berlin 1903) 482ff., Museo Chiaramonti Nr. 256, pl. 50; G.M.A. Richter, *The Portraits of the Greeks* I (London 1965) 144 fig. 782. For the Astor head, see *EA* 53f., Nr. 1188–89; and Schmidt (supra n. 23) 281–84, Abb. 32.

28. S. Reinach, "Corinne," *RA* 36 (1900) 169–75; S. Reinach, "Statues Antiques I: La Corinne de Silanion," *RA* 32 (1898) 161–66. For Amelung's doubt, see *EA* 54.

29. Schmidt (supra n. 23) 281–85.

30. Blümel (supra n. 14) 8.

31. G. Lippold, *Die griechische Plastik* (Munich 1950) 273. Compare the similar view of C. Picard, *Manuel d'Archéologie grecque: La Sculpture* III (Paris 1948) 807ff.

32. H. von Heintze, *Das Bildnis der Sappho* (Mainz and Berlin 1966) 22, fig. 11–12, n. 48.

33. See Frel's remarks in *Bulletin du Musée Hongrois des Beaux-Arts* 8 (1956)

19. W. Helbig had already queried the authenticity of the inscription: see J.J. Bernoulli, *Griechische Ikonographie* I (Munich 1901) 88f.; cf. G. Daux, *Contributions à l'Epigraphie grecque* (Prague 1969) 33.

34. Von Heintze (supra n. 32) 23, fig. 13–15, n. 51.

35. Blümel (supra n. 14) 8.

36. See Amelung (supra n. 27) 482.

37. G. Schmidt, "Der Brunnsche Kopf," *Antike Plastik* X (Berlin 1970) 29–38, fig. 1-5, pl. 51–52; B. Vierneisel-Schlörb, *Klassische Skulpturen* (Munich 1979) 438–45.

38. See L. Alscher, *Griechische Plastik* III (Berlin 1956) 81–83, fig. 69.

39. See Vierneisel-Schlörb (supra n. 37) 420.

Schliemann the Archaeologist

Hartmut Döhl

THE NAME OF HEINRICH SCHLIEMANN produces many diverse reactions. One thinks of such descriptions for him as treasure hunter, adventurer, linguistic genius—with all of these flavored with a dash of the Wild West. Many people today, especially academics, wonder if they can regard Schliemann as a prominent scholar. If one believes what is written about Schliemann in a standard book on the history of archaeology, one can lose all admiration for him. According to Michaelis, normally a very level-headed, rational archaeologist,

This is the complete version of the lecture I gave at Boulder in February 1983; the quotations have been verified and notes added. This is not the place to discuss the question of Schliemann the fraud and prevaricator. Such a discussion should take into account the psychoanalytical approaches to Schliemann, which may prove to be quite useful, but till now have been very badly done. It is also essential, I think, to deal first with Schliemann the archaeologist, showing his aims, his archaeological development, his seriousness of purpose; these points must form the context in which any argument alleging his fraudulent manipulation of data is viewed. My study of Schliemann convinces me that any thorough examination of Schliemann's archaeological work will prove him to have been seriously interested in archaeological problems. If we find Schliemann inaccurate or deceitful in his archaeological statements, we should measure him by the same standards we apply to other archaeologists of his day. Nevertheless, any correction of Schliemann's archaeological accounts is useful, but should be made *sine ira et studio,* born of a longing for greater knowledge. Many of these problems are discussed more fully in my book *Heinrich Schliemann: Mythos und Ärgernis* (Munich 1981). Accordingly, I have restricted myself in the notes to those absolutely necessary. [Some of the points made by Professor Döhl have been brought into question by research published since his article was written. Thus, for instance, Schliemann's claims to have tried to run around the acropolis site at Bunarbashi and to have excavated there in 1868 only with the goal of proving that it was *not* the site of Troy now appear to be untrue; see Traill, "Further Evidence of Fraudulent Reporting in Schliemann's Archaeological Writings," *Boreas* 7 (1984) 295–316—Edd.]

It was just 'a blissful credulity,' that gave Schliemann a 'divining rod' to coax the hidden treasures out of the earth. Without any talent and without any academic background, Schliemann was absolutely ignorant of any kind of scientific method; he was without any sensibility for art; his interest was confined to primitive times, curiosities, and vague ideas. He was a dilettante without method or knowledge, a dilettante in architectural and archaeological matters, a dilettante in excavation, without the slightest idea that there existed proper methods and techniques for excavation.[1]

Luckily for Schliemann, when this harsh view was first published, he had been dead for eighteen years.

Born in 1822, Schliemann lived his first forty-five years practically without any contact with archaeology. At the age of forty-six, in 1868, he visited Greece and northwestern Asia Minor for the first time. As a consequence of this visit, he apparently decided "to do archaeology," and thus in 1870 he made his first —illegal—campaign at Troy and in 1876 the excavation of Mycenae. During the last decade of his life, he was closely connected with Troy. He died suddenly at Naples in 1890. His archaeological activities thus cover some twenty years. In the middle of this period, in 1881, he published an autobiography,[2] which has caused havoc and which has been the reason for so many nebulous and contrary views of his work.

After Schliemann's death, this autobiography was entrusted by his widow to the archaeologist Alfred Brueckner with the request that he update it for the years 1881–1890. It was published in 1891 as an "autobiography" of Heinrich Schliemann, though this title is inaccurate for the last ten years, the most important years for Schliemann as an archaeologist. In Germany, this little booklet has been reprinted at least twelve times, whereas only two of Schliemann's own archaeological publications have been reissued.[3] It is this pseudoautobiography that has ignited the new campaign against Schliemann, in which he has been accused of fraud and forgeries. It has obscured the need for an objective analysis of Schliemann the archaeologist and scholar and is the source for often repeated misleading statements, such as the assertion that Schliemann, after having been a miserably poor boy and leading the life of a pauper, found great financial success.

The constant repetition of this theme makes it sound as if Schliemann were only capable of excavating Troy and the other sites that are to his credit because he came from a background of grinding poverty.

96

This is an unjustified moral. One has only to think of Sir Arthur Evans, who certainly came from a wealthy background and excavated Knossos (a site Schliemann also wanted to dig at), or D.M. Robinson, the American archaeologist, who excavated the city of Olynthus near Thessaloniki. It seems to me that this moralizing approach is designed for children, to instill in them a conviction that if you try, you will succeed. But, alas, this view of Schliemann is not restricted to children's books. A prominent German classical dictionary,[4] issued in 1933, devotes fifty-four lines to Schliemann; of these lines just *four* describe Schliemann's excavations—in my opinion his true and lasting achievement—while *seven* lines are devoted to Schliemann's visit to Mecca, including the circumcision he claims to have undergone just in case his status as a Moslem pilgrim was ever questioned.

I mentioned above some labels that were attached to Schliemann. We may add some more: destroyer, dreamer, odd ball, gold seeker, dilettante with no sense of history, blind follower of the words of Homer, fraud, and prevaricator. Confronted with such a contradictory clutter of labels and associations, we would do better to forget the "autobiography" for a moment and look at the actual archaeological activities of Schliemann. In this paper, I want to focus on three points: 1) Schliemann and Homer; 2) Schliemann and history; and 3) Schliemann the excavator.

SCHLIEMANN AND HOMER

As for the romantic story that the little boy Heinrich wanted to excavate Troy, we have only Schliemann's own account.[5] We can follow his career and his scholarly progress by first examining his travels. His first major journey in 1858–1859 did not lead him to Greece, but to the Orient; on a second major trip (1864–1866), this time around the world, he visited Tunis, Egypt, India, Java, China, and (for the second time) America. The motives for these travels were not so very different from those of many a modern tourist: he wanted to see those sites he thought connected with famous people or events. During the first trip to the Orient, he visited in the Hebron the graves of Aaron, Abraham, Isaac, and Jacob. He toured the ruins of Gomorrha and wrote letters "sitting under the four-thousand-year-old cedars, whose timber King Solomon used to build his famous temple."[6] Local guides must have been delighted with this kind of tourist! In China he went to the famous Great Wall, like most visitors. But unlike typical tourists, he carried back with him a three-foot-long tile from this wall. To him, this was history in tangible form.

He was more sophisticated on his first trip to Greece and Turkey (1868), perhaps because he had done some sort of university study at Paris beforehand. He published the results of this trip to Greece and Asia Minor in early 1869.[7] His concept of "tangible history" becomes most clear in the fourth chapter of this book: He was on the island of Ithaca, the home of Odysseus, and started his first excavation there. We recall his comments about the cedars of Lebanon when he speaks about the aims of this excavation: he is looking for the famous olive tree whose timber—according to Homer—Odysseus used for the construction of his marriage bed and around which he built his bedroom. Such an overabundance of naiveté was not blessed by the goddess of good fortune, and Schliemann stated, with great disappointment, that he found "nothing other than fragments of tiles and potsherds and reached the virgin soil at a depth of 2 feet." He abandoned even the slightest hope of finding at this place any "archaeological object."[8] As far as I know, this is the earliest documentation of a specific kind of terminology used by Schliemann: archaeological objects are equated with objects dating from the heroic age described by Homer.

Proof for this equation of "archaeological" and "Homeric" is to be found in several later reports. It appears in extreme form in the diary notes of his excavation at Motya in Sicily (1875). He first describes the excavation of a building with several columns and a good deal of pottery, which he dates to the fifth century B.C., and then continues abruptly: "There being nothing to find and no historical riddle to solve, I shall not continue the excavation." Similarly, in the next year at the acropolis of Cyzicos, he notes: "found nothing at all, not even a single characteristic potsherd."[9]

But back to the year 1868 and his travels. His trip culminated in the visit to the Trojan plain and the search for Troy. Knowledge of the exact location of the city of Troy had been lost in antiquity. Since the Hellenistic period scholars disputed this problem. At the time of Schliemann two hill sites were discussed. In search of the correct hill Schliemann carried his copy of Homer with him and tried to compare Homer's descriptions with the local topography. He was convinced that it had to be possible to run around the correct hill, since Hector had been chased by Achilles three times around the city walls. So, Schliemann tried to run around the hills in question. At this point in his archaeological career, his belief in the poet Homer was as strong as his belief in the reports of the historian Herodotus.

Two years later, in 1870, he conducted the first excavation at the site of Hissarlik. It was an illegal dig, which was stopped after thirteen days. In 1871 he conducted his first real season of excavation, in 1872 his second, and in 1873, his third, during which he discovered what he thought was the double Scaean gate (described so often by Homer), the palace of King Priam, and Priam's treasure.

Meanwhile, his view of Homer had begun to change, especially his notion of Homer as an eyewitness. In May 1873 he reported that the Troy (only 360 feet at its maximum dimension) he had discovered was perhaps too small for the events of the *Iliad*. But Homer had poetic license to exaggerate things. The main point was that now—by means of his excavations—there was proof that Troy had once really existed and that the basis of the Homeric epic was actual history.[10] Two years later, when dealing with the famous Treasure of Priam and the problem of whether or not it was Priam's, he remarked: "I found it (the treasure) in the ruins of the palace of the last king of Troy, who is called Priam by Homer and all classical tradition, and therefore I will also call him Priam, till it is proved that the fellow had a different name."[11] Compared with the naiveté demonstrated over the cedars of Lebanon and the marriage bed of Odysseus, this statement exhibits far more analytical reasoning.

In 1876 Schliemann discovered within the citadel of Mycenae the famous shaft graves. Two years after the excavation he commented in a letter that "it never occurred to me to say that I had found the graves of Agamemnon and his companions. I just tried to prove that they are the graves reported by Pausanias to be the graves of those heroes."[12] He sounds even more sceptical in *Mycenae:* "I therefore believed that Homer had only known the siege and destruction of Troy from an ancient tradition commemorated by preceding poets, and that, for favours received, he introduced his contemporaries as actors in his great tragedy [the *Iliad*]."[13]

This is a most exciting statement by Schliemann, since it shows the beginning of a distinction of three different avenues of scientific investigation: 1) the archaeological findings; 2) the literary tradition; and 3) the historical facts lying behind a literary report. The main goal of the archaeologist or the historian (it is difficult here to make a clear distinction) is to bring these three approaches into one synthesis. That Schliemann in his day could not reach modern standards does not matter. In terms of method he was very modern!

SCHLIEMANN AND HISTORY

The man who trusted Homer so blindly at the beginning of his career inclined more and more to an archaeological-historical evaluation later. But until the end of his life Schliemann claimed that his main aim was to work in "Homeric archaeology," or, as he sometimes phrased it, the "prehistoric antiquities of Greece." In this he was a specialist and for this reason refused to dig in such areas as Montenegro, Yucatan, or Mecklenburg, Germany. In his choice of particular sites for excavation he was led less and less by Homer and more and more by the historical knowledge he gained from his own excavations. When he dug the Mycenaean shaft graves, he noticed that the potsherds he found there were older than the potsherds found around the Lion Gate. He further observed that the sherds from Troy II (Homeric Troy for Schliemann) were even older than those from both of these areas.[14] From an archaeological point of view this was quite correct: the Lion Gate and the circle enclosing the graves are later than the shaft graves; Troy II is older than the shaft graves.

For several years he tried to get permission to excavate at Knossos in Crete. Visiting the site, he had noticed pottery of the Mycenaean type on the surface. Because of this he expected much older sherds to be found in the deeper strata of this site (and later on, Evans even found neolithic sherds here).[15] The local pottery of Troy made him look at ancient Sardis, which had similar pottery; at Ephesos he advised the excavator to make deep soundings in search of prehistoric strata, and he offered the same advice at Olympia. Besides prehistoric sites he now also investigated historical sites, such as the tomb of the warriors who fell at Marathon, the tomb of the warriors who died at Thermopylai, the citadel of Sphacteria mentioned by Thucydides, and the palace of Cleopatra in Alexandria. And even while traveling he preferred historical routes, as when he followed the march of the Persian king Xerxes with the great pathologist Rudolf Virchow in 1879 and 1890.

He liked to view landscape in its historical context and would climb mountains to have a wide view. On his last trip through the Peloponnese (in 1889) he climbed up the four-hundred-foot-high hill at Mantinea: "The view from there over the lower-city whose circular enclosure is precisely demarcated by the city-wall with its hundred towers, is beautiful beyond description and particularly interesting when one recollects the important historical events that took place in and near the town."[16]

Hills and mountains fascinated him, and, during his first trip through Italy and Greece in 1868, he climbed Acrocorinth: "From this point you can see the most important places of Greece. . . . Since I carried my copy of Pausanias with me, I read at the top of the hill the description of Old Corinth—and it was hard to believe that there had been once in the plain . . . which offered a prospect of only ruins and desolation, a most important and famous city, the pride of Greece and the center of its trade."[17]

He was motivated by historical interest—even in situations remote from his beloved prehistoric times—when he offered to dismantle the Frankish tower on the Acropolis at Athens; the costs would have amounted to twelve thousand francs, but they would have been worth it in the interest of scholarship since many ancient inscriptions had been reused as building material in the walls of the tower. He was not allowed to carry out this project himself, but he was allowed to pay the costs when the Greek Archaeological Society later dismantled it.[18]

In an essay on Heinrich Schliemann, the famous historian Sir Moses Finley wonders why Schliemann did not seek closer contact with ancient historians, since these scholars regarded him more seriously than did the archaeologists.[19] The answer is perhaps twofold. One reason may be that Schliemann had had very bad experiences with German historians, especially with the most famous of them, Ernst Curtius. Schliemann's quarrel with Curtius took place at the very beginning of his excavation of Troy. It centered on the scholarly dispute over which of the two hills, Bunarbashi or Hissarlik, concealed the ruins of ancient Troy. Nearly all nineteenth-century scholars favored the hill of Bunarbashi, especially since the Austrian J.G. von Hahn excavated at this site in 1864.[20]

In 1871 (after the very first excavation at Hissarlik) Schliemann met Curtius at Berlin and learned that he would soon visit the plain of Troy.[21] Schliemann was pleased, since he expected that the great authority would prove him right, but he was badly disappointed. Fortunately, we have documents from both sides—Curtius as well as Schliemann and Calvert.

In a letter, Curtius reported that on his visit to the plain of Troy, he and his companions went to Bunarbashi and were astonished when they saw the great walls that von Hahn had excavated, especially one particular wall, which von Hahn had called the "Curtius-wall." The next day, Curtius visited Bunarbashi again and walked "to the springs, where the Trojan women washed their clothes. You can still see those places cut out of the rocks in the shape of a washing trough. Around them even to-day springs issue out of the earth, which remind me of the paper mills at Göttingen, with green meadows and many trees around,—a marvellous place and the main proof that the most important settlement was also here in ancient times."[22]

A "Curtius-wall" and the paper mills of provincial Göttingen[23]—there was really no chance for the few walls Schliemann had dug up at Hissarlik in a few days in 1870! Curtius wrote concerning them: "Schliemann has discovered some walls here, that he thinks to be the foundations of the palace of Priam. And all the Calverts are fighting for this idea, which to us seems absurd."[24] Further experiences with Curtius and other German professors brought similar encounters with arrogance and ignorance. For Schliemann, the result could only have been personal disappointment. He, himself, on the other hand, gained with every excavation a more distinct idea of what history was all about and what it should incorporate. We must keep in mind that Schliemann excavated mainly at sites that were really prehistoric.

Another reason he was isolated from ancient historians may be that Schliemann started out with a very peculiar view of history (the olive tree of Odysseus). But even then he did have some very modern ideas that show he was a pragmatist. Two hills, Bunarbashi and Hissarlik, were in the center of the debate as to the site of Troy. Schliemann's idea was to *excavate* to uncover the historical truth. It is most interesting that his first dig in the plain of Troy (in 1868) did not take place at the hill which he was convinced was Troy, but at the hill he was convinced was not Troy. He wanted to disprove the Bunarbashi theory. He accordingly dug thirty small trenches at widely separated locations on the hill. He explained his action thus: "Normally people excavate at places which offer the prospect of antiquities. Though I was absolutely convinced that here nothing of this kind could be found, I gladly undertook the costs. . . . I had merely the public-spirited aim of extirpating the absurd and erroneous idea that Troy was situated on the heights of Bunarbashi."[25] His first dig in the plain of Troy was thus intended to furnish a negative proof! To the best of my knowledge, Schliemann is the only archaeologist who has excavated just to find nothing (nothing, that is, in Schliemann's sense!). Today we would call this the method of disproving a hypothesis. This is not the only occasion when Schliemann excavated to disprove certain ideas. The method was to test archaeological-historical situations and developments with the spade. Schliemann's historical barometer was pottery.

Again and again Schliemann's written documents show how shocked he was that nobody else seemed to realize the scientific possibilities of excavation. In a letter, dated in 1873, he wrote: "I don't understand how it is possible that people dealt with the greatest and most important of all historical puzzles, 'where was ancient Troy situated?' . . . in such an off-hand manner . . . when it would have taken just one hour of time and just one man digging (sc. to disprove the Bunarbashi theory)."[26] The spade is the instrument for solving historical questions or problems, as Schliemann often claimed. He saw himself as a historian working with a spade.

From this perspective, what are we to make of his spectacular finds of gold and other treasures? From the excavations of Mycenae he reports "wonderful results," but then instead of offering a list of treasures, he continues that "no ancient writer mentions that Mycenae has been reinhabited after its capture and the expulsion of its inhabitants [by the Argives in 468 B.C.]. But I have brought to light most positive proofs that it was reinhabited, and that the new town must have existed for a long period, and probably for more than two centuries, because there is at the surface a layer of rubbish of the Hellenic time, which extends three feet deep . . . down to the second century B.C."[27] For Schliemann, excavating and history were interconnected.

Schliemann sometimes had a very peculiar way of expressing himself. He wrote several times that a particular place urgently expected him, Schliemann, with hoe and spade. Hoe and spade for Schliemann were the instruments with which to reveal history. For him they were the same as ink and pen for the archival historian.

In discussing Schliemann as an excavator, I shall concentrate upon three points: 1) stratified excavation; 2) the meaning of the site; and 3) pottery.

Stratified Excavation

Usually it is claimed that the famous architect Wilhelm Dörpfeld taught Schliemann archaeological method, specifically, how to dig stratigraphically at Troy. Dörpfeld was the hero, Schliemann the fool. "Schliemann's most important discovery was Dörpfeld" is an oft-repeated bon mot. But Dörpfeld was added to the Schliemann team only in 1882. By this time, Schliemann had already decided to excavate the rest of the hill of Troy layer by layer, from top to bottom.[28]

That there were several different superimposed strata, Schliemann realized even before his campaign of 1872.[29] He distinguished five different layers and explained to a visitor in 1873 that "the lowest stratum dates from a time nearly 1000 years before the Trojan war (11–16 m). From 7–10 m are the Trojan remains with the 'Scaean gate,' the 'palace' and the treasure. After a catastrophe this town was covered with a debris of ashes and ruins up to 3 m. Above this stratum arose a new town, that was ruined some centuries later. Above those ruins was founded a new town by inhabitants that were still non-Greek, and above that followed the Greek colony of historic times."[30]

In 1881 Schliemann distinguished seven different layers, as shown in a schematic diagram in *Ilios*.[31] It does not matter that the modern division of the strata is different. It is important that he realized that there was a continuous sequence of cultures that flourished on the hill of Hissarlik. Schliemann, I believe, is the first excavator in the Mediterranean area to have recognized this fact and to have considered the consequences. If we put aside the German archaeologist Ludwig Ross, who observed strata on the Acropolis in Athens as early as 1833,[32] there is only one serious predecessor of Schliemann, and he realized the importance of stratigraphy before the end of the eighteenth century. This predecessor was, surprisingly, U.S. president Thomas Jefferson.[33] Thus, Schliemann did not need Dörpfeld to teach him about the value of stratification, for he was about to begin stratigraphic excavation on his own anyway!

Unlike other archaeologists or excavators and in spite of alleged lies about his personal life, Schliemann was remarkably candid in his publications. He often wrote about his earlier mistakes and misinterpretations. In 1889 he even produced a list of the errors made in his former publications for a scholarly biographer.[34] One would like to come across another scholar doing the same.

Similarly, we do not need others to accuse Schliemann of being a destroyer. In a letter to perhaps the world's most brilliant excavator, the Italian Giuseppe Fiorelli, Schliemann accused himself in 1873: "I thought at the beginning that Troy must be situated on the virgin soil, and thus I destroyed all the Trojan houses that came to light at a depth of 7–10 m, till in August 1872 I discovered the great tower; but of course since realising my great error, I have preserved them."[35] And in a letter to another prominent archaeologist and excavator, the German Alexander Conze, he wrote: "I had a new world before me in the depths of Ilium, and I had to learn everything by myself."[36] Also, in a speech at the Berlin Anthropological Society in 1882, he claimed with great relief that "on the testimony of my architects I can now assure you that I erroneously believed that nine years ago I had destroyed the temple of Pallas Athena; it was just the substructure of a Roman stoa."[37] (Of course, today we would not like to hear even this.) Vertical stratigraphy was only one part of Schliemann's concept of excavation. Careful observation of the site itself was another.

The Meaning of the Site

Unlike the ruins of the classical period, which were mostly visible at the surface, prehistoric remains are totally hidden beneath the earth. Thus, the archaeologist must determine whether remains are in fact concealed at any given spot. Once a possible site is found, trial trenches must be dug. Schliemann opened thirty such trenches in 1868 at Bunarbashi; in 1870 at Hissarlik he started with twenty; in 1874 on the acropolis of Mycenae he opened thirty-four in a trial dig; and in 1876 at Tiryns he dug twenty. The results of those trial trenches at Mycenae led him to the famous shaft graves. It was, therefore, not sheer luck but a methodical approach that brought the rich harvest of results for Schliemann. Not only was he interested in treasure. Schliemann was also concerned about the wider context of a find spot. The best documentation of this is the plan published in *Orchomenos*. The goal of the campaign was the excavation of the treasury of King Minyas (that is, a Mycenaean tomb). The plan indicates all the ruins at the site.[38]

Pottery

Schliemann's greatest contribution lies perhaps in his very careful observation of pottery. In his day, objects in pottery were as a rule only important for display in museum show cases. It was Schliemann who relentlessly maintained over and over again that pottery—including fragments of even unpainted coarse ware—constituted a historical document, a historical clue. He realized the value of pottery for chronological and stratigraphical questions. In a newspaper article dated 13 September 1873, he wrote: "At any place, where there have been human settlements, we find lots of potsherds, which are far more durable than city-walls or fortification-walls. . . . They give us two termini for the date of the enclosing walls: they can neither be older than the oldest potsherds, nor later than the latest."[39] When in 1868 he proved that Bunarbashi could not be the site of Troy, he based his argument on potsherds: he found no potsherd older than the fifth or sixth century B.C.

Over the years, Schliemann became more and more convinced about the value of pottery and its fundamental importance for archaeology. It is only consistent that in his most famous work, *Ilios,* he started his interpretation of the finds with the following words: "In treating of the objects of human industry found in the *débris,* I begin with the most important—Pottery—because it is the cornucopia of archaeological wisdom for those dark ages, which we, vaguely groping in the twilight of an unrecorded past, are wont to call pre-historic."[40] Just as we saw him at Mycenae comparing the sherds from the shaft graves with the sherds from outside the shaft graves and then comparing those with the sherds from both Troy and Knossos, so we see him developing a sound system of comparison for pottery. In an analogy to philological methods, he applied the term "comparative archaeology" to his system as early as 1880. He pointed out in a letter: "In its way comparative pottery is as important as comparative philology."[41]

At Tiryns and at Mycenae he had found a characteristic type of pottery of a typical Mycenaean shape, the so-called stirrup jar. After what was to be his last season of excavation at Troy (1890) and a few months before his unexpected death, he wrote to King George I of Greece from Troy:

> I have the honour to inform you that we have found the ruins of the culture of Mycenae and Tiryns . . . here very near the surface. The pottery of Mycenaean and Tirynthian type, especially the stirrup-jar, seems to be imported from Greece, since we find it together with the typical monochrome grey pottery, which was once spread over the Troad for many centuries . . . and which must be of local manufacture. This stirrup-jar is datable, for it first appears in graves from the time of Ramses II in Egypt (ca. 1350 B.C.); thus the stirrup-jar can serve as a tell-tale sign for the chronology of the upper levels at Troy.[42]

And since he had also discovered in these upper levels (the former sixth stratum from the bottom) the ruins of another building of the megaron type, it was just a matter of time before Schliemann would have published his realization that the Homeric Troy, the Troy of Mycenaean times, lay not in the second level from the bottom, but in the sixth. At the crucial juncture he died, and Dörpfeld published the new findings and emerged once again as the great hero.[43]

To conclude this study of Schliemann the archaeologist, I turn to the words of his friend Rudolf Virchow who summed up Schliemann's contributions in his memorial address: "He [Schliemann] had great aims and he achieved many of them. What he did achieve, he brought about by the force of his strong will. In all the fortunes and misfortunes of life he remained true to himself. His only constant aspiration was his longing for higher knowledge.—Let us honour his memory."[44]

NOTES

1. Adolph Michaelis, *Ein Jahrhundert kunstarchäologischer Entdeckungen*[2] (1908) 210 ff.

2. *Ilios* 1–20. An earlier, shorter autobiography appeared in *Ithaka* xix–xxviii.

3. In the United States nearly all archaeological publications of Schliemann have been reprinted at least twice since 1960.

4. H. Lamer, E. Bux, and W. Schöne, *Wörterbuch der Antike* (Leipzig 1933) 597 ff.

5. Cf. J. Irmscher, "Über Heinrich Schliemanns erstes Trojaerlebniss," *EAZ* 21 (1980) 659ff. G.S. Korres, *Bibliographia Errikou Sliman* (Athens 1974) 21, published a newspaper article about a speech of Schliemann in 1877 in which he told the same story.

6. *Briefe* 108 (26 May 1859). Even more curious is a note in a letter of 30 May 1859, accompanying "two new shoots of cedars of Lebanon, offspring of one of the four-thousand-year-old cedars" and "a piece of Madame Lot, that is, a piece of the pillar of salt into which she was changed when she turned around" (*Briefe* 110).

7. *Ithaka* was first published in French in Paris in 1869.

8. *Ithaka* 29.

9. Unpublished part of Diary No. 15 at the Gennadius Library in Athens, 50 (22 September 1875), 53 (April 1876). But, of course, he found many fragments from later times.

10. *Briefwechsel* I, 230.

11. *Briefe* 145f. (24 April 1875).

12. *Briefe* 151 (August 1878).

13. *Myc.* 335.

14. *Myc.* Chapter X.

15 Cf. *Briefe* 254f. (13 June 1886).

16. *Briefe* 286 (24 April 1889). There are not a "hundred towers" to be seen from the hill. Is this another case of prevarication?

17. *Ithaka* 84f.

18. Cf. *Briefwechsel* I, 267, 270 (2 July 1874 and 6 August 1874).

19. M.I. Finley, "Schliemann's Troy: One Hundred Years After," *ProcBritAc* 60 (1974) 401.

20. J.G. von Hahn, *Die Ausgrabungen auf der homerischen Pergamos* (1865).

21. *Briefwechsel* I, 186 (12 August 1871).

22. Ernst Curtius, *Ein Lebensbild in Briefen,* ed. Friedrich Curtius (Berlin 1903) 607 (5 September 1871).

23. Curtius had been a professor at Göttingen from 1856–1868! There was not only a "Curtius-wall" at Bunarbashi; von Hahn gave many walls and parts of his excavations the names of such famous scholars as Reyer, Prokesch, Spratt, Leake, Ziller, Finlay, Welcker, Brönstedt, Forchammer, and Calvert. His plan looks like an address book of archaeologists.

24. Curtius (supra n. 22) 608; cf. letter from Calvert to Schliemann in *Briefwechsel* I, 187 (13 September 1871). A thorough investigation of the archaeological activities of the Calvert family is overdue; their archaeological activities are far from being derisory.

25. *Ithaka* 151f. This excavation must have taken place about 10 August 1868. See *Briefe* 111 (22 August 1868).

26. *Briefwechsel* I, 240 (13 September 1873).

27. *Briefwechsel* II, 54 (9 September 1876).

28. *Briefwechsel* II, 140 (6 March 1882). Dörpfeld had not yet arrived at Troy; Schliemann expected him to arrive one week later.

29. *Briefwechsel* I, 199 (6 January 1872), 203 (7 February 1872). The first schematic diagram of the five layers is published in *TroyR* 10.

30. Cf. G. von Eckenbrecher, "Ein Besuch bei Schiemann auf der Städte

des alten Troja," *Daheim* 10 (1874) no. 16, 253. Eckenbrecher arrived at Troy in the early evening of 1 June 1873: "It was, we learned later on, the evening on which he (Schliemann) transported the treasure of Priam to Athens. This had to be done with great care. His wife . . . was not there, she had already left for Athens." If Eckenbrecher is correct, the treasure must have been found before 1 June 1873.

31. *Ilios* vii.

32. Ludwig Ross, *Archäologische Aufsätze* (1855) 88, pl. V.

33. Thomas Jefferson, *Notes on the State of Virginia* (1788).

34. *Briefe* 257 (21 November 1886). The list, handed over to Dörpfeld, was then given to Carl Schuchhardt; see Carl Schuchhardt, *Schliemann's Ausgrabungen in Troja, Tiryns, Mykenä, Orchomenos, Ithaka im Lichte der heutigen Wissenschaften* (1889), published in English as *Schliemann's Excavations: An Archaeological and Theoretical Study,* trans. by Eugénie Sellers (London 1891).

35. *Briefe* 135 (24 June 1873).

36. *Briefwechsel* I, 247 (17 January 1874).

37. See also H. Schliemann, *Troja: Researches and Discoveries on the Site of Homer's Troy* (1884) 206–207.

38. H. Schliemann, *Orchomenos* (Leipzig 1881) pl. III. The very same type of plan was made for other sites like Troy, Mycenae, and Tiryns.

39. *Briefwechsel* I, 239.

40. *Ilios* 213.

41. *Briefwechsel* II, 267 (10 April 1887).

42. *Briefwechsel* II, 359ff. (16 May 1890).

43. He must have already realized the historical consequences of his discovery of Mycenaean finds in Troy VI in May 1890 when he wrote to King George I of Greece. The final publication of the 1890 excavation, finished and edited after Schliemann's death by Dörpfeld, shows a different picture. It is Dörpfeld who is still convinced that Troy II must be the Homeric Troy. He wonders if the Mycenaean pottery could not have been produced as late as the eighth century B.C.; cf. H. Schliemann, *Bericht über die Ausgrabungen in Troja im Jahre 1890* (Leipzig 1891) 60. Not until 1893 did Dörpfeld change his mind in favor of Troy VI.

44. R. Virchow in *ZFE* 23 (1891) 58.

"Priam's Treasure": Schliemann's Plan to Make Duplicates for Illicit Purposes

David A. Traill

IN LIGHT OF THE RECENT RESEARCH on Schliemann it is now indisputable that Schliemann's account of the discovery of what he called "Priam's Treasure" is a lie.[1] In December 1873 he admitted the following in a letter to Sir Charles Newton, then Keeper of the Department of Greek and Roman Antiquities of the British Museum:

> On account of her father's sudden death Mrs. Schliemann left me in the beginning of May. The treasure was found end of May; but, since I am endeavouring to make an archaeologist of her, I wrote in my book that she had been present and assisted me in taking out the treasure. I merely did so to stimulate and encourage her for she has great capacities. So f. ⟨for⟩ i. ⟨instance⟩ she has learned italian here in less than 2 months.
>
> If you wish to visit now my diggings at Troy I give you all my maps and plans by which you find every thing. You find there also the labourers and servant who struck the treasure and assisted me to get it off.[2]

Later, however, Schliemann begged Max Müller to refute the testimony of his servant, Nikolaos Yannakis, when it appeared in an article in *Fraser's Magazine* of February 1878.[3] Yannakis insisted that Sophia was in Athens when the treasure was discovered, that it was he, not Sophia, who had helped remove it from the trench, that the "key" had been found two hundred yards from the rest of the pieces, and that the treasure had indeed contained many bronze pieces "but that his memory was hazy as to the rest."[4] Schliemann assured Müller: "Nicholas never came into the trenches and never saw the treasure or the key of copper which was found together with the treasure, precisely so as I described it in my book. Mrs.

Schliemann of course was present and assisted me; she never left me."[5] When we compare the unequivocal statements in the letter to Müller with those in the letter to Newton we see how faint was Schliemann's passion for what he was frequently disposed to call "the sacred truth." Several other instances of fraudulent reporting in Schliemann's archaeological works have now been exposed.[6] His extraordinary letter to Beaurain of 28 June 1873 should be considered in the light of what is now known about Schliemann's character.

When Schliemann returned to Athens on 25 or 26 June 1873 from his excavations at Troy, he was in a quandary. He naturally wished to make a public announcement of the spectacular treasure he had discovered, or claimed to have discovered, in the closing days of his 1873 campaign. He was afraid, however, that if he did so, the Turkish authorities would immediately demand their share of the find.[7] At this point Schliemann wrote a letter to P. Beaurain, his agent in Paris, who managed his apartments and other business interests there, outlining his predicament and proposing solutions. This letter and some explanatory notes follow.[8]

Privée

Athènes 28 juin 1873

Cher Monsieur Beaurain:

Il paraît que la Providence divine m'a voulu récompenser largement mes longs et pénibles travaux à Troie, car, quelques jours avant de partir j'ai trouvé le trésor de Priam dans lequel figurent 60 boucles d'oreille, 2 immense {sic} parures de tête une grande bouteille & 3 gobelets en or massif et une masse d'objets d'argent d'un valeur inestimable pour la science.

Si je publiais sur ce trésor un article dans un journal j'ai grandement peur que le gouv't turc ne pense à réclamer de moi la moitié du trésor par voie judiciaire {sic}. Et pourtant je serai bien forcé de le publier dans mon livre qui paraîtra en quelques mois. Je trouverai bien moyen de me défendre devant les tribunaux grecs en disant que j'ai acheté le trésor et que uniquement pour la gloire j'ai publié que je l'ai trouvé dans le palais de Priam. Mais pourtant j'ai peur et je vous prie donc de me dire s'il y a à Paris une orfèverie {sic}, d'une confiance à toute épreuve, d'une confiance telle que je pourrais lui confier tous les objets ⟨ . . . ⟩ avec une apparence d'antiquité et naturellement sans y aposer {sic} son timbre? Mais il faudrait mieux qu'il ne me trahisse pas et qu'il fasse le travail à un prix modéré. Peut-être pourrait-il aussi reproduire les vases d'argent en cuivre galvanisé qu'il ferait noircir.

En prenant des informations, veuillez parler d'objets trouvés en Norvège et par Dieu ne dites pas le nom "Troie."

111

Je vous repète que l'orfèvre auquel vous vous adressez doit être d'une
confiance illimitée et à toute épreuve. Agréez, cher monsieur, mes salu-
tations empressées.

H. Schliemann

J'ai ici de grands travaux de sorte qu'à mon grand regret je désespère
pouvoir venir à Paris avant fin Août.[9]

It will be noted that in his description of "Priam's treasure" here
Schliemann mentions only the gold and silver pieces. This is unusual.
Among the many letters written in July and August 1873, in which he
describes the treasure, Schliemann never omits mention of the bronze
pieces, which after all constituted the bulk of the treasure.[10] This omission is significant. Schliemann presumably was not interested in having
duplicates made of the bronze pieces.

In the beginning of the second paragraph of the letter, Schliemann's
dilemma is succinctly stated. He does not want to honor his agreement
with the Turkish government (see note 7).

His proposed defense, namely, that the pieces constituting "Priam's
treasure" were purchased rather than excavated, is, to say the least,
surprising. The whole context of the letter, of course, implies that they
were in fact excavated at Hissarlik, and Hissarlik seems their most
likely source, for all the gold and silver pieces are appropriate for
Early Bronze Age Troy. Even more remarkable, however, is the casual way in which he puts forward this option. There is no apology, no
prevarication. Schliemann seems to feel no qualms about resorting to
these tactics.

The words "Mais pourtant j'ai peur et je vous prie donc" form the
transition to the main subject matter of the letter and show unmistak-
ably that there is a close connection between Schliemann's apprehen-
sions about the outcome of the expected lawsuit with the Turkish
government and his need for duplicate copies. This rules out the possibility that Schliemann merely wanted bona fide copies for distribution
to museums.[11]

A line and a half (about twelve words) are lost after the word
"objets" near the end of the second paragraph. At this time the copies
of Schliemann's outgoing correspondence were made in "Penn Letter
Books." These books comprised five hundred pages of transparent
copy paper. Letters were written in a special, slow-drying ink and
placed under a sheet of copy paper, thereby creating a generally legi-
ble copy.[12] In this instance, however, the copy becomes illegible at the

112

bottom of the page, creating the lacuna. Attempts to restore the missing words should take into account the sentence that follows it, which seems to imply that "tous les objets" does not include the "vases d'argent." Probably then "tous les objets" was qualified by "d'or." The absence of reference to the bronze pieces in the opening paragraph has already been noticed. While exact restoration of the lacuna is probably impossible, the general sense most probably ran along these lines: "d'or pour qu'il fasse des copies exactes de chacun." The word following "faudrait" in the next sentence is hard to read. It is probably "mieux" but may be "moeurs." Neither reading is very satisfactory.[13]

Near the end of the letter, Schliemann's repeated insistence on the absolute discretion of the goldsmith supports the suspicion that his intentions were illicit. The designation "Privée" at the top of the letter, which is rarely found elsewhere in Schliemann's correspondence, even on letters that one would consider strictly confidential, also points in this direction.

Although Schliemann ends his letter with the note that he would not be able to come to Paris before the end of August, he did not go that year at all. In fact, due to his work on *Trojanische Alterthümer* and then the trial with the Turkish government, Schliemann appears not to have left Greece between June 1873 and April 1875. All the published letters for this period were written in Greece.[14]

Beaurain replied promptly:

Paris le 8 juillet 1873

Monsieur,

J'ai l'honneur de vous accuser réception de vos deux lettres des 26 et 28 juin.

Déjà quelqes jours avant la réception de la première j'avais visité les locaux vacants & aujourd'hui je me suis occupé de l'objet de la seconde.

Je suis heureux que vos efforts énergiques & persévérants ont été couronnés de succès & je comprends votre joie.

Je pense que Monsieur Froment-Meurice orfèvre jouailler, connu du monde entier, doit présenter toutes les garanties & la sécurité discrète que vous cherchez; je suis allé le voir sans lui donner aucune indication précise & il m'a dit qu'il pouvait se charger de reproduire n'importe quel objet d'art dans des conditions moderées.

Bien entendu je vous dis ce que je ferais pour moi-même sans vouloir prendre aucune responsabilité & j'ajouterai que pour une affaire de cette importance & de cette nature, il serait préférable à tous égards que vous la traitassiez personellement lorsque vous viendrez ici.

113

J'aurais beau m'entourer de toute la discrétion & de toute la prudence possible, s'il arrivait par hasard que votre quasi-secret fut livré.
Vous pourriez supposer que je n'ai pas pris toutes les précautions
désirables & je serais désolé qu'une pareille idée vous vînt.

Voilà bien franchement mon impression; mais je n'en suis pas moins à
votre disposition pour exécuter vos instructions dans la limite du possible.

Il va de soi que les objets reproduits ne pourront jamais passer pour
des originaux mais pour de simples copies??? Je ne peux savoir si vos
craintes à l'outrance du gouvernement turc sont fondées ne connaissant
nullement la législation du pays.

Je n'ai rien autre chose à vous communiquer aujourd'hui.

Nous possédons le Roi des Rois & à cette occasion l'on nous promet
de grandes fêtes; tant mieux car ça fait travailler & arriver un peu
d'argent chez nos commerçants qui en ont bien besoin.

Et recevez, Monsieur, l'expression de mes sentiments devoués.

P. Beaurain[15]

It is obvious that Beaurain is uncomfortable with Schliemann's
whole proposal but does not wish to antagonize his wealthy client. He
adduces reasons why it would be better for Schliemann to handle the
matter himself but then professes himself at Schliemann's disposal. It is
clear, however, that "dans la limite du possible" is a polite but firm
refusal to become entangled in anything illegal. His question about the
proposed use of the duplicates shows that Beaurain has made the
natural inference from Schliemann's letter that the fakes were to be
passed off to the Turkish government as authentic. Tact and his relationship to Schliemann, however, prevent him from saying this directly. One forms the impression on studying Beaurain's carefully
worded letter that he was a lawyer. This impression is strengthened by
his remark about being unfamiliar with Turkish legislation.

While there is considerable doubt over the details, the overall purpose of Schliemann's letter is clear enough. Faced with the prospect of
being sued by the Turkish government once he announced his discovery
of "Priam's treasure" and probably being forced to surrender half of it,
Schliemann is toying with the possibility of arguing that the treasure had
been purchased rather than excavated. He is reasonably confident that
this argument will prevail in Greek courts. As a backup, however, he
wants to have duplicates made. Exactly what he intended to do with
these duplicates Schliemann does not make clear, but, given the context
and Schliemann's known penchant for fraud, it would be perverse not to
conclude with Beaurain that he meant to pass off these faked duplicates

114

to the Turkish government as authentic pieces. It was an ingenious plan. If the Turks subsequently tested the pieces and found them to be fakes, then it would appear that Schliemann had been telling the truth all along and that he had been taken in by an unscrupulous dealer. The plan had one serious drawback, however. By publicly alleging that the pieces had been purchased, Schliemann would discredit the find by which he hoped to make a name for himself.

Naturally, Schliemann continued to explore his options. A few days after writing to Beaurain he learned, presumably from some lawyer in Athens, that the Greek courts had no jurisdiction over his dispute with the Turkish government.[16] Schliemann in fact prevailed with this argument at the court of the first instance in May 1874, though this ruling was overturned on appeal.[17] It seems then that as of July 1873 Schliemann's first line of defense became the jurisdictional issue. Whether he pursued his plan to have duplicates made is unclear. I have searched the Schliemann archives for correspondence with Froment-Meurice but have found none. This in itself, of course, does not prove that Schliemann did not conduct business with them, since any business of the kind contemplated in his letter would probably have been conducted in person, as Beaurain recommended. On the other hand, Schliemann appears not to have left Greece between June 1873 and the conclusion of the suit with the Turkish government in April 1875. No duplicates of the major pieces have ever turned up and it seems fairly safe to conclude that none were ever made. Two considerations, however, give us pause:

1. It was widely believed in the academic establishment that some, if not all, of the pieces of "Priam's treasure" had been manufactured by an *Athenian* goldsmith on Schliemann's instructions. Evidence for this comes from a very interesting letter of Frank Calvert, published in the *Guardian* (11 August 1875) 1024:[18]

> Dr. Schliemann says—"Mr Calvert's assertions (on a particular point which I shall presently notice) have just as much value as the insinuations he repeatedly made in 1873, both to a great luminary in archaeology in London, and in the *Levant Herald,* that Priam's treasure had been made, by my order, by a goldsmith in Athens." Now, Sir, had I done anything of the kind I could readily have sheltered myself behind the remark that I but shared the general *scepticism* with which the *savants* of Europe notoriously received the first announcement of Dr. Schliemann's *trouvaille,*—a scepticism which was already prevalent with regard to his

previous discoveries, and that, thanks to the hyperbolical terms in which the doctor chose to record them. *But* it so happens that, on the contrary, I stood almost alone in maintaining from the first a belief in the genuine character of the great Trojan "find," and I am happily in a position to prove the fact upon the very evidence which Dr. Schliemann cites against me. By the term "great luminary of archaeology in London," he evidently alludes to his and my friend, Sir John Lubbock, with whom I was at that time in correspondence on scientific subjects. I have only to reproduce here what I wrote (4th Nov., 1873) on this particular head:—
"A portion of the press ridicule the idea that Dr. Schliemann has brought to light the so-called Priam's Treasure—and even go so far as to insinuate it to have originated in the *ateliers* of Athens. Although I have not seen the objects themselves—only photographs of them—*I believe that Dr. Schliemann did discover a number of gold and silver ornaments at Hissarlik.* Still, I do not agree with him in identifying them as the property of the Trojan king.

2. Among the treasures found by Schliemann in his subsequent excavations at Troy are a number of pieces of jewelry identical to items in Priam's treasure. For instance, in his next season of excavation at Troy (fall 1878), Schliemann found no less than thirty-three shell earrings in three separate "treasures" (D, E, and F). Of the earrings in D, Schliemann reports: "The jewels contained 20 gold earrings, of which 16 are precisely similar to those found in the large treasure, which are represented under Nos. 694 and 695."[19] The earrings in E and F are also said to be like Nos. 694, 695, and 754–64 (also in Priam's treasure).[20] Of these thirty-three earrings only twelve were extant in the Schliemann Collection in Berlin when Schmidt made his catalogue.[21]

Whether or not Schliemann actually had copies made of some of the pieces of Priam's treasure and enhanced the finds of subsequent excavations at Troy with them is probably no longer susceptible of proof and certainly cannot be inferred from the letters discussed here.[22] Schliemann's letter, however, is of great importance, for it provides cogent proof that he was prepared to have duplicates of ancient artifacts made for illicit purposes. Since Korres has already shown that Schliemann claimed to have found in his own excavations objects which he had in fact purchased, the time is now ripe for a critical examination of all of Schliemann's finds. Is it not possible that the explanation for the extraordinary wealth of the shaft graves of Grave Circle A at Mycenae may be that they contain a fair number of forged duplicates and purchased items?[23]

116

NOTES

1. See Traill, "Schliemann's 'Discovery' of 'Priam's Treasure,' " *Antiquity* 57 (1983) 181–86 and a fuller version of the same article at *JHS* 104 (1984) 96–115.

2. This letter, dated 23 December but with no indication of the year, is preserved in the Department of Greek and Roman Antiquities of the British Museum. I am indebted to Miss J. Lesley Fitton of the Department for bringing the letter to my attention and to the Keeper of the Department, Mr. B.F. Cook, and the Trustees of the British Museum for kindly granting permission to publish it. In December 1873 Newton was in Athens to examine "Priam's treasure," which, despite published statements to the contrary, Schliemann had offered for sale to the British Museum in the summer of 1873. Naturally, he was interested in establishing the exact circumstances of the find. No doubt he asked Greek scholars their views of Schliemann and learned from them that Sophia had been in Athens from the early part of May and could not have witnessed the discovery of the treasure at the end of May. He would then have questioned Schliemann about this and may well have insisted on a written statement. This at any rate is the scenario suggested by the opening of the letter: "The greek professors try in every possible way to run the trojan treasure down. They do it for two reasons: 1) because they are exceedingly jealous of my discoveries and could crucify me and 2) because they are very anxious it should remain in Greece and are afraid you might take it away. But the truth shall and will be known. I am *now* decided to exhibit it in Naples or Paris if I can get the permission to place it into the goldroom of some museum or some other perfectly secure spot. Would you kindly give me the direction of Mr Gladstone?"

Indications that this letter belongs to 1873 are:

a) It was placed with other 1873 correspondence in a file of loose letters from Schliemann to Newton shown to me in July 1984.

b) The references to May, when the treasure was discovered, are without indication of the year. The natural inference is that the letter was written in the same year as the treasure was found.

c) Other letters written at the end of 1873 show that Schliemann was thinking of exhibiting his collection at Naples at this time; cf. the letter of 30 November 1873 in *Briefwechsel* I, 343.

d) What appears to be Schliemann's first letter to Gladstone is dated 28 December 1873; see *Briefwechsel* I, 244.

The words "and servant" near the end of the letter were added as an afterthought. They refer unambiguously to Nikolaos Zaphyros Yannakis, who acted as Schliemann's cook, personal servant, and paymaster for the workmen. See *TroyR* 63.

3. W.C. Borlase, "A Visit to Dr. Schliemann's Troy," *Fraser's Magazine* 17 (February 1878) 228–39.

4. Borlase (supra n. 3) 235f.

5. E. Meyer, "Schliemann's Letters to Max Müller in Oxford," *JHS* 82 (1962) 98.

6. See D. Traill, "Further Evidence of Fraudulent Reporting in Schliemann's Archaeological Works," *Boreas* 7 (1984) 295–310.

7. In his formal proposal to the Turkish government, dated in Constantinople on 18 June 1871, Schliemann agreed to share any valuable finds with the Imperial Museum on an equal basis; see *Briefwechsel* I, 185f.

8. I am indebted to Mrs. S. Papageorgiou, Librarian of the Gennadius Library, American School of Classical Studies, Athens, for permission to publish these letters.

9. The translation of this letter is:

Athens 28 June 1873

Private
Dear M. Beaurain:

It seems that Divine Providence has seen fit to recompense me generously for my long and arduous labors at Troy, for a few days before my departure I found the treasure of Priam, which includes 60 earrings, 2 huge headdresses, a large bottle and three goblets ⟨all⟩ of solid gold and a mass of silver objects of inestimable value for science.

If I were to publish an article on this treasure in a newspaper, I am very much afraid that the Turkish government would decide to reclaim half of the treasure from me through litigation. And yet I will be forced to publish it in my book, which will appear in a few months. I will certainly be able to defend myself in the Greek courts by saying that I bought the treasure and that it was only for glory that I published that I found it in the Palace of Priam. But still, I'm afraid, and so I beg you to tell me if there is a goldsmith's in Paris in which one could place absolute confidence, confidence such that I could entrust to him all the objects ⟨ . . . ⟩ with an appearance of antiquity and naturally without affixing his stamp. But it is absolutely essential that he not betray me and that he do the work at a moderate price. Perhaps he could also reproduce the silver vases in galvanized copper, which he could blacken.

In the course of your enquiries please speak of objects found in Norway and in God's name don't mention the word "Troy."

I repeat that the goldsmith to whom you address yourself must be someone in whom one can place unlimited and absolute confidence.

Yours faithfully
H. Schliemann

P.S. I have a great deal of work to do here so that to my great regret I despair of being able to come to Paris before the end of August.

10. Compare, for instance, the letters in *Briefe* 133–37 and *Briefwechsel* I, 233–36.

11. In 1872–1873 Schliemann had several casts made of the Helios metope, which he distributed to various museums; see, for instance, *Briefwechsel* I, 217, 222, and H.A. Stoll, "Die Heliosmetope," *Klio* 37 (1959) 273–84.

12. For more on these copybooks and an excellent account of the entire Schliemann archive in the Gennadius Library see D. Easton, "The Schliemann Papers," *ABSA* 77 (1982) 93–110.

13. Suggested restoration of lacuna: "in gold so that he could make exact

copies of each, providing them . . . " "Faudrait mieux" (a slip for "faudrait bien") means "it is absolutely essential." "Faudrait moeurs" would mean "he must be a man of such character."

14. See *Briefwechsel* I, 233–82; H.A. Stoll, *Abenteuer meines Lebens: Heinrich Schliemann erzählt* (Leipzig 1958) 243–52; *Briefe* 132–46; and Meyer, *JHS* 82 (1962) 82–86.

15. Translated, this letter reads:

Paris, 8 July 1873

Dear Sir:

I have the honor to inform you that your two letters of the 26th and 28th of June have been received.

A few days before the reception of the first I had already visited the vacant apartments and today I concerned myself with the object of the second.

I am happy that your energetic and persevering efforts have been crowned with success and I understand your joy.

I think that M. Froment-Meurice, goldsmith-jeweller of worldwide fame, should offer all the guarantees and the discreet security which you require; I went to see him without giving him any precise information and he said that he could undertake to reproduce any art object on moderate terms.

Of course I am telling you what I would do myself without wishing to take any responsibility and I will add that for a matter of this importance and of this nature it would be preferable from all points of view if you were to handle it personally when you get here.

It would be of no avail for me to use the utmost discretion and prudence if it somehow or other turned out that your quasi-secret were released. You would suppose that I had not taken all necessary precautions and I would be most upset if you were to entertain such an idea.

These quite frankly are my impressions; but I am nonetheless at your service to carry out your instructions to the extent possible.

It goes without saying that the objects reproduced will never be able to pass for originals, but only for simple copies??? I cannot be sure if your worst fears of the Turkish government are well-founded, being completely ignorant of the country's legislation.

I have nothing else to communicate to you today.

We have the King of Kings here and for this occasion we are promised great fêtes; so much the better, for that creates work and brings a little money to our merchants, who certainly need it.

Yours faithfully
P. Beaurain

Froment-Meurice was the name of a distinguished family of goldsmiths working in Paris from the eighteenth to twentieth centuries. In 1873 Emile Froment-Meurice was the head of the firm, which employed numerous craftsmen and was located at 372 rue St. Honoré; see *Dictionnaire de biographie française* (Paris 1933–) XIV 1362f.

16. In his letter to Brockhaus of 5 July 1873, published at *Briefe*, 133, he writes: "Nach eingezogenen Erkundigungen kann mir die türkische Regierung

wegen des Schatzes keine Unannehmlichkeiten machen, denn weder hier noch in anderen Ländern, ausserhalb der Türkei, ist ein Gericht kompetent, zwischen 2 Fremden zu entscheiden." ["According to information I have received the Turkish government can cause me no trouble over the treasure, for neither here nor anywhere else is a court competent to decide an issue between two foreigners."]

17. On the course of the trial see S. Comnos, "Hissarlik and Mycenae," *Athenaeum* (8 August 1874) 178: "The tribunal of the first instance having declared itself incompetent to decide on disputes between foreigners, the question was submitted to the Royal Court, which . . . declared the Greek tribunals competent to decide on disputes between foreigners. . . . After the decision of the Royal Court Herr Schliemann . . . appealed to the Areopagus, or Court of Cassation." See also *Briefwechsel* I, 266, 282. The suit finally ended with a settlement, whereby Schliemann paid the Turkish authorities fifty thousand francs (two thousand pounds sterling) and they renounced all claim to the treasure; see *Briefwechsel* I, 282.

18. Calvert had reviewed Schliemann's excavations of Hissarlik in the *Levant Herald* of 4 February 1873. He pointed out, with remarkable acuity, that the excavated material should be dated before 1800 B.C. and after 700 B.C. but that nothing was attributable to the period between these dates. Since the missing period included the time of the Trojan War, these findings enraged Schliemann. His response was to ridicule Calvert's views and misrepresent his role in the excavation of Hissarlik. This attack appears in *TroyR,* 270–75; for a discussion see Traill, "Further Evidence of Fraudulent Reporting in Schliemann's Archaeological Writings," *Boreas* 7 (1984) 295–316. Calvert responded in a long letter, which was published in the 7 and 14 November 1874 issues of the *Athenaeum*. Schliemann countered in the *Guardian* of 31 March 1875. It is to the charges in this letter that Calvert is responding in the letter quoted here. Unlike Schliemann, Calvert was, as far as I have been able to determine from extensive reading of his correspondence, scrupulously truthful. See also Chapter 2.

19. *Ilios* 490. There is some confusion over the types of rings in "Priam's treasure" (now more scientifically known as Treasure A) and the numbers of each type. If we restrict ourselves to the evidence of the plates in the *Atlas* of photographs, which supplements *Trojanische Alterthümer* (Leipzig 1874), and H. Schmidt's catalogue, *Heinrich Schliemann's Sammlung Trojanischer Altertümer* (Berlin 1902), which seem to be consistent with one another, a fairly clear picture of the fifty-six earrings emerges. There appear to have been:

a) Thirty plain shell earrings—twelve with three lobes (Schmidt 5882–93), seventeen with four lobes (Schmidt 5894–5910), and one with six lobes (*Atlas* pl. 196, no. 3540 and pl. 208).

b) Twenty shell earrings with studs—two with four lobes and seven studs (Schmidt 5911–12) and eighteen with six lobes and sixteen studs (Schmidt 5913–32).

c) Six lunate-shaped earrings with granulation (Schmidt 5929–32).

Schmidt catalogues only fifty-one rings. Missing are one plain shell earring with six lobes, two shell earrings with six lobes and sixteen studs (reported by Schmidt to be in Athens), and two lunate-shaped earrings with granulation. At *TroyR* 337 Schliemann divides the thirty plain shell earrings as follows: ten with three lobes and twenty with four lobes. These figures, however, cannot be reconciled with plates 196 and 207–209 of the *Atlas* or with Schmidt's catalogue. *Ilios* nos. 694 and 695 illustrate plain shell earrings with six and five lobes respectively. No. 695, having five lobes, does not in fact appear to have belonged to Priam's treasure, as the above discussion demonstrates. For further discussion of these and other items of Treasure A see D. Easton, "Priam's Treasure," *Anatolian Studies* 34 (1984) 141–69.

20. Treasure E contained, according to Schliemann, "14 ear-rings of the common Trojan type, like Nos. 694, 695, 754–764" (*Ilios* 494). Treasure F included "3 others ⟨that⟩ have the usual Trojan form of Nos. 694, 695, and 754–764" (*Ilios* 498). Nos. 754–64 illustrate plain shell earrings with three, four, and six lobes.

21. Under Treasure D Schmidt (supra n. 19) lists twelve plain shell earrings—one with three lobes (5976), four with five lobes (5977–80), and six with six lobes (5981–85). He also notes (237 n.) that these earrings are to be distributed over Treasures D, E, and F.

22. The pieces were lost, along with "Priam's treasure," in the latter days of the Second World War. For a recent account of the fate of the collection see G. Saherwala, "Die Geschichte der Sammlung trojanischer Altertümer," *Troja—Heinrich Schliemanns Ausgrabungen und Funde* (exhibition catalogue), ed. G. Mahr (Berlin 1981) 39–48.

23. This hypothesis is developed in my introduction to Schliemann's Mycenae diary below.

Part Two

THE MYCENAEAN DIARY

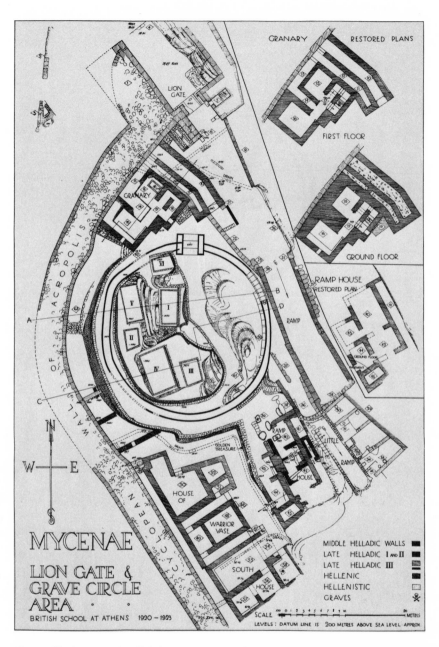

Grave Circle A and adjoining structures. (Wace, *Mycenae;* courtesy of the British School at Athens.)

Introduction

David A. Traill

SCHLIEMANN'S EXCAVATION OF MYCENAE in the latter half of 1876 ranks among the most significant developments in the history of archaeology. It did indeed, as he never tired of pointing out, open up a new world for archaeology. The shaft graves, far more then the prehistoric remains on Hissarlik, revealed an Aegaean civilization of remarkable wealth and sophistication, whose very existence had not even been suspected. A century of archaeological activity has considerably enhanced our knowledge of the Mycenaean world and has enabled us to see Schliemann's discoveries in perspective. In particular, the discovery of Grave Circle B at Mycenae has helped solve some of the problems posed by Grave Circle A.[1] Many problems, however, remain unsolved. Emily Vermeule closes her recent study of the shaft graves with some typical questions: "How does the Middle Helladic set of designs, essentially abstract and only feebly pictorial, connect with

I would like to record my thanks to various institutions and individuals who made this study possible. I am deeply grateful to the staff of the Gennadius Library, American School of Classical Studies, Athens, for courteously assisting my research there, and, in particular, to the librarian, Mrs. Sophia Papageorgiou, for granting me permission to publish the text of Schliemann's 1876 Mycenae diary; to Professor G. Mylonas, president of the Archaeological Society in Athens, for kindly letting me examine the Stamatakis correspondence in the possession of the society; and to the University of California at Davis for providing travel grants to facilitate my study in Athens. I am further indebted to numerous friends for assistance on many points, particularly to Professors G. Korres, University of Athens, S. Spyridakis, University of California, Davis, W. M. Calder III, University of Colorado, and Morton Smith, Columbia University, and to Samuel S. Foulk, Esq. of San Francisco.

such a rich world of animal imagery as we find in the Shaft Graves? How is the influence of Crete so great, so swift, and so acceptable?"[2] Behind these looms a larger question, which has perhaps merely been exacerbated by our increased knowledge. It is bluntly posed elsewhere by the same scholar: "How did the princes of the Shaft Graves get so rich?"[3] This has never been satisfactorily answered.[4] Now that we know that Schliemann's archaeological reporting was not always honest, we need to look at this question afresh. But first it will be useful to review briefly the history of Schliemann's association with the site.

Schliemann first visited Mycenae at the end of August 1868. His diary report of the visit, which lasted about three hours, is based on the excellent section on Mycenae in John Murray's *Handbook for Travellers in Greece* (London 1854). Schliemann's detailed description of the sculpture above the Lion Gate and of the interior of the Treasury of Atreus and most of the measurements he provides are clearly taken from this source. He shows as yet no interest in locating the heroic tombs to which Pausanias refers (2.16.6) or indeed any awareness that Pausanias had commented on the site at all. In short, the diary account reveals no knowledge of the history or significance of the site that cannot be attributed directly to Murray's guide. This tends to support the view, articulated more fully elsewhere, that Schliemann's interest in excavating Homeric sites, so far from being a lifelong dream, probably only began in the summer of 1868.[5] On the other hand, there are in the diary a few typically perceptive observations for which Schliemann is not indebted to the guidebook. For instance, he notes the abundance of sherds on the acropolis and deduces from this that the site was inhabited and probably, therefore, Agamemnon's capital, as traditionally believed.

An expanded account of this visit appears in *Ithaque, le Péloponnèse et Troie*.[6] This was written up in Paris in the last three months of 1868, when Schliemann seems to have immersed himself in the study of Troy and Mycenae. He now offers an interpretation of Pausanias 2.16.6 which postulates that most of the heroic tombs seen by Pausanias were located within the extant city walls. What led him to this unorthodox view is unclear, but he may have been influenced by local gossip and what were, fairly obviously, signs of clandestine digging within the walls. He reports: "comme j'ai eu l'occasion de le voir dans une fosse, creusée par un paysan dans un but que je n'ai pu connaître, on trouve de ces débris jusqu'à une profondeur de six mètres."[7]

Most of 1869 was spent in divorce proceedings in Indianapolis and in courting and eventually marrying Sophia Engastromenos in Athens.[8] Once free to devote his energies to archaeology again, Schliemann conducted a brief excavation at Hissarlik in April 1870 without the consent of the owners of the land. He was soon stopped. In the same year he had also planned to excavate Mycenae. However, at this time bands of brigands were roaming unchecked in Greece, and he decided that excavating Mycenae would be too risky an undertaking.[9] He then had three seasons of excavation at Hissarlik in 1871, 1872, and 1873. His account of his discoveries appeared in German and French editions in February 1874.[10] At the beginning of March 1874 Schliemann requested permission from the Greek authorities to excavate Mycenae and then, without waiting for a reply, set off to begin digging. He hired some workmen and over a period of five days dug thirty-four trial trenches in different parts of the site.[11] In most cases, he reached bedrock in less than a meter. Within the Lion Gate, however, he dug six trenches, which went much deeper, reaching bedrock only at depths of fourteen to twenty feet. Various accounts of these excavations are published.[12] Schliemann reports that he found only a great deal of pottery and, in particular, a large number of clay figurines. When the minister of culture learned of Schliemann's illegal activities, he sent an irate letter to the ephor of the Argolid to see that these excavations were stopped forthwith. He also ordered that any finds should be confiscated. A lively account of this episode, which draws on otherwise unpublished official documents, is to be found in Emil Ludwig's biography.[13]

Schliemann finally received permission to excavate at Mycenae on 29 March 1874.[14] He was unable to resume excavations, however, because a lawsuit was brought against him by the Turkish government in April 1874. The Turks demanded their half share of the treasure that Schliemann claimed to have found at Hissarlik. In April 1875 the matter was settled when Schliemann agreed to pay the Turkish government the sum of fifty thousand francs (two thousand pounds sterling) in lieu of their share.[15] During the rest of 1875, Schliemann spent most of his time lecturing to learned societies and visiting major archaeological collections throughout Europe in search of objects to compare with the artifacts he had unearthed at Troy and Mycenae. He also conducted brief excavations at Alba Longa and Motya.[16]

In the following year, after four months of intensive lobbying in

Constantinople, he finally obtained, on 5 May, a *firman* to resume excavations at Hissarlik. However, violent disagreements with the governor of the Dardanelles, Ibrahim Pasha, and the agent appointed by him to supervise the excavations, Isset Effendi, led to Schliemann's abrupt departure from the Troad at the beginning of July before excavations had even begun.[17] By 20 July he claims to have applied for and obtained permission to conduct excavations at Tiryns, Mycenae, and Orchomenos.[18] It seems, however, that the permit was awarded not to Schliemann but to the Greek Archaeological Society. W. Simpson observes: "The right to excavate at Mycenae was given, if I am rightly informed, to The Archaeological Society of Athens and not to Dr. Schliemann; but as he had been applying for such a right, the Archaeological Society engaged him to carry on the explorations under the inspection of M. Stamataki {sic}, one of their body, and who was to receive the objects as they were discovered during the excavations."[19] The finds, of course, in accordance with Greek law, were to be the property of the state. Shortly after the close of excavations, the finds were taken to Athens. With few exceptions they are housed in the National Museum there.

It is unclear what restrictions the Archaeological Society imposed on Schliemann other than appointing Stamatakis to receive and guard the finds. Stamatakis also represented the general ephoria of the Ministry of Culture as supervisor of the excavations. Excerpts from his reports to both the ephoria and the society are published in Ludwig's biography.[20] From what can be inferred from these documents, it appears that Schliemann exploited to his own advantage the lack of both a specific contract between the ephoria and himself on the one hand and of clear-cut restrictions imposed on him by the society on the other. Thanks to the ambiguity of his position and to appeals to higher authorities in the government and the society, Schliemann successfully thwarted Stamatakis's attempts to restrict the number of workmen and the number of places being excavated simultaneously. Most of the time, Schliemann had workmen digging at the Lion Gate, at the grave circle, and at the Tomb of Clytemnestra. For considerable periods, too, he had workmen excavating the buildings north and south of the grave circle. In one letter Stamatakis complained that Schliemann was excavating in seven different places.[21] Occasionally, as, for example, on 2 November, Schliemann took a group of workmen to dig at a site some five hundred meters from the Lion Gate. When it is recalled that

Schliemann often had over 120 workmen, one can readily sympathize with Stamatakis's complaints that his task of providing adequate supervision of the workmen had been rendered very difficult. Moreover, besides keeping an eye on the workmen, Stamatakis and his assistant had to receive, clean, and catalog the finds, keep a daybook up to date and make periodic reports to both the Ministry of Culture and to the Greek Archaeological Society.[22] Their task was not made any easier by Schliemann's tendency to fly into a rage whenever Stamatakis tried to exercise his authority and, for instance, stop the removal of a slab before it had been properly examined. Accordingly, if Schliemann had made some arrangement with his workmen to dupe Stamatakis—for example, that he would pay them well for every piece of gold they passed on to him without Stamatakis's knowledge—it is easy to see how this could have been carried out. It is worth recalling that Schliemann's foreman, Spyros Dimitriou, had also worked with him at Troy, where some such arrangement was no doubt made to hide the most valuable finds from the eyes of the Turkish official.[23] Given the admittedly conscientious but nonetheless clearly inadequate supervision of Schliemann's excavations at Mycenae, it is now appropriate to look with a more skeptical eye at the enormous wealth of the shaft graves.

The *richest* graves in Grave Circle B and the *poorest* in Grave Circle A (Graves I, II, and VI) are comparable in wealth.[24] But they are completely outstripped by the splendor of Graves III, IV, and V in Grave Circle A. Of the approximately 14 kilograms of gold objects from the six graves in Grave Circle A, 13.4 kilograms come from these three tombs, with more than half of that from Grave IV alone.[25] Vermeule's question can therefore be put more precisely: "Why are Graves III, IV, and V so rich?" In 1876 they astonished the world with their wealth. More than one hundred years later, though familiarity has dulled our reaction, they still astonish. R. Hope Simpson's *Mycenaean Greece* lists more than eight hundred Mycenaean sites in Greece.[26] Not one has produced a tomb with even one tenth of the weight of gold ornaments found in Shaft Grave IV. This fact is surely as remarkable as the wealth of Grave IV itself. When one recalls how unscrupulous Schliemann was, one cannot help but wonder if the facts were quite as Schliemann has presented them. The parallel with Troy is suggestive. "Priam's treasure" is the richest single find from any Early Bronze Age site in Western Anatolia. Recent research suggests that it is probably a composite assembled by Schliemann from several tomb finds made over the preceding months of excavation.[27] Is it possible that the authentic grave goods of Shaft Graves III, IV, and V were similarly augmented?

It should be stated clearly at the outset that the diary provides us with no evidence of large-scale fraud of this kind. It does reveal a number of errors, confusions, and mistaken attributions. But one would expect to find this in any excavation, particularly in an early one in which there had been a large number of workmen inadequately supervised. It seems likely too that toward the end, the finds came in such quantities that neither Schliemann nor Stamatakis had time to record them accurately. Yet, there are some minor discrepancies which do not appear to be innocent mistakes. When one recalls Schliemann's proclivities, it is hard to escape the conclusion that at Mycenae, too, he deliberately distorted the archaeological record.

We shall first examine instances in which deliberate misrepresentation of the facts seems certain and then proceed to a discussion of various hypotheses that seek to explain the immense wealth of Graves III, IV, and V by positing on Schliemann's part the kind of behavior we find at other stages in his career.

In the diary entry of 19 September Schliemann claims to have found a serpentine gem with an engraving of two horses and two human figures, which he describes in some detail. In his sixth report to the *Times* (*Times* VI), Schliemann specifies that this gem was found along with two others, at a depth of sixteen and a half feet, "on the north side of the large cyclopean house" (apparently one of the buildings south of the grave circle). One of the other gems had a representation on it of a "cow-head with very long horns." At *Mycenae,* 362, however, Schliemann states categorically that both these gems (*Mycenae* nos. 539 and 541) were purchased from villagers in Chonika. Why then, one might fairly ask, did he represent them as genuine excavation finds in the diary and the *Times*? An innocent mistake seems unlikely. Our suspicions are increased by the presence of an asterisk—the only one in the excavation notebook proper—beside the description of the find. Perhaps we should pose the question in a different form: why did Schliemann feel compelled to tell the truth about these gems in *Mycenae*? On this, of course, we can only speculate. Consideration of analogous discrepancies, however, offers some guidance.

In *Times* VII Schliemann reports that Dom Pedro visited the sally port of the northeast extension. The diary confirms that Dom Pedro visited the site on 29 October, but also indicates that the sally port was not discovered until 8 November. It is hard to see how the misinformation in the *Times* could be an honest mistake, especially if, as seems likely (diary note 142), Dom Pedro never went near the sally port. Even harder to see as a slip is Schliemann's claim that Dom Pedro rather than Drosinos, Schliemann's engineer, actually discovered it. While these statements might be dismissed as harmless puffery, they do show a disconcerting disregard for truth. More relevant to our immediate purpose, however, is the fact that these untruths are studiously avoided at *Mycenae* 144f.

Another discrepancy concerns Sophia. In *Times* X Schliemann describes how, once they had reached the level of the burials, Sophia and he would get down on their hands and knees in the mud and pry out the jewelry with knives. The passage occurs in his description of Grave IV, but he is speaking generally of their procedure in all the tombs. The Nauplion newspaper, the *Argolis,* however, reports that Sophia departed from Nauplion on the same steamer by which Professor Phinticles arrived from Athens. It is clear that Phinticles reached Mycenae on 27 or 28 November.[28] Probably, then, Sophia left Nauplion on 27 or 28 November, or possibly 29 November, and, if so, would certainly not have participated in the excavation of Grave V and probably not in the greater part of Grave IV. This appears to be confirmed elsewhere in the *Argolis,* where it is reported that Schliemann, Stamatakis, and Phinticles were working in the mud with their knives, but no mention is made of Sophia.[29] In the corresponding passage at *Mycenae* 214, Schliemann makes no claim that Sophia was working in the mud with her knife. The "Mrs. Schliemann and I" of *Times* X has been replaced by a vague "we,"[30] perhaps because Schliemann knew that Stamatakis and Phinticles, though unlikely to read the *Times* reports, would certainly read his book. Similar considerations could have forced him to a more accurate account of Dom Pedro's visit. The need for accuracy in *Mycenae* about the provenience of the gems is less obvious. Perhaps, however, Schliemann recalled that Stamatakis knew that these gems had been purchased or simply that they would not appear in Stamatakis's daybook. The enigmatic asterisk in the diary entry of 19 September could have been intended to remind him of this.

The above argument suggests that the discrepancies between the *Times* and *Mycenae* accounts are attributable to Schliemann's perception of his audience and of its ability to control the accuracy of his statements. The critical factor appears to have been whether he thought Stamatakis and a few others would form part of that audience. If this analysis is correct, it follows that on matters in which Schliemann had successfully duped Stamatakis and the others there would be no need to change his story in *Mycenae*. Thus, the substantial agreement between the diary, the *Times,* and *Mycenae,* while seeming to confirm the integrity of Schliemann's excavations, cannot be considered sufficient proof of this. False claims in *Troy and Its Remains* are supported by false claims in Schliemann's 1873 diary.[31]

There are some striking similarities between Schliemann's 1871–73 Trojan campaign and the 1876 excavation of Mycenae. Both were preceded by illegal trial diggings in which Schliemann was not supervised by competent authorities.[32] In both campaigns, finds of precious metal are sparse until the last two weeks, when they suddenly come in great profusion. At Troy almost all the gold and silver found in 1871–73 was found in "Priam's treasure." At Mycenae almost all the gold was found in the shaft graves and 95 percent of that came from Graves III, IV, and V between 23 November and 2 or 3 December. Yet, Schliemann had found a gold-covered button under the stelae above Grave V as early as 19 September. He abruptly abandoned the excavations on 2 or 3 December, with the grave circle incompletely excavated, and returned to Athens. No explanation for his precipitous departure has ever, to the best of my knowledge, been put forward. The following year Stamatakis discovered and excavated Grave VI.[33] Could it be that Schliemann knew that there was little more to find because everything that had been planted had already been dug up?

The finds of Graves III, IV, and V could have been enhanced in any or all of the following ways: 1) with finds from undisclosed graves discovered elsewhere in the grave circle; 2) with pieces found by local villagers and purchased by Schliemann; or 3) with modern copies. We shall examine these possibilities in turn.

1. Scholars are generally agreed that Schliemann found more tombs in Grave Circle A than he reports in *Mycenae.* It is assumed that these tombs were much less impressive than the shaft graves and that Schliemann dug through them unawares. Some of these, such as the Middle Helladic graves east of Shaft Grave III (see diary note 211), are unlikely to have produced much in the way of precious metals. On the other hand, what were presumably Late Helladic III burials under the overhang in the center of the grave circle, may well have produced some

valuable grave goods. Even Schliemann himself suggests as much at *Mycenae* 164: "as so many small objects were found just below the dangerous rock, two of my workmen always returned to the spot." Their zeal is explained by Schliemann's practice of paying a bonus for every trinket found. Yet, the only valuable object he reports being found under the overhang is a bronze dagger. Evidence that Schliemann found other tombs either within or close to the grave circle occurs here and there in the diary (e.g., 15 September entry). On 21 August Schliemann reports the discovery of a bronze sword, one of the most impressive of the early finds. Yet there is no mention of it in the early *Times* reports. It appears to resurface in *Times* VI, where a sword is associated with the find of an alabaster pommel of a sword handle. At the corresponding diary entry (25 October), there is no mention of a sword. Yet this fairly clear instance of "saving" a valuable find for later deployment is exceptional, and some will see it as an innocent error. On the other hand, it is likely that if Schliemann had made rich finds which he wished to put aside for adding to the royal graves which he was determined to discover, he would probably have said nothing about them in his diary. His Trojan diaries record none of the several tombs which were presumably excavated prior to the end of May 1873 and whose grave goods went to make up "Priam's treasure."[34]

2. The research of G. Korres has already shown that Schliemann bought antiquities and passed them off as finds from his own excavations.[35] As we have seen in the case of the gems discussed above, Schliemann indulged in this behavior at Mycenae, too. Though in this instance Schliemann corrected in his final report the false information recorded in his diary and disseminated in the *Times,* it is sobering to reflect that if Schliemann had died before writing *Mycenae,* we would have no reason to doubt the provenience assigned these gems in *Times* VI. The question inevitably arises whether the shaft graves were salted with purchased items, whose real provenience Schliemann saw no need to disclose in *Mycenae.* There are indications that many people, particularly Greeks, believed this. P. Gardner, who visited Athens early in 1877 and examined the finds, and A.S. Murray, of the British Museum, report rumors to this effect.[36]

3. Rumors circulated in Schliemann's lifetime that some of his "excavated" finds had in fact been manufactured by a goldsmith in Athens.[37] It is now clear that in 1873 Schliemann seriously considered having

duplicates made of some of the gold and silver pieces in "Priam's treasure" with the intention of passing them off as authentic finds.[38] Accordingly, these rumors of 1876–77 should not be too readily dismissed. Objects in gold leaf are the easiest fakes to make and, until recently, the hardest to detect.[39] If Schliemann found five identical copies of an object in gold leaf, he could have had another fifty copies made with little fear of detection, since the five original examples authenticated both the appearance of the object and its occurrence in multiple copies. Accordingly, if there are any fakes among the shaft grave finds, they are most probably to be found among those objects in gold leaf which occur in multiple copies, such as the gold discs, buttons, and cutouts. These invite suspicion not only because of their superabundance in Graves III, IV, and V and their comparative rarity elsewhere in the Mycenaean world but also because of their strange distribution within these tombs.[40]

A few unique objects are suspicious for other reasons. Among these must be reckoned the so-called Mask of Agamemnon.[41] As G. Kopcke has pointed out in his recent study of the masks, the Mask of Agamemnon is stylistically akin to two masks from Grave IV (Karo 253 and 254) and the electrum mask from Grave Gamma.[42] Yet there are some striking differences. These include the treatment of the ears, which are partially detached from the rest of the mask; the eyebrows, which form two arches, not one, and are chamfered rather than engraved; the lack of eyelashes; and the greater definition in the handling of the mouth, nose, cheeks, and chin. Finally, the facial hair on the "Agamemnon" mask is, as Karo well observes, "ganz singulär": a beard running from ear to ear, a handlebar mustache, and an imperial. Of these three types of facial hair the mustache and imperial are unattested elsewhere in Minoan or Mycenaean art; the beard, on the other hand, while unparalleled on the other masks, is remarkably similar to that seen on the gold inlaid heads on the silver cup from a chamber tomb at Mycenae.[43] In particular, the manner in which the hair is combed down under the mouth suggests a typically Mycenaean V-shaped (or goat's) beard under the chin, of which the mask affords us only a partial representation. Thus there are excellent reasons both for suspecting and for presuming the mask's authenticity. The overall effect of the mask appeals to a modern sense of aesthetics and conforms to nineteenth-century notions of an authoritarian figure. Not surprisingly, it has always been regarded as by far the best mask by scholars and the general public alike.

If Graves III, IV, and V contain genuine Mycenaean objects, which were either found elsewhere in the grave circle or purchased from villagers and then planted in these tombs, their presence will be difficult to detect, given the extraordinary heterogeneity of Mycenaean art and our limited knowledge of its development.[44] Some pieces, however, seem more likely than others to fall into this category.[45] In the only case where it is certain that objects reported from a shaft grave do not belong where they were allegedly found, scholars have found innocent explanations for the anomaly; yet, there can be little doubt that Schliemann reported two terra-cotta figurines from Shaft Grave I in order to support his own theories.[46] Modern gold fakes, on the other hand, can be easily detected without harmful effect to the object, thanks to a technique developed by G. Devoto of the University of Rome, which was successfully used in M. Guarducci's brilliant exposure of the Praenestine fibula as a fake. It is to be hoped that a study based on this technique will confirm or refute the authenticity of these artifacts in the near future.[47]

Finally, there is the mysterious Leonardos affair. Leonidas Leonardos was the chief of police at Nauplion.[48] It seems clear that he suddenly acquired a considerable sum of money in November 1876, which provoked the jealousy and suspicions of his peers. The diary entry of 3 November, in which Schliemann expresses his indebtedness to Leonardos, gives us reason to suspect that Schliemann, not Dom Pedro as was generally believed, was the source of his sudden wealth. Schliemann's failure to indicate the nature of Leonardos's service invites the suspicion that it may not have been legitimate. Had Leonardos acted as Schliemann's agent in procuring from local villagers objects that they had found in clandestine excavations of tholos tombs and other likely spots? Had he assisted in seeding Graves III, IV, and V? Closely bound up with the Leonardos affair is the question of the Corinth connection. Why did Schliemann plan to "return" to Corinth on 25 November, in the middle of the most exciting days of his excavations? When was he there last? Why would Leonardos be interested in this trip? Could it be to make more purchases? Did he know a goldsmith there? The diary does not answer these questions, but Schliemann's diaries are apt to be less than candid.[49]

135

NOTE ON EDITING THE DIARY

In the notes to the diary my principal aim has been to make it more readily intelligible to the reader. I have sought to identify, with references primarily to Schliemann's *Mycenae* and Karo's *Schachtgräber*, and occasionally to other authorities such as Wace and Mylonas, the principal objects mentioned. I have not generally attempted to correct his misidentifications or to offer an archaeological commentary, tasks for which I am quite incompetent. In referring to the shaft graves, I have consistently followed the numbering system in use since Schliemann's day rather than Schliemann's own. Thus I = Schl. II; II = Schl. V; III = Schl. III; IV =Schl. IV; and V = Schl. I.

Schliemann's record of his 1876 excavations of Mycenae occupies pages 61–136 of Diary No. 15. The diary also contains, amongst various travel notes, accounts of Schliemann's excavations at Mycenae in 1874, at Motya in 1875, and at Cyzicus and Tiryns in 1876.[50] Schliemann kept his diary record of the 1876 excavations at Mycenae in English. His choice of language probably reflects his determination to present his findings first to the English-speaking world, preferably in the *Times*. He appears to have reached this decision because his work at Troy had met with derision in the German press, whereas in Britain the reaction had been much more favorable.

Schliemann's spelling and punctuation have been preserved throughout. Occasionally, "{sic}" is used to indicate a misspelling that might surprise. Editorial changes are indicated by angle brackets ⟨ ⟩ for additions and square brackets [] for deletions. Other editorial matter is enclosed within braces {}. The numbers in the margins indicate the pagination of the diary. A slash in the body of the text marks the beginning of a new page. Slashes are also used to separate the Julian and Gregorian dates for a given day; see diary note 17.

OTHER SOURCES

The last diary entry records the activities of 28 November. The excavations continued, however, until 3 December. Accordingly, some reports published in Greek newspapers are appended to supplement the diary. During and immediately after the excavation period, Schliemann sent a series of fourteen reports to the *Times*. Many of these reports differ little from the corresponding passages in *Mycenae*. As a result, only reports VI to XIII, which contain significant discrepancies, are reprinted here.[51]

Unfortunately, the letter copybook containing copies of Schliemann's outgoing correspondence for the latter half of 1876 is lost. However, the original letters he sent to Max Müller in this period have survived and are preserved in the Gennadius Library. A selection of these invaluable letters has been published by Ernst Meyer.[52]

NOTES

1. Mylonas, *Kyklos B.*
2. E. Vermeule, *The Art of the Shaft Graves* (Cincinnati 1975) 50.
3. E. Vermeule, *Greece in the Bronze Age* (Chicago 1972) ix.
4. O.T.P.K. Dickinson, *The Origins of Mycenaean Civilization, SIMA* 29 (Göteborg 1977) 6: "I readily admit that in some topics, such as the sources of Mycenae's early wealth, my argument is tenuous, and would welcome a more convincing theory, but I hope to have shown that there is, at least, difficulty in accepting other views often put forward."
5. See Traill, "Schliemann's Dream of Troy: The Making of a Legend," *CJ* 81 (1985) 13–24.
6. *Ithaque* 94–109; *Ithaka* 88–101.
7. *Ithaque* 100; *Ithaka* 94.
8. On his divorce see Traill, *CJ* 77 (1982) 336–42.
9. *Briefwechsel* I, 161.
10. *Trojanische Alterthümer* (Leipzig 1874) and *Antiquités Troyennes* (Paris 1874).
11. *Briefwechsel* I, 256, 258.
12. *Briefwechsel* I, 253–56, 258–59; *Briefwechsel* II, 33–36.
13. Emil Ludwig, *Schliemann* (Boston 1931) 156–160.
14. Meyer, *Schliemann* 281. This date is presumably derived from the text of the official document, part of which Meyer quotes in German translation (282), and may be Julian. The corresponding Gregorian date would be 9 April. The 1874 agreement gave Schliemann permission to excavate the acropolis of Mycenae (but not the Treasury of Atreus) and the rights to the first publication of his discoveries; the General Ephoria of Antiquities was charged with the supervision of the excavations and Schliemann was required to consult with its representatives regarding the commencement of the excavations, the number of workmen, the duration of his right to first publication, etc. All finds, of course, in accordance with Greek law, were to belong to the state.
15. *Briefwechsel* I, 265, 282.
16. *Briefwechsel* I, 290–96. The Motya sections of Schliemann's diary are

published in B.S.J. Isserlin and Joan du Plat Taylor, *Motya* I (Leiden 1974) 108–10. Schliemann seems to have clashed with the authorities here too; see B.S.J. Isserlin, "Schliemann at Motya," *Antiquity* 42 (1968) 144–48 and Antonio Casca et al., *Mozia I, Universita di Roma, Centro di Studi Semitici, Studi Semitici* 12 (Rome 1964) 13f. n. 3.

17. *Briefwechsel* II, 41, 47f., 50.

18. *Briefwechsel* II, 52: "Um nun hier nicht still zu sitzen habe ich die Erlaubnis nachgesucht u erhalten Tiryns, Mykene u Orchomenos auszugraben." ["So as not to be sitting doing nothing here I have sought and obtained permission to excavate Tiryns, Mycenae and Orchomenos."]

19. W. Simpson, *Fraser's Magazine* 16 (December 1977) 692. Confirmation that this was indeed the arrangement is to be found in unpublished reports of Stamatakis in the possession of the Greek Archaeological Society. I am grateful to Professor G. Mylonas, President of the Society, for kindly letting me examine this correspondence.

20. Ludwig (supra n. 13) 167–72.

21. This unpublished letter, which is dated 5–17 September and addressed to the General Ephoria of Antiquities, is in the possession of the Greek Archaeological Society; see note 19.

22. This emerges from another unpublished letter of Stamatakis, dated 15–27 August, to the General Ephoria of Antiquities. It, too, is in the possession of the Greek Archaeological Society; see notes 19 and 21.

23. *TroyR* 357.

24. Vermeule (supra n. 3) 88; Dickinson (supra n. 4) 40.

25. Karo, pp. 166–68.

26. It is not intended to suggest that all these sites have been excavated, though Hope Simpson observes (216): "Almost all of the obvious major Mycenaean centres have been more or less fully excavated." Still less would I imply that all these sites might reasonably be expected to produce tombs to rival those of Mycenae.

27. See Traill, *Antiquity* 57 (1983) 181–86 and *JHS* 104 (1984) 96–155; for a reply, see Easton, *Antiquity* 58 (1984) 197–204, and *AnatSt* 34 (1984) 141–69. For a reply to Easton, see Traill, *AnatSt* (forthcoming).

28. See Greek newspaper excerpt no. 19. In his letter of 27 November to Max Müller, published by Meyer at *JHS* 82 (1962) 93, Schliemann seems confident that the excavations will resume the following day: "But, at all events, I hope to continue the work tomorrow and finish it this week." Perhaps Phinticles had already arrived; the diary entry of 28 November ("Only today resumed work on arrival of Mr Phendicles") does not preclude the possibility that he had arrived the preceding evening. There seems no suggestion that the day's work was delayed while they awaited his arrival.

29. John Murray (publisher), *A Handbook for Travellers in Greece* (London 1872), describes the steamer service as follows: "Steamers run from Athens to Nauplia and back, once a week, remaining about 10 hrs. at Nauplia." It is unlikely that Sophia would want to be down on her hands and knees

in the mud shortly before her departure for Athens. If she ever did this at all—and this must remain dubious—it is more likely to have been in the excavation of Grave III; see the diary entry for 23 November and note 247. For the *Argolis* report see Greek newspaper excerpt no. 12.

30. Readers of the *Times* would naturally take this to refer to Sophia and Schliemann, whereas those who knew the truth could take no exception to it. In her speech before the Royal Archaeological Society in London on 8 June 1877, Sophia claimed, in language reminiscent of the *Times* report, that "on our knees in the mud, my husband and I had to cut out the pebbles, to cut away the layer of clay, and to take out one by one the precious jewels." Even if Sophia did write most of her own speech, this section at least is probably attributable to Schliemann. On the disputed authorship of the speech, see Lynn and Gray Poole, *One Passion, Two Loves* (New York 1966) 196; for the complete text of the speech see Poole 285–86. The same phenomenon occurs with Orchomenos. In the newspaper accounts Sophia has a prominent role in the discoveries; in the book her role is sharply reduced; see Poole 226.

31. *Antiquity* 57 (1983) 181–86 and *JHS* 104 (1984) 96–115.

32. For Troy in 1870, see Meyer (supra n. 14) 252–55; for Mycenae in 1874, Meyer 279f.

33. See Appendix A: Reports in Greek Newspapers, no. 21.

34. See Traill, *JHS* 104 (1984) 96–115. Similarly, his Indiana diary (1869) betrays no hint of his attempts to circumvent the prior residence requirement, though this was the main impediment to his obtaining a divorce in 1869 and was in the forefront of his thoughts. In fact, Schliemann explicitly denies that there was any such requirement; see Traill, *CJ* 77 (1982) 337–42.

35. "Epigraphai ex Attikes eis Katochen Herrikou Sleman," *Athena* 75 (1974–1975) 54–67 and 492 (French résumé).

36. P. Gardner, "Henry Schliemann," *Macmillan's Magazine* April 1891 (No. 3781) 479: "Greeks smiled at his madness and made him the subject of daily scandal. Some declared that he first bought and buried the antiquities which he afterwards found." A.S. Murray in his review of Schliemann's *Mycenae* in the *Athenaeum* of 22 December 1877 819: "we may not, perhaps, wonder that some of the emulous or unsympathetic seemed half inclined, upon first announcement, to hint that 'he who hideth can find.' " It is noteworthy that two reputable scholars saw fit to refer to such rumors in print.

37. In a letter, which was published in the *Guardian* of 31 March 1875, Schliemann takes issue with Frank Calvert, referring to "the insinuations he repeatedly made in 1873, both to a great luminary in archaeology in London and in the *Levant Herald,* that Priam's Treasure had been made, by my order, by a goldsmith of Athens." In his reply, published in the *Guardian* of 11 August 1875, Calvert denied the charge, observing, however, that "had I done anything of the kind I could readily have sheltered myself behind the remark that I but shared the general scepticism with which the *savants* of Europe notoriously received the first announcement of Dr. Schliemann's *trouvaille.* "

38. See Chapter 5.

39. A. Furtwängler, *Neuere Fälschungen von Antike* (Berlin and Leipzig 1899) 28.

40. Dickinson, (supra n. 4) 50 notes that Grave Circle B produced no gold cutouts or gold-covered buttons. In Grave Circle A all the more elaborately decorated disks—a total of 701, comprising, however, only 14 types—are confined to Grave III. Though hundreds of buttons were found in both Graves IV and V, there were none, apparently, in Grave III. Large numbers of animal cutouts were found in Graves III and IV, but none in V.

41. As Dickinson (supra n. 33) 164 rightly points out, it was not Schliemann who so identified this mask.

42. G. Kopcke, "Zum Styl der Schachtgräbermasken," *AM* 91 (1976) 3.

43. Karo 624. I draw my conclusion regarding the uniqueness of the mustache and imperial from S. Marinatos, *Kleidung- Haar- und Barttracht, ArchHom* I B 24f. Even if one grants that there is a mustache on the round mask from Grave IV (K. 624), a view which Marinatos calls "fraglich," it is of a radically different type from that on the "Agamemnon" mask. For an illustration of the silver cup see Mylonas, *MRIG* 25.

44. Dickinson (supra n. 4) 53 and Vermeule (supra n. 2) 1 and passim attest to the heterogeneity of Mycenaean art, and throughout her book Vermeule stresses our limited understanding of it. Both problems may have been exacerbated by Schliemann's contamination of a core of authentic shaft grave finds (1600–1500 B.C.) with finds from later tombs.

45. Here one may note that all excavated parallels for the three inlaid daggers from Graves IV and V are of fifteenth-century date; see R. Higgins, *Minoan and Mycenaean Art* (London 1981) 140. The Thera fragment illustrated at Vermeule (supra n. 3) pl. XIIIC does not come from a supervised excavation and its provenience is therefore dubious.

46. See diary entry of 16 November with note 212 and *Boreas* 7 (1984) 312–16.

47. The technique is described in M. Guarducci, *La Cosidetta Fibula Prenestina: Antiquari, Eruditi e Falsari nella Roma della Ottocento, MemLinc,* ser. 8, vol. 24 (1980) 546–54; see review of A. E. Gordon, *CJ* 78 (1982) 312–16. Through the offices of the American School of Classical Studies, Athens, I applied in 1982 and again in 1983 for permission for Professor Devoto and myself to examine selected Mycenaean artifacts to test the hypothesis that some of them might be fakes. Both applications were unsuccessful. I regret that the rather startling hypothesis advanced here is accordingly unsupported by the scientific evidence with which I had hoped to substantiate it.

48. In the 3 November diary entry Schliemann implies that Leonardos was chief of police at Argos. Elsewhere, however, as in Ludwig (supra n. 13) 177, he is described as "police superintendant at Nauplia."

49. See Traill, *CJ* 77 (1982) 340f. For the complicity of Greek police with tomb-robbers see the 1896 letter of the dealer John Marshall in Osbert Burdett and E.H. Goddard, *Edward Perry Warren* (London 1941) 200: "The tomb-

robbers are usually half-starving; a find comes and for a month they are rich. The police are watching round, not to stop the work but to share the plunder."

50. For further details of this diary and an excellent account of the Schliemann papers see D. Easton, "The Schliemann Papers," *ABSA* 77 (1982) 93–110.

51. Full references to all the reports are given in the introduction to that section.

52. Friedrich Max Müller (1823–1900) was a distinguished oriental scholar and historian of religion at Oxford University; see *DNB* XXII (suppl.) 1023–29. Schliemann started corresponding with him in 1873. E. Meyer, "Schliemann's Letters to Max Müller in Oxford," *JHS* 82 (1962) 75–105, esp. 88–96.

⑦

The Mycenaean Diary, 1876

Heinrich Schliemann

Charvati 5 Augst: We left Tiryns this morning and spent today all day in the Acropolis of Mycenae.

Nauplion 6 Aug: Visited this morning the sites of the old and the new Heraeon and the Treasury or tomb recently discovered near it; went thence to Argos, where we visited the remains of a large cyclopian building attributed to the substructions of the brass-tower of Danae.[1]

Mycenae 7 Aug: I returned here tonight. Dimitry has worked here today with 22 workmen, opening on the W. side of the acropolis a ☐ exc 10 m broad & 20 m long.[2] There were found on the top the remnants of dwellinghouses of the Roman period and immediately below them objects of the Alexandrine time, such as a splendidly executed Leda of coarse and evidently painted clay, but without head.[3] She is evidently at work with the godly swan, for she extends with her right arm her mantle in order that the thing might not be seen. To the same period may belong a coarsely made seline holding / in his lap the Bacchus child with a Phrygian cap; further a pretty well made terracotta head and a broken terracotta-tablet with the inscription:[4]

this inscription has evidently been much longer. There was also

found a rusted copper coin. These remains were inter-

mixed with *prehistoric* remains, among which I mention
a) a splendid axe of diorite
b) 2 whorls of green stone
c) an idol without head, evidently belonging to a *male divinity;*
     holding the arms across on the breast
d) 2 heads of Hera idol
but all these latter objects must have been washed down from the
steep rock by the winter rain.[5]

Mycenae 9 Aug: Yesterday the feast of the Pantelamon and no
work. Today 50 workmen, of whom 10 from Phichtia at 2 1/2 dr
and 40 engaged by Dimitri who works at 1 dr the metre. But I do
not think he has as yet removed more than 200 cubic metres by
65 day wages, so that he does not seem to profit much by the
bargain. Nothing was found today except potsherds, among
which the fragment of an idol and 2 stone implements or
weights.[6] I have put my 10 men to work from the side of the gate,
so that the entrance will be free in a few days. Already now we
know that from the gate proceed 2 para⟨l⟩lel walls.[7]

Mycenae 10 Aug: I had today 15 labourers of whom 5 worked in
the *treasury*[8] to clear the entrance and *10* in the Lions gate;
Dimitry had *41*. No great progress has been made, because the
latter is anything but an overseer. By the objects and particularly
by the beautiful idols of the good Hellenic period it is certain that
the acropolis of Mycenae has been inhabited, if not immediately
after the capture by the Argians, at least from the Alexandrine
times up to far into the Middle Ages.[9] That the surface of the
Acropolis is strewn with fragments of prehistoric pottery and that
these are found intermixed with the Hellenic and Roman remnants to a depth of more than 4 feet, is no proof to contrary, for
for ages the prehistoric things have been washed down / from the
slopes. We came to⟨day⟩ near the wall to the calcinated remnants
of a large dwelling house;[10] the fire must have raged fearfully, for

143

even the stones of the Cyclopian wall had suffered greatly. found were

a) masses of fine potsherds with the most beautiful archaic designs in red, yellow, brown, etc.
b) a number of greenstone whorls large & small; 1 with a treble cross
c) a[n] cowhead with horns[11]
d) the upper part of a Junoidol with breasts
e) an enormous iron key with 4 teeth, which may be the key of the gate[12] At the other end is a ring for suspension
f) 1 iron knife[13]
g) a 19 Ctm long copper nail which served as hairpin
h) an axe of porphyr {sic}
i) stone weights
j) a piece of blue colour
k) the foot of a large coloured goblet
l) millstones of lava[14]
m) an ὑδρία
n) 3 archaic vases, one of which very wonderful

it is black.[15] We struck on huge stones just inside before the gate.

Mycenae 11 Augst: I had today 16 workmen, of whom 6 in the treasury and 10 in the gate. Dimitri had 40. We are getting deeper and have now in one excavation an average depth of 2 m. The quantity of objects found increases daily. Today were collected:

a) 7 cows
b) 1 idol and 1 basis of an idol
c) 7 whorls of blue or green stone, of which a large one with 6 engraved ⊙ on the flat side

d) 2 glasslike buttons, which must have served as ornaments
e) 1 such   do.   of petrified bone
f) a small but highly interesting key
g) hammers and weights of stone
h) many handmillstones of Trachitestone[16]

144

i)   a vast quantity of highly interesting potsherds, amongst which one with 2 suns and signs like characters

{Workmen's receipts dated 12 August, 31 July, and 5/17 August 1876.}[17]

Mycenae 11 August: I had today 6 workmen in the treasury & 10 in the gate; besides 32 occupied by Dimitri. I measured tonight the cubic of rubbish taken out by Dimitri and found it to be abt 500 m, for which he had to receive dr 500, which hardly covered his expence {sic} and wages for him at 4 dr daily. But, if he were a better commander he would have done a better business. There were found today

a)   17 idols or fragments of idols of Juno; on the top of the polos of one of them was painted a cross of branches of trees
b)   several fragments of pottery with *men*
c)   do.   do.   "   do.   "   4 animals
d)   8 whorls of stone & 2 of clay, also 1 of glass

The many large blocks and smaller stones just inside the gate seem to have been hurled at the assailants in 468 B.C. and to have remained ever since in situ, for the rubbish between them is hard like stone, and intermixed with but few if any potsherds.[18]

Mycenae Monday 12 Aug. I had today 7 workmen in the Treasury and 12 in the gate. Dimitri had 43. We found

1)   wall ornaments of baked clay with beautiful impressed or painted ornaments[19]
2)   fragment of very rude primitive pottery with incised ornaments
3)   2 splendid horseheads ornamented with black lines on a dead colour of a light red
4)   two cows
5)   10 idols of Juno
6)   a long arrow of copper[20]
7)   many whorls of blue or green stone & some of terracotta
8)   Hundreds of splendidly painted prehistoric fragments of pottery
9)   A stupendous head of an iron nail, which must have served as ornament

145

10) several prehistoric vases
11) 3 coins, of which 1 of silver

Mycenae Tuesday 13 Aug. Had today 7 workmen in the Treasury
& 12 in the gate. Dimitry had ⟨   ⟩[21] We found
1) 16 idols with polos
2) 3 cows
3) a small column, perhaps a priapos.
4) ″ do   saw (brown) of silex
5) ″ fragment of a bronze bell
& many most interesting potsherds, of which the most wonderful
are those painted outside and inside. Strange to say the inner
paintings of a vase often exceed in beauty those on the outside.

Mycenae 16th Augst Wednesday. Today 7 workmen in the Treasury and 12 in the gate, where immediately to the right in enter-
ing the gate is a recess formed of huge stones joined by means of
small ones. This small chamber is but partly filled with earth.[22]
More and more large stones turn up in the passage which from
the gate leads to the first gallery. These stones seem to have been
hurled down on the assailants when the fortress was stormed and
the gate must ever since have been out of use. Found today
a) a wooden comb
b) a very curiously ornamented piece of bone, evidently the
                                    fragment of a lyre
c) ″ do   do   small bronze wheel[23]
d) a round and flat piece of wood with a small incision all

around for suspension ; one side, which is very pol-

ished, seems to have once been covered with wax, in which
were incised some 4 or 5 of which are still visible in the
wood[24]
e) 17 idols ⎱ with black or
f) 14 cows ⎰ red ornaments
g) 8 fusaïoli of green or blue stone
h) a very large quantity of outside and inside painted beautiful
    potsherds

i)   a large fragment of alabaster with incised ornaments

The walls come now out more and more and as they rise perpendicularly they present a really colossal aspect. The cyclopean house[25] leans on the wall, and, as the rubbish sticks in the interstices between the stones, both the housewalls and the fortress wall appear as if their stones had been joined with earth. There was found tonight

j)   *1 idol with a bare bird's head and large protruding birds' eyes, very compressed face and the arms hanging down; no cowhorns.*

k)   a plate with 2 handles

l)   an entire vase with painted ornaments

Close to the cyclopean house are several upright standing large flat stones, but probably without significance.[26]

Mycenae 17 Aug Thursday: Had today 8 workmen in the Treasury, where I found by 2 P.M. the triangular space above the entrance, which may be 8–9 metres below it. But on acct of the great rudeness and the insults of Stamatakis,[27] I stopped the work there altogether. In the principal excavation / the cyclopean house, one room of which is 5 m 13 Ctm long & 2.83 broad, having walls 93 Ctm and 1 m 87 Ctm thick, comes out more and more, and the prolongation of this building now appears. Very curious are the many tombs marked by large unpolished tablets of white chalkstone in a depth of 3 1/2 m. I have now brought 8 of them to light, but have not yet dug deep enough to know what these tombs contain, or whether they are tombs at all.

There were found:

a)   11 idols, some of which with a bare bird's head, large birdeyes and the hands joined on the breasts. This sort of idol[s] appears to be the most ancient.

b)   1 *arrow* of bronze of the *pyramidal Phoenician form* like in Motye.[28]

c)   9 cows of terracotta of various colours

d)   a figure (entire) 15 Ctm high, all over with black and brown ornaments on light yellow dead colour; bare head with black ornaments; long female hair indicated on the back and most likely a female figure was intended to be represented, probably a priestess, old and ugly; the features are neither *Assyrian nor Greek.*

e) 2 bronze knives, one of which with part of its bonehandle
f) a fragment of blue *crystal* vase with carvings
g) 12 fusaïoli, of which 10 of blue stone and 2 of terracotta.
h) 4 ornaments of blue stone in form almost of fusaïoli
i) 1 babys {sic} feeding bottle, black on light yellow
j) 1 weight of lead
k) 1 large fragment of a splendid in the Assyrian style ornamented vase found in *2 m;* it has 2 breasts each with a cross.

Mycenae 19 Aug Saturday: Had today no other workmen than those of Dimitry, say 43; I went to Nauplion and during my absence but poor progress was made. There is cyclopean house by house and tomb by tomb; also a cyclopean *waterconduit,* [29] 1 tomb formed of 6 large tablets and 10 or 12 upright tombstones, which probably mark the site of graves. All are of a [30]

{Workmen's receipts dated 8/20 August 1876.}

Mycenae 21 Aug. Today Dimitri had 43 and I had 5 workmen and 1 cart. Besides 27 men from Charvati are working by the metre. We found today
1) 1 beautiful double sword of bronze with the nails of the handle[31]
2) 1 leaden ball with iron hook
3) 11 *Juno idols*
4) 9 *cows*
5) 10 stone whorls
6) 1 formstone[32]

Mycenae 22 Augst Tuesday. Had today Dimitri 42 workmen; I 5 and one cart and the Charvatians had 27 men. Found:
18 cows
17 idols
14 whorls
1 whetting stone

Mycenae 23 Augst Wednesday: Dimitri had today 41. I had 5 and the Charvatians had 26 men; the latter make rapid progress. found
1) 19 idols
2) 16 cows
3) 1 *idol with a cow's head*
4) 1 cow-idol open on all sides
5) many remarkable fragments of pottery.

Mycenae 24 *Août,* 1876. Dimitry had today 40, I had only 5 and a cart; the Charvatians were 26; besides I took 14 men from Fichtia to dig a trench into the treasury. Found
1) a large fragment of a tablet, probably a tombstone, with spiral ornaments on the top and on one side.[33] Besides a number of idols and cows. Among the latter are some large heads of cows, which seem to belong to a woman's body.

Mycenae 25th Augst. Dimitry had today 40, I had 5 and *no* cart; besides 26 Charvatians were working. Among the many interesting finds today is
1) a goblet, in the form of a modern champain-glass {sic}, with a handle
2) a small well painted basin of terracotta, with 4 feet, probably for burning incense
3) a disk with a 5 double painted cross[34]
4) 50 cows
5) 60 idols, one of which, only having 2 breasts and no indication of a face, but all over covered with written characters, &
6) 1 hatchet of stone
7) a hard stone with two series of spiral ornaments
8) a block of red prophyr with same kind of spirals[35]
9) a fragment of Hellenic pottery representing Apollon or Orpheus playing the lyre
10) quite a treasure of bronzen objects;[36]
   a) 1 long knife or sword .27 Ctm long
   b) 1 crooked one   .18 Ctm   "
   c) 3 small knifes
   d) a sheath or scabbard, for a lance, 10 Ctm long

e) 2 small wheels, which however can never have served as such, each 9 Ctm in diameter

f) 2 two edged hatchets 22 Ctm long

g) hair pins

h) 2 half ruined vases

i) remnants of 4 more vases

I found today, *26th Aug, Saturday,* close to the 2 other tombs with bas-reliefs, another tombstone with sculptures, and, 10 feet further W. a fourth one and only 10 feet further W. I think to have found a fifth tomb with sculptures. The length of the 3 tombs is 4 m 10;[37] of the first   1.20 m

              "   " second   1.02 m

              "   " third   1.01 "

between the 2 first tombs the space is 30 Ctm; between the 2nd & 3rd, 42 1/2 Ctm.

{Workers' receipts dated 14/26 August 1876.}

{Drawing of tomb bas-relief (*Myc.* no. 140, Karo pl.V); see p. 151 below.}

{Drawing of tomb bas-relief (*Myc.* no. 24, Karo pl. VII); see p. 152 below.}

{Workman's receipt dated 14/26 August 1876.}

All the payments together were today dr 13464.50. The bas re-liefs I found are very important.

27th Augst Sunday. I accompanied today the painter to Mycenae to get sketches made of the yesterday discovered sculptures. The large trench with the 6 metres high perpendicular cyclopean wall, the 5 m high cyclopean house and the numerous tombs present a curious aspect. S.W. of the cyclopean house are 3 rows of to-gether 46 tombstones,[38] all of them fixed in the virgin soil in 4 1/2 to 5 m depth. These tombstones are 3 to 6 feet high and 3 to 4 ft

broad; until now only 6 tombstones with sculptures were found; but of two of them only large fragments remain. Each has 2 divisions. In one a man in a chariot drawn by one horse, of which he holds the lines.[39] Another man who stands before the horse seems to oppose its progress; he holds horizontally in his hand a long lance of very curious shape which he seems to thrust into the body of the man in the chariot. Both men are naked. Neither the harness nor the thongs of the leather by which the horse draws the chariot are indicated; behind the chariot is the head of a lance. In the division below are 2 circles, each with 3 ornaments in spiral lines which are joined. Below this are 3 horizontal parallel lines. The other tombstone is divided in 3 partitions, in 2 of which are represented large serpents.[40] To the E. of the cyclopean house is a series of 9 tombs, each 2 m high and formed of 5 tablets of a calcareous stone; each tomb is covered by several small tablets.[41] These tombs can impossibly be those mentioned by Pausanias, for, when he visited Mycenae (170 A.C.) even the posterior Hellenic city had probably already nearly 4 centuries ago disappeared;[42] it had left a 1 m thick layer of rubbish and the lower terrace of the acropolis was just as full of rubbish as it is now. Thus the tombs were at his time buried 4–5 m deep in the rubbish just as they are now. And / yet, what he says abt the tombs of Agamemnon and his compa[g]nions killed by Aegisthos and Clytaemnestra can leave no doubt in any body's mind that he saw all the tombs in and not outside the acropolis. The great antiquity of the tombs is proved as well by the very primitive basreliefs as by the circumstance that the tombstones stand in the virgin soil. Besides⟨,⟩ the 3–5 m thick layer of prehistoric rubbish⟨,⟩ by which the tombs were covered, had evidently accumulated gradually by the remnants of the successive households. A glance at the talus can leave no doubt whatever in this respect. The gradual accumulation cannot be better shown than by the most ancient handmade pottery on the virginsoil; this pottery is rudely made, is monochrom and the monochrom is produced by the oxyd. of iron in the furnace, but nevertheless the strange form of these vases, their high polish, lustrous colour etc makes that they do not lack a certain elegance, in particular the black ones.

Thursday 31 Augst 1876. I have today 50 workmen, of whom
25 from Charvati in the trench commenced by them
4 above the treasury to remove the rubbish
14 in   ″   do   (all from Fichtia)
7   ″   ″ cyclopean house.
*All the painted potsherds we dig up in 3–4 metres depth in digging
the trench before the treasury must be older than the latter or at
least of the time of it.* I dig out today the Cyclopean house, which
is nothing else than a tomb; it is filled with calcined ruins. The
inner chamber is 5.08 long; 2.84 broad; the E. wall is 1 m thick,
the N. wall 95 Ctm; against this latter leans a 1 m 95 Ctm thick
wall of which only the N. side is 1/2 m thick walled and the rest
filled up with small stones. The W. wall of the house is 85 Ctm
thick; the S. side consists of 2 distinct walls, of which the outer
one is 1.10; the inner 1 m thick. Found in the tomb:[43]
1) remnants of bones
2) mutilated cows
3) a very curious female idol, with a crown on the head, in a
   sitting posture; it has 3 irregularly placed breasts, which have
   evidently been patched there after the idol had been made;
   one / of the breasts may mean the female organ.
4) a curious weight of black jasper with a handle for suspension
   and the fragments of a splendidly painted vase of a light yellow with black lines. Particularly curious are there two eagles
   much resembling the Russian arms and many other.
    Also other broken vases were found and a portion of wheat
and λαθούρια (Wicken, vetches or lens), but much burnt.[44] A
door was found on the N. side, but shut up by the 1 m 95 thick
wall, which shows that it is a tomb. There is on the S. side a small
opening, as a window. Thus the Treasuries must be treasuries
and not tombs, the more so since the pottery found in this tomb
is much older than that found before the treasury.

Friday 1 Septbr. I had today 57 workmen, of whom 25 of Charvati worked separately. The excavation of the tomb continues.[45]
There is brought out a certain number of whorls of green or blue
stone, large quantities of broken pottery of all kinds and particularly of light green deadground with ornaments of black colour,

representing swans, antilopes {sic} etc. I can however not give a greater age to these latter, they being intermixed with the usual pottery which shows red, brown or black ornaments on a light red colour. A regular door is now discovered in the N. corner of the house; it is below 1 m 32, higher up only 1 m 14 broad; as the entrance passes through the thick wall it is 2 m 40 long.[46]

Saturday 2 Sept. I had today 54 labourers and made the fatal discovery that we have for a long time been digging in the virgin soil; that all the tomb stones stand on one side to the top in the virgin soil whilst on the other there is an accumulation of household remains and particularly a large quantity of potsherds.[47] Thus it is evident that the tombs were dug E-W in the virgin soil ⟨;⟩ in the tomb was deposited the dead body, which was probably put facing the W. because on the E. side is always the tombstone. Until now all the bones of the dead had disappeared, at least but a few were found and no skull. In one of these tombs were found a number of a kind of beautiful glassbuttons[48] as well as an entire Juno idol with 2 horns and a polos. Later in the day another such entire Juno idol was found, as also a very primitive and exceedingly rude one in the treasury or better in the trench before the treasury. Instead of a "polos" there is a sort of a crown on the head, which has very large eyes; these seem to have been plastered on when the figure had already been made; the hands are protruding and two breasts are indicated. There can be no doubt that this idol is the most ancient yet found and, as it has nothing whatever to do with the cow, it appears that Juno's relation to the cow is of a posterior date; this appears also to be confirmed

{Workmen's receipts dated 21 August/2 September 1876.}

by the fact that no cow idols are found on the virgin soil. In a depth of 2 m. were found in the trench before the Treasury three steps, probably belonging to a Greek theater, for they are bent and evidently form a circle.[49]

Mycenae, Tuesday 5 Sept 1876. I had today 112 workmen & 2 overseers viz 27 men from Charvati, 13 from Phichtia, 40 from

Cutzopodi and 32 from different parts. I had given to the men from Cutzopodi a separate field & they have done an enormous work.[50] In their field, which borders on that which we first dug up & where all the tombs are, are the ruins of not less than 6 Hellenic houses.

A tomb I have dug out today but found it full of beautiful potsherds—also one coin—among which some entire vases also some gobelets {sic}; there were besides found in the tomb bones of animals, but no human bones.[51] As nothing has been found yet in any one tomb it appears certain that all tombs have been rifled of their contents / in antiquity.[52] This seems particularly to be the case with the Cyclopean haus {sic},[53] which contained but few human bones, but a great many bones of animals. In the house is the natural rock protruding. In the aforesaid tomb was found a tablet of stone on which was grossly engraved the following:

In the same tomb was found a copper medal, seemingly with an *encensoir*.

I am working here with picks and baskets only; no carts. There are three rows of sepulcres {sic}, all of which surrounded by a small cyclopean wall.[54] We preserve all cut stones, but remove all those which are unhewn; the latter are often very large and roll down from the mound with a thundering noise.

It was blowing quite a gale today and we suffered cruelly from the dust, which was continually blown into our eyes. But still I proclaim that there is nothing in the world sweeter than excavation particularly in remnants of prehistoric times, where every potsherd reveals a page of history.

The *Latomia* or *Quarry* where all the stones for the Cyclopean walls and all the stones for the numerous treasuries were cut, is evidently at the village of Charvati itself, where the shape of the rock shows for a long distance that large masses of it w[h]ere cut away.

The name of Charvati derives from the Arabian خرابتي

ruins, which has passed over into the Turkish language and received there the plural (خراباìت) which in Arabian does not exist. Thus this village is named by the ruins of Mycenae, though it is 1/2 hour's ride from it.

Wednesday 6 Sept: I had today 107 workmen, of whom 29 from Charvati (of whom 3 at 2 dr); 13 from Phichtia; 40 from Cutzopodi and 25 of difft villages.

It is a very strange fact that all the tombs are full of potsherds among which some entire vases.[55]

In the compartment given to the men from Charvati I struck the virgin soil in 5 m.

I am working here with baskets, picks and shovels.

On Monday 4 Sept. I had the visit of The Rev. Gerald S. Davies, M.A. Charterhouse. Godalming. (England).[56]

The 3 rows of sepulcres are surrounded by a cyclopean wall, which is however much *posterior* to the tombs, for it is composed of all sorts of stones, well cut stones, tombstones and uncut stones. In many places this wall is straight, in others it rises under an angle of 65 to 75°.

Nearly every day, and particularly in the afternoon, we have a terrible tempest here, which continually throws dust into our eyes and blindens {sic} us. But in spite of all the hardships I endure and the heavy expence I encur {sic}, I cannot imagine anything sweeter than to excavate Mycenae, because every potsherd is a new page of history.

Thursday 7th Sept. Last evening a splendidly sculptured porphyr block was found. The sculpture is certainly not like any piece of ancient art ever found in Greece and decidedly shows Asiatic taste. Also a Doric triglyph block: 52 Ctm broad & 1 m long & 28 thick was found; but the metope shows no sculpture.[57]

I had today 111 workmen, of whom 13 from Phichtia, 29 from Charvati (between these 3 at 2 dr.), 29 of difft villages & 40 from Cutzopodi. The wall around the tombs is only 5 m distant from the great circuit wall.

A beautifully *inscised* {sic} *perforated transparent brown stone* of a necklace was found;[58] also some 4 or 5 very archaic vases with one handle were found; besides *one of the usual goblets with 2 handles and this is the* δέπας ἀμφικύπελλον.[59] *But the most interesting thing of all was a cowshead on a long neck ornamented with a treble necklace and this can only have belonged to an idol. Very curious vases were also found* ornamented outside with the usual *designs of fishbones and inside with fish. In the excavations before the treasure {sic} was found a very strange male figurine in the Asiatic style, having a diadem with a / star on the head, a long aquiline nose, very large eyes and an immense protruding Assyrian beard.*[60]

Also a fragment of a vase was found with an oxhead with long horns beautifully modelled on it.[61]

It is a great problem why all the Treasuries were so deeply buried in the ground;[62] this question is the more perplexing since they are masterpieces of architecture and the 6 m broad *dromos* which leads to them can evidently only have been made to serve as ingress and can impossibly have been destined to be buried 33 feet deep in *stone hard rubbish*. I think that, since the⟨y⟩ evidently served as treasuries, they were covered in a great danger, perhaps in the time of the Doric invasion. But, if so, real treasures ought to be contained in them; but, as far as I know and hear from old men who still remember the excavation of Atreus' Treasury by Veli Pasha in 1810 nothing was found but a marble table, some bronze plates and sculptured stones and I hardly anticipate to find more in the present tomb.[63] Further it is a riddle to me why I find here in the stone hard rubbish with which the entrance is covered the very *oldest potsherds and idols*, in fact so ancient as none turned up in the acropolis, also the tomb must in

all probability belong to the third epoch

in the heroic age, viz to the time of the Lionsgate. The treasures are always in domelike form, with a ⟨   ⟩ feet high Δ above the door to lessen the weight on the traverse of the door. The stone-hard rubbish is further mixed with potsherds of the same kind of most ancient Attic vases with birdheaded men and storks as in the Ministry of public instruction.

Friday 8 Sept 1876. I had today 39 men from Koutzopodi; 29 from Charvati, 15 from Fichtia, 30 from difft villages; in all 113 workmen and in spite of all my endeavors I have not reached yet the virgin soil near the wall and it may be 8 m deep; I have now reached 7 m. The pottery of difft *prehistoric* ages are mixed up there.

The second inner *fortress wall,* of *smaller stones* joined with earth, was evidently built in great haste when the town was in great danger to be taken by the enemy; this is the more apparent as the great cyclopean circuit wall was on the S. side for a distance of 14 m destroyed and on its innerside a similar *support* wall of smaller stones joined with earth was built.[64]

A great many more idols of *cows* & women with *cowhorns* or full moon disk were found; also *another cowhead with horns on a female body as far* as the breasts⟨;⟩ in the middle of the skull is always a round hole; the necks are always richly ornamented with necklaces; these things are evidently *handles of vases.*[65]

There was *however also found a perfectly flat idol with large eyes with cowhead but without horns* showing *the figure from both sides in profile.*

A Doric marble triglyphblock, 1 m long, 52 Ctm broad, 28 thick was found near the surface.[66]

Also 1 *cow without horns and female Kopfputz* was found.

Much time is always lost by the large boulders being moved to the edge of the mount, when the men leave the work to see how with a thundering noise the[y] stones roll down.

The older the *Juno-idols the more compressed is always* the head; the polos in form of a *bowl* and having often inside a +.

In the excavation of the Charvatians, in a depth of 5 m a cyclopean house with several rooms comes to light, 12 m long, 11 broad; the coating of the inner walls is of mud, which seems to prove that chalk was still unknown and at least *not* used. In the same trench are the ruins of another, 14 m long cycl. house.[67]

I see more advantage if I give to each village a different trench.

In the Treasury part of the dromos has been brought to light, which shows a breadth of 5 m 90 or only of 11 inches

{Drawing of tombstone bas-relief (*Myc.* no. 141, Karo pl. VI lower section); see p. 161 below.}

smaller than the Treasury of Atreus. The Δ window and part of the entrance has been dug out. Unfortunately the large slab, which roofed the entrance, is broken and it has to be replaced or substituted by an iron bar before the work of excavating the interior of this Treasury can be commenced with.

Saturday 9 Sep no work.

Monday 11 Sept. I had today 120 workmen.

Tuesday 12 Sept I had today 120 workmen. Found today a strange terracotta cow with a handle over the back.

The entrance of the Treasury is now so far cleared the great block which roofs the door is brought to light, and as I see on it traces of ornamentation, I hope to discover the sculpture which must have adorned the Δ . In the latter also are signs of the sculpture once having been there. The door is 2 m 46 broad ⟨;⟩ the block which roofs the entrance is 5 m 60 long. We have worked all day to bring to light the whole of the "dromos." Very *ancient* painted pottery and *no* more cows or horned females are

found there. In the upper diggings I have been digging the 3 ranges of tombs without yet reaching the virgin soil.

Close to the Cyclopean wall I found the rock in 7 m 70. A piece of agath of brown transparent colour was found; it is ciselled {sic}; a deer with 2 horns is lying; before it is a lotus flower behind it a plant with its root; the stalk branching of⟨f⟩ into 3 flowers.[68]

Chalk was known: a lot of remnants of wall coating of chalk with spiral ornaments.

In the excavation of the Charvatians a large cyclopean house is coming out more and more.

{Drawing of tombstone bas-relief (*Myc.* no. 142, Karo pl. VIII, 1430); see p. 163 below.}

{Workmen's receipts dated 7 and 8 September 1876.}

{Workman's receipt dated 1 September 1876.}

Wednesday 13 Sept: I had today 118 workmen, of which 25 in the Treasury. In the Δ above the door are many small stones and besides many very archaic potsherds, thus there can be no doubt that the Treasury has been filled up in high antiquity. The Δ is 2 m 60 broad and 3 m 60 high. To the right & left of it are protruding tablets, which may have served to put statues upon. Just 12 m from the entrance are three circular steps of calcareous stone tablets, the lowest one of which is just above the *dromos.*[69] The dromos at the entrance is 5 m 86, at 10 m distance 5 m 90 broad. The steps belong to a Hellenic building, which is 20–25 m from the Treasury. The large standing tablets, which I have considered as tombstones must be such, because to the N.E. side of them are ⟨   ⟩ m deep ⟨   ⟩ m broad trenches cut in the rock;[70] but, except broken potery {sic} and 1 or two needles of bone or ivory and some rare bones, among which I cannot recognize human bones. Quite a number of curious idols was found, among which a strange female idol with a phrygian cap and protruding hands, the lower part resembles an arrow; the head a birdshead. A Greek potsherd with incised[71]

TO☐ERoo⟨⟩)EM τῷ ᵍ/ᵖⁿ̈ ⁿ̈ . . . ..

Thursday 14 Sept I had today 119 workmen, of whom 25 in the Treasury. In the Treasury, or rather before it, were found very beautiful archaic potsherds and an idol of Juno with cowhorns. Besides 6 beads of a necklace; a large bead ⊖ of glass two smaller ones (⊖——⊖) of topaze and three others ⊖⊖⊖ of the same transparent bluish stone; but all of them / [them] were drawn on a thin wire of copper or bronze.[72]

In the other diggings were found a small fish of wood, and in 6 m depth, a beautiful white transparent gem with splendidly engraved animals.[73] This is a masterpiece and of inestimable value. Some cow and horned female idols were found also and a much ruined sculpture with spiral ornaments.

Today came the mayor of Argos Spiridon Calmuchos & the mayor of Mykenae Panagiotis Nesos. My diggings now show that all along the rows of the tombstones are cut in the soft natural rock broad ditches abt 1 m deep.

{Workmen's receipts dated 4 September 1876.}

{Workmen's receipts dated 4 September 1876.}

Friday 15 Sept. Had today again 119 workmen & 2 carts. Examined again the gem, which represents 2 pregnant *stags female* (deer) each one with its young one which is ⟨   ⟩ from the mother's ⟨   ⟩;[74] it is admirably done. It has been a fingerring, but the ring is broken and only the incision with part of the ring remains. There was found today quite a number of idols, also a fish of wood. Several oystershells and shells.[75] Found today a stone with these signs:

164

Saturday 16 Septbr: Today was worked with 32 workmen in the Treasury, where the most ancient idols continue to be found. So e.g. a female idole {sic} without a head, 2 breasts, below which

the hands are joined. On the breast is the sign

This idol is *unpainted* and one of the oldest I saw yet. Further a human head much resembling one of a cat. This head is painted.

{Workman's receipt dated 5 September 1876.}

Tuesday 19 Sept. Today 91 workmen. Stamatakis wanted to conserve the three steps in circular form, which had been built just above the dromos and evidently belonged to a villa,[76] of which some ruins may be seen further down in the dromos. But, when he tried to tunnel them they fell in, and had therefore to be taken away.

In the "chantier" of the Charvatians has been brought to light a large Cyclopean house, 6 m below the surface. There is a long water conduit and seemingly a cistern in this trench.[77]

In another trench was found a 3 1/2 Ctm long, at one end 2 1/2 at the other 2 Ctm broad piece of green stone, on which is rudely carved a human face, with a very broad nose, large mouth, Egyptian eyes, and altogether *Egyptian features.*[78] On the neck I see three leafs, probably meant to indicate the necklace.

The door of the Treasury is 2 m 47 broad; that of the Treasury of Atreus is ⟨ ⟩ m ⟨ ⟩ Ctm broad. We have brought to light the other 1/2 circle of tombstones; but here are two 1/2 circles, the one parallel (separated 75, 80, 90, 100 & 1 m 10 from each other) with the other; both rows stand inclined in the same direction.

In 4 1/2 m was found in the Charvati trench a splendid, but broken vase, whose handles terminate in *lizards;* [79] the whole vase is covered with warriors of a dark red color on a light yellow dead ground; the men wear cuirasses and are armed with long lances, in abt the middle of which is attached something in the shape almost of a Trojan idol and the same sort of thing must figure on the lance of the man on the bas relief. The warriors are all of the same type; long faces and particularly long noses; the representation is very primitive. The inside of this vase is uniform red; the terracotta is very deficient. Further found: the bead* of a necklace with 2 horses of which are indicated only the hindlegs on which they stand upright against each other;[80] there being no place for the heads, these are / represented as turned backwards; the horses {sic} anatomy, also their manes are well indicated. Between the 2 horseheads are 2 very small human figure⟨s⟩; the one that of a man with a long pointed Persian cap, the other a female with uncovered head; the stone is serpentine.

A large Juno idol with horns was found; further the head of a *cow* with a human face well modelled, aquiline nose, a small mouth small chin; ears indicated, but very *low;* painted red.

The rooms of the Cyclopean house are cut out 40 Ctm deep in the rock; afterwards walled. In the tomb belonging to the tablet representing a man with a horned animal, was found a good deal of ash, probably of human ashes, and a button of bone covered with a small blade of gold, on which is marked a circle and in it a triangle containing the representations of three long & broad knifes, the handles of which are in form of a beautiful spiral.[81]

20 Septbr Wednesday: I had today 92 workmen. The Cyclopean house in the trench of the Charvatians, in 6 m depth, has 5 chambers and 4 corridors; one of these latter, and I think all, are 1 m 16 Ctm. broad; the one room is 5 m 55 long, 4 m 10 broad; its E. side is 50 Ctm deep cut out in the rock. Below this room is a cistern and a much larger one below another chamber, the floor of which is 1 1/2 m higher; this latter cistern appears to be larger & deeper. The cyclopean walls still retain part of their coating of mud.[82] Of small very fine pots, in the shape of cups, with one handle, were found 40; they are of the 4th century B.C.[83] All were found in one place.

Of curious objects today were found a sitting cow, without horns, the head with a headdress like that of a woman; through the neck is a hole for suspension with a string.

I viewed once more the large fragments of a vase found yesterday with representations of warriors, who have κνημῖδες, a round

shield, long lances with a near the end, helms with

Helmbusch and something protruding from the front part of the helm in the shape of a horn. The handle, of which there must have been two, is *double* and terminates in a lizard or rather a crocodile. A *formstone of jasper* with most fantastic types for casting bronze ornaments, or perhaps silver or gold ornaments, was found;[84] there are types on all 6 sides; it has even a type for [those] those curious objects of a glassy substance in form of a helix, which have on either side of the button 2 holes for suspension with a string. There were found besides

2 beautiful green axes[85]

abt 40 whorls

26 idols in form of a woman

13 cow-idols

also a lion of terracotta;[86] further

a *handle representing a woman with a cowhead.*

Among the many idols is a fine head with earrings, polos & breasts; further was found a small tripod with a handle above.[87]

Thursday 21 Sepbr.: Today 80 workmen, I have changed now the 13 Fichtiotes in the Treasury against as many selected Charvatians, who have made wonderful progress. But except 3 cows and a certain quantity of fragments of primitive painted vases with painted decorations representing *cranes* and an oyster nothing was found. I am very much afraid of this work for there is much danger for the poor workmen. But still there was found of baked clay a man on horseback, much like those horsemen found in Boeotia, and holding with both hands the horse's head.[88] It is of very primitive manufacture.

In several places, in 3 m depth were found certain quantities of the painted chalk coating of internal housewalls.[89] These mural paintings are very pretty indeed; there is the usual Roman orna-

mentation with red colour on a yellow dead colour and blue borders with spiral designs.

A piece of bone was found, like a Trojan idol,   on

the one side is protruding a piece, probably with a perforation, so that it could be used as a breastpin.[90]

The row of the *two parallel lines of white tablets,* which stand oblique, cannot be a waterconduit, because near the wall it stands on the red virgin rock and is there by 2 m higher than in the opposite part of the circle. It has threatened today all the day with rain.

Friday 22 Septbr: I had today 82 workmen. The work in the Treasury is progressing. The *door* is 13 feet from the entrance; its hinges are 5 inches deep, and thus this is the length of the passage at the thres[h]hold. Except a small marble plate with spiral ornaments nothing was found.[91]

Between the 2 parallel lines of tombstones the rubbish is in several places mixed with thousands of small long *shells,* the origin of which I ignore. Has not the double line encircled a garden?[92]

The other large tombs are very irregularly made; the one is small & short the other long & larger.[93]

{Workmen's receipts dated 11/23 September 1876.}

{Workmen's receipts dated 11/23 and 12/24 September 1876.}

Saturday 23 Sept: I have had all these days 5 more workmen than I thought; thus today 87 men.

I have been making a new road for the cars; have also been making good progress on the piece of hill above the large trench of the Charvatians, where the accumulation of Hellenic rubbish is large and has 2 m depth.[94] This accumulation is much deeper still to the S. of the gate, where it seems to exceed 6 metres.[95] Very remarkable is the great Cyclopean wall S. of the gate, which has now been brought to light by one metre near down to the rock on which it rests; it is ⟨   ⟩ feet high. It is built in the way of the Tirynthian walls.

Along the parallel rows of tablets are found quantities of bones and ashes *of burned bodies,* together with frequent *large sea snails.*[96] {Added in margin: May not the parallel rows have served for libations or flowers to honour the dead?} A small perforated paralellepipedon {sic} of jasper was found, evidently belonging to a necklace.[97] It has at each end a +, on 2 opposite sides 2 fields each with one eye, and the other 2 opposite fields each with / ![blacked out]. Further a sort of whorls {sic} of baked clay perforated in a strange way ![drawing of whorl]

The soil in the acropolis having been again and again disturbed by the building of walls, the *layer of primitive pottery certainly is not* in its place and *I begin to feel strong doubts that the acropolis* was built in the time of the handmade pottery. If a few of those primitive potsherds turned up in the Treasury, that proves nothing, for some huts may have existed there in prehistoric times. But, I repeat, handmade pottery was found in the acropolis, and particularly in a great depth, but together with posterior potter's wheel fabricate and not making up a stratum like in Tirynth.

{Workman's receipt dated 12/24 September 1876.}

Wednesday 27 Sept 1876. I had today 101 workmen and have been all the day, with 26 of them, busy to deepen the "dromos" of the Treasury so that the carts may load in the very building. 75 workmen have been busy in the acropolis. *It is deserving particular attention that the fragments of pottery found in the "dromos," though every bit of it prehistoric, is by far posterior to the terracottas collected just before and in the treasury.*[98] *Cuttings in the walls on either side of the entrance leave no doubt that the latter has been flanked by two quadrangular columns.*[99] In a very great many cases I see the stones of the "dromos" with fresh breakings and thorough crevices (crévasses), because the stone having been buried for thousands of years in the damp air, it breaks in being / exposed to the sun. It is all τιτανόλιθος. The entrance passage just below the Δ is roofed by 4 mighty slabs. I see no holes or nails in the stones of this Treasury.[100] Found today:

1) a splendid axe of black jasper
2) an enormous quantity of bleustone whorls
3) small terracotta disks with impressed ornamentation

4) most *extraordinary are always to me the fragments of glancing yellow or green glazur* {sic} pottery, which every one, at the first glance, will take for Turkish pottery, but, in examining it, and seeing its super so quality and its *glazur & colour on both sides,* one sees the mistake.

5) *fragments of the internal chalk coating of the ancient houses, with varied painting, are daily found.*[101]

6) a puncher of stag's horn

7) a quadrangular bone needle with ornaments

8) a small tablet of black glass with 2 perforations, and thus evidently serving as an ornament; on it a large flis {sic} splendidly represented by an impression when the matter was weak or liquid.

9) in one place a great many perforated blue glass beads, whorls of blue stone and a number of idols were found.

10) In the same place a small handmade pot with 2 ears or handles & painted ornaments.

I had today the visit of the *engineer* Χαρίλαος Σουΐδας, who, to my joy found the walls of the treasury solid enough and was of opinion that the Lionsgate could be cleared.

Thursday 16/28 Sept: I had today 104 workmen. Worked with 20 men in the treasury, where I deepened the road so that the cars might reach the treasury. Besides the usual cows & idols were found:

1) a very primitive *un*painted idol with masculin⟨e⟩ features, immense eyes, aquiline nose; the head covered by a cap in form of a turban, no mouth; elbows protruding far above the shoulders. It was found in a depth of 2 m and must therefore have been washed down from the mount by the winter rain.

2) another very primitive idol with a birds face, *no mouth,* uncovered head, 2 ears, the two hands on the breast but not joined, the face a little looking towards heaven as if in an attitude of prayer; the lower exremity solid.[102]

Friday 17/29 Sept: I had again 104 workmen & 4 horse carts. In the Treasury the work goes on rapidly. It deserves particular attention that in the Treasury and for 20 metres in the "dromos" the potsherds are the most ancient yet found in Mykenae, whilst farther down they are more modern though still prehistoric. The aspect of the Treasury from the "dromos" is grand in the extreme. In the excavations in the acropolis 2 more tombstones have turned up, belonging to the row of tombstones without sculptures. We continue to be much annoyed by the ruins of Hellenic buildings, which, in some particular sites, as e.g. to the left of the Lionsgate, have left 4–6 m rubbish and a vast number of well cut building stones. Found:

1) 2 *hatchets,* one of *beautiful black jasper, the other of splendid green* stone
2) a *knife of obsidian* [103]
3) a great many cow- or female idols of Juno

It deserves particular attention that the accumulation of household-rubbish {sic} is not in successive layers here as in Tiryns. Here it certainly appears as if, after a long succession of households, the layers or strata had been dug up and mixed together. Besides it should be particularly remarked that the *most ancient* painted vases, as are *only* found in the Treasury, are here of rare occurrence.

Saturday 18/30 Sept I had today 104 workmen and was particularly occupied to open a trench before the Lionsgate.

Findings of all sorts, and even potsherds, become very rare. We hardly find anything at all & I would propose that the internal

{Workmen's receipts dated 18/30 September 1876.}

coating of the rooms, consisting of chalk (τίτανος) covered with peintures murales, derives from framehouses, for in cyclopean houses it could hardly be preserved. Besides in the cyclopean houses I never yet found anything else than a smoothed *coating of earth.* Thus the *chalk coating* with *paintings* must belong to an epoch approaching the destruction of the old city. It can impossibly be very ancient. [104]

In the Treasury only fragments of very ancient painted pottery with *cranes,* with *meander* etc, are found; also the head of a female idol with large eyes and rather a birds head; of course no mouth. But since there are *no cranes* in Greece, I would suggest

171

that the pottery with figures of cranes must have been fabricated in a country where there are cranes, and imported here.[105]

The Charvatians have made 1639.78 metres

have received 1335.50 drach

have still in credit   304.28 do

Tuesday 3 Octbr: I had yesterday abt. 80 and today 110 workmen; yesterday 2 carts, today 5 carts.

Having broken down yesterday the cone of earth which I had left standing in the trench of the Charvatians, I continued to excavate the adjoining chamber and found there, besides a vase handle, running out in a crocodile's head, an immense bronzen {sic} tripod (καβάν), but little damaged, and a bronze casserolle of much smaller size; besides lots of beautiful potsherds. I have dug out this chamber abt. 3 m deep and as there is neither a door nor a window either in this or in any other of ⟨the⟩ house's chambers, I now believe that every one of the house's chambers served as a particular tomb. This seems also to be confirmed by the many bones found there. But I am at a loss to explain how two large cisterns happen to be just beneath 2 rooms of the house.[106]

I have also continued the excavation E. of this trench, but found there hardly any thing at all. The most interesting object found there was a Juno idol with *no* polos, a very compressed face, large black eyes, necklace, high protruding breasts, long hair indicated on the back.

The heads of the 2 lions above the gate must have been but very small and high protruding, for there is no space for them; and it has been found necessary to fasten them for in each of the places where they are missing can be seen two borings, one from above and the other horizontally.[107] Perhaps, by some accident, they were broken when this fastening was found necessary.

In the trench close to the gate great progress has been made, but only 2 arrows were found, one of copper with long barbs, and one of iron.[108]

Wednesday 4th Octbr. I had today 120 workmen and nearly succeeded in opening the passage of the Lions' Gate, obstructed by thousands ⟨of⟩ large & small stones which appear to have been

172

hurled against the Argians who stormed the acropolis in 468 B.C. The entrance is besides protected by a labyrinth of walls in order to facilitate the defense. To the left of the entrance is a wall of huge stones, which is far from solid & makes me afraid for the life {sic} of the workmen. The space between the stones has evidently been filled up by the detritus of plants and the dung of the cattle, which has been washed down from the height by the rains.

In the cyclopean house I have continued the excavation of the chamber and only struck the rock in 7 m below the surface. I found there a beautiful vase, of that kind which has on the top 2 handles and a tube; besides⟨,⟩ a splendid idol with *2 feet,* uncovered birds head, large eyes, necklace; hair well indicated on the back; on the head is the sign ⟨ ⟩ ; the garment well indicated with red colours on the back; the hands are protruding; no mouth. Among many other highly interesting potsherds were found there large fragments of vases with very primitive representations of warriors, some of whom have a helmet in form of caps with thorns or Stacheln; all of them have very long faces, very long noses, cuirasses, helmets with long Helmbuschen; from the forepart of each helmet is protruding something in form of a horn; *assyrian beards,* yellow shields; the objects on the lances

may.[109] All the features of the warriors are perfectly of the same cast.

On some other vases are painted *swans* or lifeless but highly interesting objects. The rock at the bottom of this room is 7 m below the surface. Where the double row of large tablets reaches the slope the slabs are of enormous size;[110] there it suddenly goes down. I have excavated there all the day and found there a great many interesting fragments & lots of idols.

Thursday 5 Octbr. I had today again 120 workmen. Great difficulties in the removal of the great number of large stones in the Treasury for want of machinery. Wrote therefore to Nauplion to send the necessary instruments and t⟨w⟩o able men.

Three more fragments of vases with letters were found this morning; also a fragment of vase with a *small tube* for *suspen-*

sion. But though in this respect much resembling the Trojan vases, the Mycenae vase is very different from any Trojan vase by its beautiful painted ornamentation and the brightness of the colours. On this as well as on nearly all other vases we see spiral ornaments.

Before the Lionsgate was found an arrow in form of a small pyramid, like the Carthaginian arrows in Motye;[111] only this arrow was of bronze and had 4 rills all around; the point with which this arrow head was fixed in the arrow was broken off.

Friday 6 Octbr. Again 120 workmen. A vast number of Juno idols were found, for the most part inside and outside of the double row of tombstones. For the most part the central part of the body was in form of the fullmoon, but a great many idols there were too with two horns; also a vast number of cows was found and *even one with a cow head* and a *female necklace;* but, as always, this idol was on a handle. An object in form of a fish [with] with 3 feet, beautifully painted.[112]

{Workman's receipt dated 24 October (sic) 1876.}

Immediately to the right in the entrance of the Lionsgate is a large cyclopean house,[113] which is part of the cyclopean house, which I had believed to be a tomb. There are several parallel corridors one 1 m 26, another 2 m and the third 2 m broad. I cannot imagine / what for they may have served, as I see no doors, there are further two corridors in a W. direction, one of which leads straight into the single roomed house. In many places one sees the clay coating of the walls. On the top of part of this Cyclopean house had been built a Hellenic house, of which the chalk floor and large stone plates remain.[114] To the left of the entrance the accumulation of rubbish & humus washed down from the mount, so that, to sustain the talus, it has been coated with huge stones.

{Workman's receipt dated 25 September 1876.}

Saturday 7 Octb: I had today again 120 workmen. Found a certain number of idols and some painted potsherds, one of

which with representations of hegoats with long horns, found in 5 m. In one of them were letters, of which however are only preserved ⌡ Γ .
Γ

{Workman's receipt dated 26 September 1876.}

{Workman's receipt dated 27 September/9 October 1876.}

Visit of H.M. the Emperor of Brazil to Ilium[115]

Having been officially requested by the Turkish government to hasten to the Hellespont in order to accompany H.M. Dom Pedro II to the Troad, I left my excavations at Mycenae on the 9th and arrived here Friday 13th inst. H.M. arrived on Saturday 14th inst. at 6 1/2 a.m. by the Austrian steamer "Aquila Imperiale", of which {i.e. commanded by} Captain Terwig, in company of H.M. the Empress, the Countess de Barral, the Viscount de Bom Retiro, the Count de Gobineau,[116] actually French Ambassador at Stockholm and Dr Carl Henning,[117] a young German scholar, whose occupation is to assist the Emperor in his scientific researches. H.M. the Empress not being able to stand the fatigue of long rides, she and the Countess de Barral descended here at the house of the Austrian Consul Mr N. Xanthopoulos, where appartments {sic} had been prepared for the high visitors. I had the honour to accompany the Emperor and the rest of the party by the same steamer to Koumkalë at the mouth of the Scamander where horses stood ready for all of us. H.M. made there the just observation[118] that, were it not for the very strong current of the Hellespont, the alluvium of the Scamander would many centuries ago have shut up these straits and united Europe to Asia by a new / isthmus. Having left to our right the tumuli which the tradition of all antiquity indicates as the tombs of Achilles and Patroclos,[119] we forded the Scamander, which has at present but little water, it not having rained here for 10 months, and went straight on to Koumkoi where I showed to H.M. the ancient bed of the Scamander now called Kalifatli Asmak and the still very deep ancient bed of the Simois (now Dumbrak Su) which formerly ran here under a right angle into the Scamander, where as now, being branched off into several channels for the benefit of numerous watermills, it forms immense and always impassible swamps. At Hissarlik H.M. examined my excavations with the very deepest interest and delighted me by his citations from the Ilias, which he seems to know almost entirely by heart.[120] All the indications which Homer gives for the topography of Ilium were present in his mind and he found that on the whole the situation of Hissarlik agreed with them, but that in his opinion, the two large springs, the sources of the Scamander, the one with hot, the other with cold water, at which Achilles killed Hector, were necessary to establish the identity; as these two springs exist not here but at a distance of 60 m, near the summit of Mount Ida,[121] H.M. was reluctant to give at once his decision as to the identity of Hissarlik with the Homeric Ilium. I am at a loss to say what astonished me more the Emperors {sic} deep learning or his really wonderful memory. So e.g. he remembered the article "*Troy*" in the Times of June ⟨   ⟩ the author of which, who did not sign his name, ridiculizes {sic} me saying that in my books and maps I show that from the Scaean Gate a passage enters the large mansion just above it, whereas the passage is blocked up by a wall and that, consequently, what I take to be the gate cannot be a gate at all.[122] But I had no difficulty in showing to H.M. that the passage really exists that it is blocked up not by ⟨a⟩ wall of stones but by the rubbish which I had left *in situ* merely in order to prove that said large mansion is superposed by a posterior though still prehistoric palace, because I had been afraid that my statements would otherwise meet with incredulity.[123] When afterwards we came to the sacrificial altar and I showed to the Emperor its pedestal of unburnt bricks, which had been partly destroyed by the winterrains, the remnants of the large slab with which it was covered and which had been broken by the villagers, as well as the large sacrificial stone, cut out in the form of a crescent, which had been rent asunder by them and lay now on the ground half covered by the rubbish, H.M. scorned very much at the vandalism of the present Trojans, but much more at the author of the above article who perverts every way the truth seemingly because he is afraid that he will otherwise not be believed.[124]

The Emperor was very particular in fixing by his pocket compass exactly the direction of the paved road which descends from the Scaeangate to the Plain and he found it to be S.W. by W. What appeared to astonish H.M. most in my excavations was the

enormous accumulation of this solitary mount, which by the household remains of 5 successive cities had increased by 53 ft. in
height and by 132 to 265 feet in width. After having examined
and reexamined the ruins of Hissarlik for two hours with the
deepest attention the Emperor gave the signal for our departure
and we rode across the plain by way of Kalifatli to Neochori, a
village on the high shore of the Aegean sea, where H.M. wished
to see Constantine / Kolobos, of whom I have written in my
works on Troy,[125] mentioning that though born without legs, he
has nevertheless by his industry and economy, in a small village
store, accumulated a large fortune, and, what is still more astonishing, he has merely by books and without a teacher [he has]
rendered himself master of the French, the Italian and the ancient Greek languages.[126] H.M. requested him to recite him
something from the Ilias and Kolobos declaimed to us at once
with great facility nearly the whole first rhapsody. The Emperor
proceeded thence to Beshika Bay, where the "Aquila Imperiale"
was waiting for him. The steamer remained there at [at] anchor,
and next morning at 6 1/2 we started on horseback for Bounarba-
shi. H.M. is of opinion that the artificial canal, by which the
rivulet of the 40 springs of Bunarbashi is conducted into Beshika
bay must be of a remote antiquity, since the whole plain before
this gulf must necessarily derive from its alluvium. H.M. ascended the 75 feet high Udjek Tepe and found it very strange
that this tumulus should ever have been identified with the tomb
of Aesyetes, from which Polites, the son of Priamos, watches
when the Greeks storm from the ships, because this tumulus is at
a distance of 3 hr from the Hellespont, whilst no human eye can
see men at a distance of even half an hour.[127] Having heard from
me that Udjek Tepe has ⟨   ⟩ feet in diameter and is 75 ft high
H.M. at once calculated that it must contain 346175 cubic feet.
The Emperor was much pleased to see the 40 cold springs of
Bounarb, but laughed heartily at the defenders of the Troy-Bou-
narbashi theory, who remodelled them into only two sources, one
cold the other hot, in order to sustain their impossible theory.[128]
The pure virgin soil between these sources and Bounarb, in Bounarb itself and between this village and the 3 tumuli on the Balidagh as well as the pointed or abrupt and always unequal rocks
which have evidently never been touched by the hand of man and

finally the total absence of potsherds proved besides to the Emperor that no human habitation can ever ⟨have⟩ been there. H.M. examined with very great interest / the 3 tumuli on the Balidagh, one of which attributed to Hector has been excavated and found to contain potsherds of the 3d century B.C.,[129] so that the tomb cannot claim a higher antiquity. H.M. further most minutely examined the small acropolis at the exremity of the heights which has for so long a time passed as the Pergamos of Troy, whilst an inscription found by me and published by me* in my "Troy & its Remains" proves it to be Gergis;[130] but when he had seen that the average depth of the accumulation of rubbish there does not exceed 1 1/2 foot and that it only contains fragments of Greek pottery of the 2–4th century B.C., further that none of the walls can claim the denomination "Cyclopean" and finally when he considered that the distance from this acropolis to the Hellespont is 4 1/2 hours, whilst by all the indications of the Iliad, the distance between Ilium and the Greek ships was but very small and could impossibly exceed 1 h., he most peremptorily rejected the Troy Bunarb theory declaring it absurd and ridiculous.[131] After having lunched under a tree at the 40 springs we rode back to Beshika Bay & went at 4 p.m. on board the Aquila Imperiale, which, by order of the Emperor steamed for the island of Tenedos. Mr Gersaglis, the agent of the Austrian Lloyd offered himself at once as guide to the Emperor and showed him the small town of frame houses containing 5000 inhabitants and the miserable fort which appears to have been built since the Turkish occupation. In seeing fragments of Greek sculpture here and there in the pavement and in the walls H.M. pointed to them and said: Tenedos must once have been a rich and prosperous island and there must have been a time when the site of the present wooden houses was occupied by splendid houses and temples. When asked by the Emperor where the site of the temple of Apollo is Mr G. said that according to the description which Homer gives us / of its situation, its site must necessarily be in a place which he pointed out. The Emperor heartily laughed at him and wisely observed that Homer only once mentions the island of Tenedos and merely alludes to an Apollo temple there by saying that this god reigns powerfully in Tenedos.[132] We returned only by 9 p.m. to the Dardanelles, where the Emperor gave me this morning at

178

7 1/2 o'clock the very great honour to come to see me at the miserable "Hôtel de l'Hellespont," where I am lodged. An hour later H.M. embarked with his whole party on board the Aquila Imper, which left at 9 for the Pireus. The Governor General of the Archipelago had sent his first dragoman and political agent N. Didymos as well as a colonel and a captain with 8 gensd'armes to accompany H.M.

Monday 23 Oct. 1876: We returned here tonight at 11 o'clock.[133]

Tuesday 24 Oct. Today it rained and I was unable to work.

Wednesday 25 Oct: From today is to be reckoned the horse of Anagnostis. I had today 77 workmen, but did not much work on acct of the shortness of the day and the masses of huge stones in the gate and in the treasury. But nevertheless some progress has been made. Many idols were found, among which a cowshead with a very long neck attracted my particular attention; but when I asked for it to night it was no where to be found. A large piece of *alabaster* modelled in the shape of a huge door button, was found;[134] also an entire idol with cowhorns; and lots of fragments of most beautiful terracottas, one of which particularly attracted my attention for its outside & inside most magnificent ornamentation. The access to the large gate is by steps and 4 m behind the gate / is a second gate like in the Scaean-Gate; of this gate how ever only the protruding cyclopean masonry is preserved because the gate has been of wood.[135] The flat upper stone has been ciselled {sic}. The most interesting discovery made today is a large real tomb just below the basrelief with the man on a chariot before which is an animal with two horns.[136] If it does not rain tomorrow it shall be excavated entirely. I found this morning near the Treasury a well preserved idol on the surface, where it may have been lying for thousands of years; it seems to represent a masculine deity.

Thursday 26th Oct. I had today 91 workmen and 5 carts, what ⟨with⟩ the weather being wet, I have made but little progress, the more so as I had at the gate 5 carts and was continually bothered by huge stones. There was found at the gate a bronze or copper sealring, on which are engraved 2 *young naked* ladies of marvellous beauty; the anatomy is exceedingly well observed.[137] What pleases most is the simple and beautiful coiffure of the girls and their gesture. Both are sitting close to each other but looking in an opposite direction. Further an engraved transparent *redstone perforated* of a necklace with a splendidly engraved animal which turns round its head and seems nevertheless to be moving at great speed; the anatomy is here also well observed. There has been found today a female idol with 2 breasts⟨,⟩ above which protrudes on either side a long cowhorn.[138] This idol has never had a head and has formed the handle of a vase. Another female idol with a compressed head in which is painted a cross; the eyes

 are formed by deep holes; farther a mutilated cow-

idol with a large number of signs on either side, which may be written characters; the latter are of red colour on a light yellow dead colour; further a small splendidly painted tripod in form of an armchair; another tripod with painted ornaments and finally the fragment of a comb of bone.[139]

Friday 25 {sic} *Octbr:* Today Spyros has commenced the excavation of the treasury for his account in consideration of dr 900. He had / there 17 or 18 workmen and 2 horse carts. I had 88 workmen in the acropolis and besides 3 horsecarts. It began to rain at 10 and by 10 1/2 the rain became so plentiful that we had to stop work. Nothing particular was found, except some idols.

{Workmen's receipts dated 16 October 1876.}

Mycenae 28th Octbr 1876: I had today 100 workmen and 5 carts. In the Treasur[e]⟨y⟩ was found a blue marble with ornamentation of fishspines and a circle in *bas*-relief. In the acropolis nothing was found except a few idols and a *parallel[o]epipedon of terracotta splendidly ornamented with red ornaments of trees, also of 2 human figures on a light yellow dead colour. This object is perforated for suspension.* Near the gate 6 small round perforated pieces of a transparent stone, deriving from a necklace, were found.[140]

180

Mycenae 29th Octbr 1876: We had today the visit of the Emperor
Dom Pedro with his suite. Coming from Corinth he went directly
up to the acropolis, where he attentively examined my excavations.[141] The large circle of 2 parallel rows of tombstones and the
3 straight lines of tombstones—and particularly the sculptured
ones[142]—attracted his particular attention and he lost himself in
conjectures why there should have been made the parallel row
and for what purpose the space between the 2 might have been
used. The cyclopean houses and walls were also examined with
particular interest by H.M. He then examined the great gate and
the postern⟨,⟩ the treasury and repaired to the so called Treasury
of Atreus, where a splendid breakfast was prepared by the care
of the demarchos of Mycenae.[143] This meal in the midst of the
mysterious treasury seemed to please H.M. exceedingly. He
afterwards examined with very great interest at Charvati the collection formed by my collection and particularly admired the
enormous mass of differently shaped Junoidols, the incisions and
the sculptures. H.M. went hence by carriage to Argos and Nauplium and will return tomorrow to Corinth.

Mycenae 30th Octbr 1876: I had today 83 workmen and 4 carts;
Spyros had 15 and 1 cart, but he makes but little progress on acct
of the masses of huge stones he has to contend with. To the left
of the passage which from the Lions' gate leads into the acropolis
I have brought to light an ancient cyclopean wall / consisting
partly of huge, partly of small stones, which is only 1 metre east
of the posterior cyclopean wall which has been built before it. I
am digging alongside of it in a southerly direction, hoping to
[(find)] strike a cyclopean wall of huge stones which converges
from the huge cyclopean wall under a right angle to the E. Except a small silverring[144] and a few fragments of idols nothing
turned up there. In the other excavation were found several female and cowidols; also an unusually long terracotta-horn which
evidently derives from a large cow; further a perfectly *flat* cow
having only one big hind- and 2 forefeet. There was also found a
Junoidol of the usual form with a very compressed birds face, but
with a phrygian cap instead of a *polos*.[145] There were found besides several *uncovered* birdlike heads of idols with large eyes.

The tombs, whose site was marked by the sculptured tomb-stones,[146] had my particular attention. These tombs are in a ditch which has been cut into the soft red rock, but I have not been able yet to find out how they were built, for I find in the ditch only 2 rows of large slabs of calcareous stone lying the one on the other. On these slabs I found bones of a human body; also part of the jaw with 3 mill teeth.[147]

The Emperor Dom Pedro II returned today by 10 a.m. with his suite to Charvati to breakfast; but to my greatest disappointment I had not known it before and had consequently prepared nothing.[148] The Emperor charged me to send him photographs as well of the 4 basreliefs I found, as of the statue he had seen in the municipality of Argos.

Tuesday 31 Octbr Tuesday: I had today 97 workmen and Spyros had 15. I had besides 4 carts and Spyros 1. Very little was found and I could only work until 11 o'clock.

Wednesday 1 November. I had today 97 workmen and Spyros had 15: we had besides 5 carts. My confidence that the large cyclopean wall in the midst of the acropolis branches off / to the E. has been right; but of this eastern wall only some stones are *in situ;* close to this wall a cyclopean waterconduit was brought to light, which conducted the water from the mount.[149] But it [it] only reaches half the passage and has evidently been destroyed. Me now thinks that the long corridors to the right of the passage may be cisterns. We have also commenced to excavate the canal between the parallel rows of plates at its N. extremity and found there a number of idols and beautiful potsherds.[150]

We also continued the excavation of the tombs which had been marked by the sculptured slabs, but only found there cut calcareous slabs, some of which, and perhaps all, derive from more ancient monuments.[151] In the cyclopean house we found a fragment of an archaic basrelief representing a man, who is much like that one who holds the horns of the mysterious animal on the other sculpture. He is also naked and holds a line in his hand. There were also found fragments of sculpture representing a horse and a spiral ornamentation.[152]

182

Mycenae Thursday 2 Novbr 1876: I had today 98 workmen & 4 carts. Spyros had 18 and 2 carts. The latter encounters more and more stones the deeper he digs. I went this morning with 7 work-men to sink shafts in the 28 m long & 18 m broad building with cyclopean walls, on the high bank of the mountain stream, whose deep and always dry bed is on the right of the Lionsgate.[153] The building is 1/4 hour distant. But I struck there the virgin soil already in less than 1/2 m depth and in a still less depth in the adjoining field. I must say the same of two shafts I sunk on the brow of the hill to the W. of the acropolis, whereas to the N.W. of the Lionsgate I have been digging all the day without as yet striking the virgin soil and find there masses of fragments of pottery. The large waterconduit[154] discovered yesterday to the left of the entrance passage of the acropolis descends seemingly from the mount and leads into a cistern only 12 feet to the right of the Lionsgate. This waterconduit leads / all along the passage⟨,⟩ being laid on the virgin soil and a small branch of it leads into the larger of the corridors,[155] which can therefore be nothing else than a cistern; I have been excavating it for 2 days without finding yet its bottom. Just S. of same is another cistern from which a watercon-duit goes W.[156] In the close by double row of large slabs, as well as in the passage near the Lionsgate a great many terracotta-idols were found; also a large lump of lead of cylindrical form, prob-ably a weight, and a golden earring much like [the] in shape the most ancient Trojan earrings; the only difference is that the thick golden wire is here quadrangular; it is the simplest possible kind of earrings {sic}, the wire having only been twice turned round.[157] I have now nearly every where in the passage struck the natural soil, here the rock there the softer red or white virgin soil. Many fragments of splendidly painted pottery were taken out; also, *on the virgin soil,* many fragments of *handmade black pottery* with a lustr[i]ous surface. The excavation on the site of the sculptured slabs has not yielded anything yet.

Mycenae 3 November (Friday): It having rained all the night I did not work today and went to Nauplion, where I engaged Mr Δροσινὸς, ὑπολοχαγὸς τοῦ μηχανικοῦ, to make the plans of both Mycenae and Tiryns. *I am greatly indebted to the master of the police, Leonidas Leonardos in Argos.*[158]

{Workmen's receipts dated 23 October/4 November 1876.}

Mycenae 4th Novbr (Saturday). I had today 97 workmen; Spyros had 18. Heavy rain having set in at 2 1/2 P.M., I have been obliged to stop the work. I had today only 2 carts, which served until noon on the gateway and thus I have succeeded in cleaning the passage until the virgin soil. The thres[h]hold of the gate is ⟨ ⟩ Ctm *broad* and consists of one tremendous slab, which reposes on the sloping rock and is at its N.E. end ⟨ ⟩ Ctm, on its N.W. end ⟨ ⟩ Ctm thick so as to establish the horizontal line. It has on its N. side, just in the midst, a deep cutting, which must have been used for something. On both sides were found fragments of large common vases and tiles and very little archaic pottery. There are in the slab⟨'⟩s surface a number of horizontal rills in order, probably, to impede the horses slipping & falling.[159] There is besides, near the N.E. extremity a large straight furrow in the stone and another semicircular one on the opposite side; both have evidently served for the doors and perhaps also for the flowing off of the rain water.[160] Besides the entirely unpainted goblets there are near and on the virgin soil others with varied paintings or with a lustruous {sic} black surface.

Mycenae Monday 6th Novbr 1876: It having rained yesterday & the day before nearly all the day, it was so wet today that only 32 workmen could be obtained today, of whom I took 24 and Spyros 8. Yesterday morning came here the *lieutenant Vasilios Drosinos* and the Eparchos Ioannes Kontakes from Nauplium to make me a plan of the acropolis and the treasury.

Today at noon I ascended to the N. of the acropolis the steep Mount which is 2500 ft. high and crowned by an open chapel of the prophet Elias. I took a boy with me to guide me.[161] I had to leave the horse at a long distance from the top and to ascend at least 800 feet on foot. I was amply recompensed for the trouble I had taken, for not only was the panoramic view sublime, but I made there the interesting discovery that in high antiquity the summit has been fortified by cyclopean walls and that there are even at 6 to 16 m below the summit long cyclopean walls to defend all sides from which the summit is accessible.[162] The summit forms a triangle and its eastern wall is 10 1/2 the two other

184

walls⟨,⟩ which converge at a point due W⟨,⟩ 30 m long. In this latter corner is an accumulation of stones which may derive from a small ancient temple and a huge stone which shows traces of having been hollowed out, may have served as altar. The circuit walls consist of stones of no great size joined with small ones⟨;⟩ they are on an average 1 1/4 m thick and 1 to 2 m high; but the masses of stones alongside of them prove that they have once been much higher. 6 m below this W. point is a 40 m long cyclopean wall, 3 m high, of larger stones joined with small ones; it is 1 1/2 m. thick. 16 m below the summit, to the S., is a 1 1/2 m. thick, 80 m long cyclopean wall of large & smaller stones joined by very small ones. This wall is now only 3 m high, but it has, like all the other walls, evidently been much higher. Like the wall to the W. / it has served to protect the ascent to the summit. In both these walls are 1 m broad doors. The chronology of all these walls we find evidently in the fragments of pottery which are peeping out from between the stones and by those by which the summit of the mount is strewn. These fragments are either glazed green or brown Turkish, or black of the Hellenic time, or very archaic of green colour with black ornaments and these are particularly or solely found between the stones of the walls. Similar fragments are found in the acropolis only on or near the virgin soil and they therefore must be nearly as old or as old as the acropolis' cyclopean walls. In the E. wall on the summit is a 1 m. broad door and in the large stone, which forms the thres[h]hold, can be seen the holes in which once turned the hinges of the door. 20 Ctm before those holes are visible in the stone one inch deep furrows, forming a curve, in which the door must have turned. In the S.E. corner is a[n] 7 m long, 3 m broad open sanctuary of the prophet Elias, formed on the E. & S. sides by the cyclopean walls of the summit and on the two other sides built up roughly by the modern villagers. In the enclosure grows a tree which is visible at a long distance, the former has an entrance but no door. As this is the only smooth place on the summit, it is more than likely that in this very spot [has been] in high antiquity existed a small temple, which may [be] have been the most ancient shrine of Hera in the Argolis. At all events, the immense importance which was attached to this cyclopean enclosure at a height of 2500 feet just N. of Mycenae, could not have been better shown than by the cyclopean walls by which all access to it is obstructed. Every⟨where⟩ else on the summit is seen the selfgrown, very uneven rock, which appears never to have been touched by the hand of man.

Mycenae Tuesday 7 Novbr 1876: Today being the feast of St Demitrios, I had no workmen and only with great difficulty Mrs Schliemann[163] obtained 10 workmen for Spyros at 3 1/2 dr and 4 for the service of the engineer.

{Memo of payment to Spyros Demetriou dated 7 November 1876.}

Mycenae, Wednesday 8th Novbr 1876: I had today 75 workmen. Spyros had 28 and 3 carts. The Lionsgate is 3 m 19 high and the threshold is 2 m 35 large and 3 m 09 long; in the midst of the outside is a ☐ hole for the doorposts 38 Ctm long & 28 broad.[164] On the E. side is a 28 Ctm large furrow and on the W. side one which at its mouth to the N is still larger but gradually becomes more narrow; both seem to have been made only for the rain water. There are besides in the thres[h]hold 15 small straight parallel furrows to prevent men and horses from slipping. On the side facing the N. is besides, in the midst, a strange & large opening, which must have served for something, since similar ones are also in the Scaean gates. There is a distance of 3 m 46 from the 1st to the 2nd gate, which consists of 2 protruding quadrangular masonries 65 Ctm high, 61 broad & 87 long. The large deep holes for the hinges of the gate and the 4 holes to the right & left for the bolts, are highly interesting.[165] Peculiar to Mycenae appears to be the ornament on the column between the 2 lions:[166]

At the N.E. corner of the Acropolis the engineer discovered an *ogivelike passage* in the wall, which is 5 m thick and thus the passage must be as long.[167] I continued today the excavation in the place where the sculptured tombstones have been and found there, at least 1 m below the spot where the first gold button had been found, a *second gold* button on which was engraved a

circle and in it a splendid[168]/

This was in 6 1/2 m depth. The pottery found there is nearly all handmade and monochrom black or red but on both sides with a lustr[u]ous surface and as fine as the finest of the lowest city of Troy; but now and then pottery of variegated colour turns up. The tombs have evidently been plundered in a high antiquity and the earth and rubbish pêle mêle thrown back into the sepulcre. In the cyclopean house[169] the fragment of a πίθος with *burned olives* was found in 5 m depth.

The *parallel double rows of tombstones* has evidently originally been all covered with cross slabs, which were solidly fitted on them by means of 3–8 Ctm deep quadrangular cuts, which are on an average 10 Ctm broad and the cross slabs were so cut as to fit in them; many of these cross slabs are still in situ. The slabs are from 1 1/4 to 2 m 44 long. The longest are there where the[y] double row descends from the rock to the wall.[170] Inside is first a 40 Ctm thick cyclopean masonry to hold the slabs in their respective position and after that rubbish mixed with small, long snails[171] and innumerable fragments of terracottas; the breadth of the slabs is from 50 Ctm to 1 m 20.

Mycenae, Thursday 9th Novbr 1876. I had today 77, Spyros had 28 men & 2 carts. I lifted today the slabs of the tomb[172] to facilitate the excavation and worked there very hard all day. 7 small, 10–12 millimetre broad and 6–10 *Ctm* long blades of gold[173] were found there; also *4 more gold buttons,* of which one with a

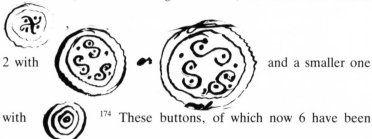

2 with ⬡ ⬡ and a smaller one

with ⬡ [174] These buttons, of which now 6 have been

found, are all of bone & covered with a golden blade. The bone
is cut in form of our shirt buttons, . Also a large pearl

of blue stone,[175] many bones among which a swine jaw. Several *of
the forms of the beautiful pottery were not yet found.* Otherwise
little was found.

Friday 10th Novbr 1876. I had today the same number of labourers. There were found today 4 more gold buttons: thus there are
now found in all *10 buttons.* All are beautifully engraved.[176]

There were besides found today a number of gold leafs and among
them a very large one, on which were impressed a number of small
circles and spiral ornaments. But all these objects are found separately and at distances of whole *mètres* from each other⟨;⟩[177] be-
sides⟨,⟩ fragments of beautiful but most ancient monochrom vases
are continually intermixed with much more modern though still
prehistoric vases made on the potter's wheel; human bones are
continually found intermixed with those of swine and other animals, and thus it is evident that either the tombs have been
plundered, or else that they were exhumed {sic} when the wall
was built which in the lower part of the acropolis sustains the
double parallel rows of white slabs, and that the tombs were re-
filled in a blunt way after having been emptied.[178] At all events the
emptying of the tombs appears to have taken place in such a rough

188

way that the gold buttons and blades passed unobserved, or else that they were thrown away as worthless. It is a strange fact that the objects of gold were only found in black calcinated ruins. The tomb in question, on which 3 of the sculptured tombstones stood, is 3 m 50 broad and probably more than 8 m broad {sic};[179] the N part of it being covered by part of the double row of tombstones, I cannot dig it up without destroying the latter; it is cut out in the sloping rock and thus the E. side is by 2 m higher than the W. side.

Among the pottery I may still mention the fragments of most ancient dark green vases with brown ribbons and those / with black ornaments on a light yellow dead colour; there was also found the fragment of a wood button and a goblet handmade, lustr[u]ous black inside and outside, with a large hollow bottom.[180]

Immediately behind these tombs are 2 upright slabs without sculptures, which I took out; they stand likewise on a quadrangular hollow cut in the rock 3 m 50 br and 6 m 25 long, which I am now emptying.[181] There were found many fragments of splendid and most archaic painted pottery and a number of idols; also a beautifully painted disk of baked clay twice perforated for suspension; it is painted on both sides.

In the Treasury we shall probably clear to night the central part & the passage of the entrance as far as the virgin rock. The walls of the building, in their lower part, being much damaged, I leave around them a broad circle to protect them.

Saturday 11th Novbr 1876: I had today abt the same number of workmen. In the 2nd line of tombstones, which are unsculptured, I continued the excavation of the 3 m 50 Ctm broad, 6 m 25 long □ tomb, on which the two first slabs stood and brought it to a depth of 2 1/2 m without striking yet the bottom; but nothing has been found here yet. I also commenced the excavation of the 2 following tombs[182] of the same line; one of the tombstones is 1 m 89 long & 1 m 20 broad; the other is 1 m 45 long & 1 m 21 broad; both have been fastened extremely well with square blocks of stone. Here was found, in a depth of 5 m, a magnificent large button of ivory of hemispherical form, on whose globular surface is engraved a cross, embellished with 5 small gold pins, each with a hole in the centre; one of the pins is in the midst of the cross, on the flat side is a small tube for being fastened with a string to the upper part of a mantle or coat.[183]

In the still much larger sepulcre below the sculptured tombstones / was found a 3 1/2 Ctm in diameter gold button, whose

ornamentation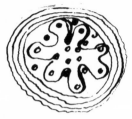

is *much like* the coils of the serpents on one of the tombstones.

Further a button with 3 parallel circles  all splendidly engraved.[184] Thus there have hitherto been found 13 buttons;[185] all are gold blades on buttons of bone; also other ornaments were found, such as a small 6 1/2 Ctm long, horn of bone

 with incised lines; on the flat side are 2 holes for fastening it to some object; it resembles a cornucopiae (ἀμαλθεια). Also two pieces of bone

having on the other side the 2 holes for the pins to be fastened to other objects.[186] In the same way another piece of bone

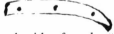

9 Ctm long. There were besides found a number of gold blades (very thin) with impressed ornaments, among which the spiral lines are conspicuous.[187]

190

{Workmen's receipts dated 31 October 1876.}

Mycenae, Sunday 13 {sic} *Novbr 1876:* I had great difficulty in getting for today 48 workmen and to procure for Spyros 25 and 2 carts. Wishing to terminate the excavations today in order to leave tomorrow morning,[188] I pursued the excavations with the utmost vigour and brought the excavation of the □ trench below the 2 unsculptured tombstones to a depth of 4 1/2 m without finding any thing at all. Only towards evening I found there, on the bones of a corpse, quite a mass of large gold leafs with impressions of numerous circles and spiral lines; one of the leafs is of tremendous proportions[189] and this seems to have covered the face of the deceased; *but no,* the body had evidently been burnt as all the bones and the gold leafs were envelopped {sic} in a mass of black ashes. Some of the goldblades, which were thicker than the rest and consolidated by a silver wire,[190] seem to have served as a crown for the dead. Both this and the other

tomb of the sculptured tombstones are 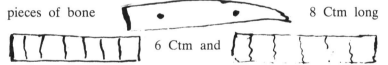 which deserves

particular attention. As yet I saw of the body only ribs. Both on the N and S sides are, at a depth of 4 m, small cyclopean walls.[191] In the other tomb, of the sculptured tombstones, only ornamented pieces of bone ⌐•————•⌐ 8 Ctm long

⎰⎰⎰⎰⎰⎰⎰ 6 Ctm and ⎰⎰⎰⎰⎰⎰ were found; all with small furrows on the other side, or with holes, for being fixed as ornament on other objects.[192] In the Treasury the virgin rock has been / found at a great depth; it slopes from the entrance rapidly towards the centre; except a stone mortar (Mörser), a fragment of a stone basan {sic} and fragments of most ancient painted vases with meanders etc., nothing was found; in the centre is a hole, which, when excavated, speedily filled with water.

Mycenae, Monday 13th November: I had today only 45 workmen; Spyros had 14. I found in digging S. of the 2 □ tombs, a strange piece of *wood,* 6 1/2 Ctm broad and a few idols.[193]

191

My first work this morning was to destroy the cyclopean wall S. of the 2 tombs; after that I removed the 2 tombstones S. of the other 2 and found below them three slabs in the following position:[194]

I found there two pieces of wood, in the form of lances, but both cleave in the air.[195] All the day I have been digging around them. In the 2nd ☐ tomb was found a 1 1/2 to 1 m 60 high wall all around the ☐ talus.[196] The body as yet examined is on the S. side of the ☐ embedded in black ashes and these are covered with a layer of large stones. It lies immediately on the virgin soil, and the ☐ being 4 1/2 m deep its virgin soil is fully 9 m below the surface of the acropolis. It is evident that all the *bodies wer⟨e⟩[y] burned.* Such a mode of burying the dead has never been discovered yet. I trust the tomb will be found to contain many bodies. With the bones of the first were found

3 *twice perforated* pieces and 9

pieces of a bone- or glasslike substance; the latter are also perforated.[197] All have evidently ornamented the dead body.

In the upper excavation was found a twice perforated pearl of bluestone / All the gold leafs have evidently been in the fire

together with the dead body.

1 leaf is	47		Ctm long	&	10		broad[198]
1 " "	47 1/2	"	"	"	6 1/2	do	
1 " "	55		"	"	6 1/2	do	

1 " " 62   " "   "   6 1/2   do
1 " " 63   " "   "   6 1/2   do
There are besides many fragments of leafs and 8 small leafs.
Also 4 circular pieces of gold blade 2 — 8   Ctm in diameter
                                     1 — 5 1/2 "   "
                                     1 — 2 1/2 "   "
There were besides found 5 splendid crosses each formed of 4
gold leafs 18 Ctm long & 4 broad.[199]

{Workman's receipt dated 2 November 1876.}

Mycenae Tuesday 14 Novbr. It having rained all the night and
today all the day there was no work.
    In the Treasury have been found 5 pieces of copper or bronze,
in the form of blades.[200]

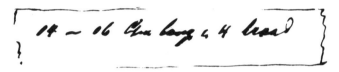

{Workman's receipt dated 3/15 November 1876.}

Mycenae Wednesday 3/15 Novbr: I had today 85 workmen: Spyros had 12. In the Treasury the work I intended to do is nearly
finished. The ground is virgin rock; it is covered with a layer of
chalk and sand. In the midst of the Treasure is a hole to which a
small channel seems to lead from the door passage. The threshhold has now been brought to light. On the same was found a
circular blade of gold. Immediately / S. of the threshold I struck a
wall of large hewn chalk stones. In the door passage was found a
half-column (fluted) of calcareous stone 1 m 27 high and 40 Ctm
in diametre.[201]

In the acropolis I have worked very hard and made great progress in the work of digging down the *circle* to the rock in order
to bring to light the tombs which may be there. In the tomb of

the 2 unsculptured tombstones were found only the calcinated remains of 2 more bodies, *each exactly with* as many ornaments⟨,⟩ 5 large leafs, 4 circular pieces of goldblade & 5 crosses formed of leafs, as the first body.[202] All of them are covered with spiral or circular ornaments. There was besides found in the tomb a much broken bronze vessel and a number of broken vases with beautiful designs; the one with 4 handles.[203] There were found in the tomb some bone-buttons with the same spiral ornamentation as on several goldbuttons.[204] In the acropolis in 6 m depth, was also found a good deal of beautiful pottery, and quite a number of fragments of vases having on each side a protruding piece with 2 tubular holes for suspension.[205] These vases are handmade and so is all the beautiful *black* pottery with a lustruous surface. Evidently all the rubbish in the circle derives from the ☐ tombs. One fragment of vase had the following signs:

Mycenae, Thursday 16 Novbr 1876. I had today 100 workmen. Sypros has stopped work in the Treasury and I have taken him with his 12 workmen. I have dug away the huge masses of rubbish with great rapidity and, to my great pleasure, I have struck the rock at a short distance (abt 5 mètres) E. of the unsculptured tombstones which are in the same line with those of the large tomb just excavated.[206] Below these third {sic} tombstones / are found others, 2 slabs lying the one on the other and, at the S. end of them, one standing.[207] Huge, abrupt masses of selfgrown rock have come to light S. of the 2nd tomb and the space has evidently been filled up with the rubbish dug up from the large ☐ graves.[208] Undoubtedly there is also a large ☐ tomb here cut out in the rock, but I have not yet found it. But I have found the ☐ tomb which was marked by the tombstone with the 2 serpents and which is just S. of the first tomb.[209] There were found, in a depth of 6 1/2 m, *5 archaic, handmade vases,*[210]

1 of a light green dead colour with ornaments of rude black
colour (2 handles)
2 light yellow
1 particularly interesting 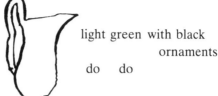 light green with black
ornaments
1 also   "   do   do

Close to the rock were found many human bodies, but of none of them the skull could be taken out without being broken; these bodies had evidently not been burnt; with one of them a *sawknife of obsidian* was found.[211] Similar knifes were collected today in large numbers and a great many broken *lustruous black handmade vases.* Of idols but a few. The 2nd tomb being now cleared out there was still found in it the fragment of a gold leaf, a silver vase with handle (φιάλη), two Juno idols with horns, *painted red* and 2 perforated pieces of a necklace, both of a hard blackstone.[212]

I have taken out tonight the unsculptured tombstone, which stood close to that with the basrelief of the 2 serpents,[213] and found it to be 1 m 80 from the 1st tomb and 3 m 50 from the double row of slabs. We had today the visit of:[214]
Dr. A. Milchhoeffer de l'Ecole Allemande à Athènes
do Alten, lieutenant d'Etat major à Berlin
Ernst Steinworth, Cand phil
Edoardo di Thraemer, Oberlehrer am Gymnasium in Felten, Livoniau {?}

Mycenae Friday 17th Novbr 1876: It having rained all night, I had but 42 workmen today, and, the path being slippery, I did no great work. Two men were working under an overhanging rock and twice I had dragged them from there to work in another place; they had hardly left the place when a large piece of rock fell and knocked them down but without hurting them. Had they loitered a moment longer they would have been killed on the spot.[215] Before this event there was found below the rock a *dagger of bronze* consisting of 2 blades, *each 21 Ctm long,* the middle part of which is soldered together so that the two edges (Schneiden) are by 6 millm separated from each other;[216] the handle is 10 Ctm long and has been inlaid with wood or bone which has been fastened by three nails.

195

The *silver vase found in the tomb is 14 Ctm wide and 7 high.* There was besides found in the tomb the mouth of a decayed bronze vase[s]; it is *gilded* and beautifully ornamented with an impressed ornamentation.[217]

In the present depth of 8 m I find almost exclusively *handmade lustrous, black pottery* or handmade light green vases *with rude black ornaments* made with black clay and with no real colour. The black pottery certainly remembers {i.e. recalls} that found in the lowest city in Troy and particularly the black goblets the bottoms of which might serve as second goblet and has horizontal flutings[218]

Some of the green (with black) vases also resemble the Trojan. There is further found an immense quantity of *obsidian* knifes in this depth. Of the 3rd tomb the *upper tombstones* were 5 m below the surface; just 1 m below these was found *a seemingly much more ancient monument of 1 upright and 2 horizontal slabs;*[219] in a similar way it was also with the *4* sculptured tombstones; that is to say 1 under the 3 sculptured slabs & one below that with the 2 serpents.[220] Nothing more than this can prove the immense importance attached to these tombs already in a very remote antiquity, than to erect / new monuments when the soil accumulated.

Describe the halfcolumn in the Treasury.[221]

{Workmen's receipts dated 6/18 November 1876.}

Mycenae, Saturday 18 Novbr: I had today more than 100 workmen and made excellent progress, in spite of the continual rain which was pouring upon us. My supposition that the double circle of white slabs has been erected in honour of the great dead, buried within its precincts, seems to be borne out by the discovery today of 3 more immense tombs cut in the rock; the one having been marked by the tombstone of the two serpents just S. of the first tomb; but besides this tombstone / and alongside with it was another unsculptured tombstone.[222] But, as in every instance, these tombstones have been placed there when the accumulation of rubbish on the rockcut tomb was already 3 m deep, because I found there the remnants of two tombstones abt 1 m above the rock. Of the other tomb,[223] S.E. of this, *no tombstone was above* at the level of the other tombs, but *there was an unsculptured one at 1 m above the rock cut tomb,*[224] which however had been bent by the weight of the dislocated large piece of rock and was now nearly horizontal. Below the third tomb also, which had been marked by the 2 unsculptured slabs below,[225] there were, 1 1/2–2 m below them, two horizontal slabs and an upright one at the S. end of them. All this proves the veneration with which all these tombs were regarded, because, though the original tombstones had for ages been covered by the accumulated rubbish, yet the precise spot of the graves was so well known that they were again marked by new tombstones. I guess there is still another tomb hidden below the dislocated piece of rock.

In the first excavated tomb was found one more piece of bone almost in the shape of a gazelle horn, with incised parallel incisions on the round side and 2 holes on the other, the flat, side to be fixed as an ornament.[226]

Between the tombs and, 6 1/2 m below the surface, was found an *almost circular cyclopean masonry,* with a large round opening, like a well;[227] it is 2 m 10 from N to S and 1 m 55 from E. to W. It is a remarkable fact that even 2 m above the rockcut tombs only the most ancient archaic pottery is found; *most* lustr[u]ous black inside & outside, handmade and of most fantastical form; or of light red dead colour with dark red ornamentation of circles or spiral lines or of light green dead colour with rude black ornaments. Remarkable are the goblets of light green or yellow dead colour with

splendid ornamentation with black colour.   *Arrows of*

silex sometimes occur at these depths of 7–8 m[228] / *no* real stone implements.

The now dislocated & incumbent large blocks of rock have evidently once been straight, the rock having been cut into from above.

{Workman's receipt dated 8/20 November 1876.}

Mycenae, Monday 20th Novbr 1876: I had today 79 workmen, but the space being very limited, they were too crowded and did not do much work. Even until now the first tomb[229] is not entirely excavated yet. At the bottom of this sepulchre[230] there is on all four sides a strange sort of a wall, formed of plates of micated slate, which are heaped up so as to go down under an angle of 45°.

The supposed well now turns out to be nothing else than a sort of a[n] sacrificial altar and to stand in the midst of an enormous sepulchre, which is by far the largest yet discovered. Below the small cyclopean walls of this altar I observe, in an obliqe position, 3 tombstones and a small column.[231] Nearly all the pottery now found is handmade, and either lustr[u]ous black, or light green with black ornaments or light red with rude dark red ornaments. But some fragments of vases with *incised* ornaments certainly turn up; so I found a fragment of a large vase.

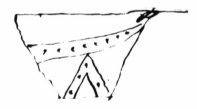

Mycenae 21 Nov (Tuesday): found in the tomb of the serpents a sword, a lance & a gold cup.[232] Only 45 labourers

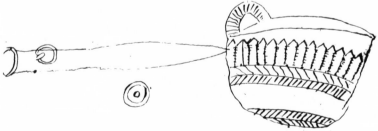

worked only till 10 on acct of rain.

198

In the same tomb was found a light green vase, handmade & 16 Ctm high and 2 series, each of three, protruding lumps and a large light red vase with black spiral ornaments and 2 women's breasts surrounded by a circle of black strokes.[233]

Wednesday 22 Nov: It rained today and there was no work.

Thursday 23 Novb: Had today 50 workmen and worked to dig up the tombs; were frequently interrupted by rain. Opened last night the small tomb which had been marked by the two large tombstones and below which I found three more tombstones.[234]

{Memo of payment to Spyros Demetriou dated 12/24 November 1876.}

The former were 3 m, the latter 5 m below the surface. The rock, which rises here under an angle of 55° (or descends under an angle of 35°), has at a depth of 6 m 40 been cut perpendicularly to make the tomb, whose E. side is thus 2 m 10; the N. side 1 m 40, the W. side 80 Ctm and the S. 1 m deep cut in the rock.[235] On the 4 sides of this tomb are 2 m high layers of slate plate, which are fixed together by means of yellow clay and rise under an angle of 45° so that they protrude 1 m 10 Ctm.[236] There is a layer of small stones on the virgin rock on which the dead bodies were burned; the ashes on the oblique layers and the marks of the fire on the pebbles can leave no doubt in this respect.[237] Thus on the first layer of pebbles lye {sic} the remains of the deceased and all the gold objects with which they were burnt. The bronze vessels, of which we found 8–9, were deposited on the N. side.[238] In this tomb were found the bones of three women,[239] whom I recognize by the smallness of the teeth and the female ornaments. The bones of the three[240] corpses, which were 1 m distant from each other, were really covered with / masses of gold, particularly the head, on which rested a tremendous crown of large splendidly ornamented leafs⟨,⟩ and innumerable smaller and larger objects of gold, particularly round gold leafs, of which there certainly were 300⟨,⟩ and smaller and larger pieces of gold, which had evidently been fastened to the rich clothes which had been burned with the dead.[241] I particularly remarked with the woman the gold ornaments representing an altar with a bird on either side; also a number of smaller and larger gold vases; a crystal in form of a lamp with 2 holes for suspension and with beautiful paintings; a man etc; further with the woman 2 sceptres with well ciselled handles etc.[242] There were also found 4, on one of the small sides open, boxes which contained charred wood;[243] the wood had been fastened inside[s] with long copper spikes; each 16 Ctm high, 22 1/2 long & 11 broad. At 1 m further N. were the bones of another *woman,* as I conclude by the necklace of beautifully incised pieces of gold, one of which represents Hercules killing the lion, and a necklace of brown agate.[244] Between the large vessels at the N. end was one

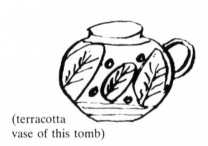

(terracotta vase of this tomb)

and a φιάλη with burned wood.[245] The gold ornaments with the last woman were less heavy and not more than 1/2 oka. The virgin soil of this tomb is 8 1/2 m below the surface. In all we may have gathered 4 1/2 okas of gold ornaments in the 2 tombs.[246] Only by noon we finished this tomb, having worked with the knifes all the morning in the mud.[247] At 1 o'clock we began the large tomb immediately W. of it, which is 7 m 18 long, by 6 m broad. The bottom of it is 10 m below ground. At 3 m above it stood the cycl sacrificial altar, below which were 2 slabs 82 Ctm long & 46 broad.[248] On the S. side of the tomb / we took out 4 large bronze vessels put one in another and also a *gold* vessel with representation of fish (dolphins).[249]

On the S. side are visible on the rock the black traces of the funeral fire and its ashes on the 2 m high embankment which slopes on the 4 sides down.

Friday 24th Novbr 1876: Today 15 workmen. We did the above work.[250]

The tomb of the bas relief with the serpents is only 70 Ctm deep cut into the rock.[251]

The cyclop waterconduit near the gate is only 2–2 1/2 feet broad and 30–35 Ctm deep and covered with slabs.

The large 1st tomb (of the 3 sculptured tombstones)[252] is 3 m 15 broad & 6 m 45 long; until now it is 3 m 65 deep.

The 2nd tomb (of the serpents)[253] is 2 m 90 br & 3 m 45 long

The 3rd ″ (without tombstone)[254] 7 m 18 long, 5 1/2 broad

The 4th ″ (with the 2 unsculptured slabs)[255] is 5 m long & 3 m 05 br.

The threshhold in the Treasury is 2 m 50 long & 73 br

Distance thence to the wall of large stone 2 m 84

Entrance passage 5 m 90 long

Space laid bare in the Treasury 5 m broad, 6 1/2 long

Door[256] 5 m 51 high

The passage is still 30 Ctm deeper

Only the upper hingeholes exist

The rubbish stands 2 m 65 high on the *dromos*

Dromos 5 m 82 br & 40 m long

Before the *dromos* of the Treasury of Atreus large cyclopean terrace.[257]

{Workman's receipt dated 13/25 November 1876.}

Mycenae 25 Novbr (Saturday) 1876: We began this morning the following tomb;[258] that one over which was the cyclopean sacrificial altar; found there at once the bones of a man and five large bronze vessels,[259] in one of which exactly 100 large & small beautifully engraved buttons representing spiral lines or ⤸ ; further a large silvern {sic} cowhead (gilded) with two long horns of pure gold,[260] which had evidently been stuffed with wood, for they were still now filled with half-rotten wood. There was further found a heap of bronze lances and swords, some still retaining part of their wooden sheath; many had still remnants of the χρυσόηλον wood of their handles, at the end of which was a bone or alabaster-button well adjusted by 4 protruding pieces and by 4 perforations; all these weapons were in a bad state of preservation and the majority crumbled away before our eyes. Many of the lance-shafts had been partially preserved; but the wood cleaves and disappears.[261] There were a very great many pieces of wood which had been gilded and a number of bronze objects likewise gilded. Also 5 vases of gold; one with a pigeon on either side⟨;⟩[262] of these vases 3 at least were drinking cups. In clearing the soil from E. to W. we found the bones of another man with immense bones; there were also 5 bronze vessels, one of which contained a number of silver vases and part of the gold vases above referred to; also 100 large & small buttons. In all were found 9 silver vases but only 3 of them—the one a beautiful οἰνοχόος, are entire.[263] There was an innumerable mass of very small and a few large gold leafs; also a massive golden belt of enormous size with the πόρπη to fasten it.[264] Very curious is the packing of the precious vases and other objects in the large bronze vessels. Very curious is it also that the bronze vessels were all stuck the one in the other.

{Workmen's receipts dated 14/26 November 1876.}

Mycenae 28 Novbr Only today resumed work on the arrival of Mr. Phendikles;[265] continued the excavation of the same tomb & found the bones of 4 more persons, thus in all 6, 2 of whom must at all events be women, as I conclude from the smallness of the teeth and the female ornaments.[266] All must be royal personages for they were all covered with gold. Found there:
2 diadems with ἔμβολον[267] and
1 large female comb of gold with teeth of bone
many bone buttons
a vast quantity of goldleafs
1 *necklace of amber*
1 large breast plate of gold[268]
3 golden masks which covered the faces of the persons;[269] one of them the face of an old woman as appears from the crooked and old teeth⟨,⟩ the comb and other female ornaments; this body also wore the great breastplate; the mask covered the head entirely, whose broken bones are saved.

202

2 small gold vessels[270]
2 gold vases with 1 handle
3 handles of swords covered with gold plates
innumerable gold buttons of diff size
3 golden girdles or belts, 1 of which of immense length[271]
1 small wine can of gold
1 large vase with 2 handles (κάνθαρος)
1 large bracelet weighing at least 100 drams[272]
1 thin do[273]
2 golden fingerrings, the one representing a hunting the other a
   battle
1 broken silvervessel
1 golden helmet[274]
1 small lion
3 large breastpins, one representing a he goat
1 vessel of lead in form of a stag with long horns[275]
large quantity of other ornaments
25 arrows of silex
1 gold ornament of a knemis
13 large kettles or casseroles[276]
many small & large swords, some with alabaster, other {sic} with
   wooden ◯ handle which had been gilded
also knifes
No trace of iron nor glass
Many brass battleaxes like those of Troy

136 {Workmen's receipts dated 18/30, 22 (Charvati), and 24 (Athens)
   November 1876.}

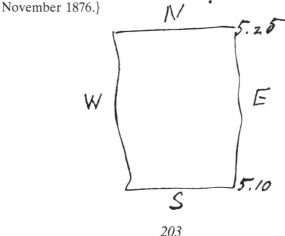

NOTES

1. At Argos, Pausanias was shown "an underground building over which was the bronze chamber which Acrisius built to guard his daughter" (2.23.7). In his commentary on this passage J.G. Frazer notes: "On the south-eastern slope of the hill Diras there is a subterranean passage which is now open for a length of 65 feet. . . . The passage leads into a small circular chamber. Curtius and Bursian think that this may be what was shown to sightseers as the prison of Danae. . . . See Curtius, *Pelop.* 2 pp. 354, 361; Bursian, *Geogr* 2. p. 50 sq." The Diras is the ridge between the Larisa and the Aspis hills. For modern discussions see R.A. Tomlinson, *Argos and the Argolid* (Ithaca 1972) 15–27 and *MG* 24.

2. Apparently, "Dimitry" is Spyros (or Spyridion) Demetriou (or Dimitriou) from Athens, one of Schliemann's foremen at Troy (cf. Schliemann, *TroyR* 357). The trench is within the Lion Gate on the site of Grave Circle A.

3. At *Myc.* 62–64 Schliemann maintains that Mycenae was uninhabited throughout the Roman period, adducing as evidence Strabo and the absence of Roman coins on the site. There is no reference to the Leda in *Myc.* This presumably reflects Schliemann's lack of interest in the later periods.

4. Neither the Selinus figure nor the inscription are mentioned in *Myc.*

5. The diorite axe is presumably one of the two hatchets of serpentine reported at *Myc.* 76. However, two well-polished axes of diorite are reported as found on the crest of the hill south southwest of the acropolis at *Myc.* 40. For the whorls of green stone see *Myc.* 77. Schliemann sometimes refers to these whorls as "fusaioli," as in the 16 August diary entry. The idol without a head is perhaps referred to at *Myc.* 72: "some idols with a bird's head, covered or uncovered, large eyes, no horns, but two well-indicated hands joined on the breast." For the Hera idols see *Myc.* 71: "Since the 7th inst. I have been able to gather here more than 200 terra-cotta idols of Hera, more or less broken, in the form of a woman or in that of a cow."

6. *Myc.* 77: "a number of weights of diorite."

7. Schliemann is talking about the passage inside the Lion Gate, where his group of ten men are working.

8. This is the tholos tomb located some 120 meters west of the Lion Gate and known as the Tomb of Clytemnestra.

9. See note 3.

10. This is the building to the north of the grave circle, now known as the Granary. See note 25. There is a tear in the page between "to" and "near," creating a lacuna of about four spaces.

11. Presumably a broken idol such as are illustrated at *Myc.* 74.

12. See *Myc.* no. 120 (bottom right).

13. *Myc.* 74.

14. *Myc.* 77: "millstones of trachyte."

15. Several complete vases are illustrated at *Myc.* 64–68.

16. For the "glasslike" buttons see *Myc.* 75f; small, interesting key: *Myc.* no. 120 (center); "handmillstones": *Myc.* 77.

17. These receipts appear periodically, generally in groups, throughout the Mycenaean diary. Usually the texts of the receipts (always in modern Greek) are written in Schliemann's own hand and signed by the workmen. The first receipt reads: "I, the undersigned carpenter, received payment for my bill of 28 drachmas. Mycenae 12 August 1876. {signed} Georgios Zerbos." Sometimes these receipts are dated, like the above example, by the Gregorian calendar. More often, like the one immediately following (dated 31 July), which was written and signed on behalf of an illiterate worker by Stamatakis, they have a single, Julian date. Frequently, like the third, they bear both dates. At this time Greece was still officially using the Julian calendar, which was twelve days behind the Gregorian. Schliemann's normal diary entries have Gregorian dates.

18. Cf. *Myc.* 62.

19. At *Myc.* 79 Schliemann so describes the objects he illustrates at nos. 137 and 139, though they appear to be seals. Buttons virtually identical in design to *Myc.* no. 137 were found in Shaft Grave IV (Karo 334). The triskele design of no. 139 is similar to that of many buttons in Graves IV and V. It is surely remarkable that artifacts so similar in design to the disks and buttons of the shaft graves were discovered in the first week of excavations. Also remarkable is their juxtaposition in *Myc.* with no. 138, a gold-covered button, though none of these is reported until 19 September. Some two hundred of these seals in the hands of a goldsmith could account for all the buttons in Graves IV and V.

20. *Myc.* 76, where two bronze arrowheads are mentioned.

21. Periodically there are blanks left by Schliemann, where he intended to fill in the appropriate numbers or words later but omitted to do so. They will hereafter be indicated by "⟨   ⟩."

22. Presumably, this is the room marked B between the grave circle and the Lion Gate of plan B of *Myc.*

23. For the wooden comb, cf. *Myc.* 79, where a terra-cotta comb is illustrated (no. 130). For the lyre fragment see *Myc.* 77f., no. 127; for the bronze wheel see *Myc.* 74, no. 120.

24. At *Myc.* 77 it is said to be of terra-cotta. This, too, is evidently a seal; cf. note 19.

25. By "cyclopean house" Schliemann means the building now identified as the Granary, which is located to the north of the grave circle.

26. These are presumably the slabs constituting the northern section and gateway of the grave circle and almost certainly identical with the "tablets" marking the "tombs" of the next entry; see note 41.

27. P. Stamatakis, the ephor of the Argolid, was appointed to supervise the excavations at Mycenae to ensure that Schliemann observed the terms of the Archaeological Society's contract with the Greek government and to receive the finds on behalf of the state. Schliemann resented the restraints imposed on him by Stamatakis. In *Myc.* he refers to him only once (352) and that by way of insult: "a government clerk by the name of Stamatakis." Schliemann's hostility

to the conscientious Stamatakis has been rather mindlessly adopted by his biographers. However, as O.T.P.K. Dickinson has recently pointed out (*G&R* 23 [1976] 161f.), "it is impossible to read the extensive excerpts from letters and telegrams dispatched by all concerned quoted by Ludwig without feeling considerable sympathy for Stamatakis, who had been given an impossible task and was only lukewarmly supported by the Ministry." An objective assessment of Stamatakis's role in the excavation of Mycenae is long overdue.

28. *Myc.* 76.

29. On plan B of *Myc.* two water conduits are indicated between the grave circle and the Lion Gate.

30. At this point the sentence breaks off. On the tombstones see n. 26.

31. Not mentioned in the *Times* reports; the first mention of a sword in *Myc.* occurs on p. 144; see note 134 below.

32. Presumably, the mold for casting ornaments (*Myc.* no. 162) described at *Myc.* 108 or possibly the one mentioned at *Myc.* 109.

33. Probably *Myc.* no. 144 (= Karo 1431).

34. Presumably similar to the one described on 16 August (d); see notes 19 and 24.

35. *Myc.* 97, no. 152.

36. This "treasure" very probably constitutes the contents of a tomb. It is described at *Myc.* 111f., where a tripod is included in addition to the objects listed here. The objects are illustrated at *Myc.* nos. 120–25.

37. He appears to mean by this the length of the line created by the three tombstones. Cf. *Myc.* 88: "thus the line of the three tombstones together is 13 ft. 8 in." The three tombstones are *Myc.* no. 24 (= Karo 1427), *Myc.* no. 140 (= Karo 1428) and Myc. no. 141 (= Karo 1429).

38. This total presumably includes the slabs constituting the northern section and gateway of the grave circle (see note 41) as well as the sculptured and unsculptured slabs within the circle.

39. *Myc.* no. 141 and Karo pl. VI, 1429. The spiral designs of the lower panel are a development of an Early Helladic design found on a sealing from Lerna; see R. Higgins, *MMA* 73, fig. 79g.

40. *Myc.* no. 142 and Karo pl. VIII, 1430.

41. Despite Schliemann's indication that they lay "to the E. of the cyclopean house," these are the slabs constituting the entrance gateway with perhaps some of the adjoining slabs. Some of these slabs are over two meters high (Karo p. 25 and drawing on p. 27). At this point Schliemann believed that they were tombs; cf. Dickinson (supra n. 27) 163. Later (e.g., at *Myc.* 80 and 340) Schliemann identified them as cisterns.

42. By "these tombs" it seems from what follows that Schliemann is referring to all forty-six tombstones mentioned above and not simply to the immediately preceding nine tombs. The reference to Pausanias is to the passage at 2.16.6, which Schliemann quotes and discusses at *Myc.* 59–61. At *Myc.* 102f. Schliemann uses the argument that these tombs must have been buried when Pausanias visited the site. With the benefit of hindsight, however, he neverthe-

less asserts at *Myc.* 101f.: "I do not for a moment hesitate to proclaim that I have found here the sepulchres which Pausanias, following the tradition, attributes to Atreus, to the king of men Agamemnon etc."

43. That is, in the Granary, which he has just identified as a tomb.

44. The jasper weight, the eagles, and the wheat and vetch are reported at *Myc.* 100.

45. That is, the excavation of the Granary continues.

46. Here, in the preceding entry, and in the corresponding passage at *Myc.* 99, Schliemann appears to be describing the room of the Granary numbered 16 on the map of Grave Circle A. Once again, Schliemann's directions are not exact. The door is at the northeast corner.

47. From his 9 September report, published in *Times* II and from *Myc.* 340, it appears that the "tombs" Schliemann is here discussing are those which he later identified as cisterns or reservoirs and which were in reality the entrance gateway of the grave circle (see note 41). In *Times* II he states: "I have not been more lucky with the tombs formed of four large slabs, for they contain nothing else than the remnants of households, and, particularly, fragments of archaic vases." Cf. also *Myc.* 100.

48. Perhaps the small disks of glazed clay described at *Myc.* 108f.; cf. notes 19, 24, and 34.

49. A few seats of this Hellenistic theater built on top of the Tomb of Clytemnestra are still in situ; see Wace, *Mycenae* fig. 54 and Mylonas, *MMA* 122.

50. The men from Cutzopodi apparently excavated the section south of the grave circle.

51. Schliemann unfortunately gives no clues as to the location of this grave. There is no mention of it or of the vases in *Myc.*

52. By "nothing" Schliemann can only mean, in view of the preceding, "no valuable objects." This sentence does not accord well with the suggestion recently put forward by H. Döhl (*Heinrich Schliemann: Mythos und Ärgernis* 92) that Schliemann was more interested in sherds than treasure.

53. That is, the Granary.

54. The small cyclopean wall supports the parapet (double wall) of the grave circle in the lower western section. As Schliemann indicates on 7 September, it is five meters from the large city wall; see map of Grave Circle A.

55. Presumably, Schliemann is again referring to the northern part of the grave circle, which at this time he believed to be a row of tombs. That Schliemann thought it strange that tombs should be full of potsherds and some entire vases is a striking reminder that, despite a rather remarkable veneer of knowledge, he was still, in 1876, quite ignorant about some of the most basic facts of archaeology.

56. The name and address are written in a different hand, presumably Davies's.

57. The "porphyr block" is illustrated at the end of this entry and at *Myc.* no. 151. It presumably came from the dromos of the Tomb of Clytemnestra;

cf. Wace's reconstruction of the facade of the Treasury of Atreus in his *Mycenae* pl. 51. The "Doric triglyph block" is presumably a fallen fragment of the classical and Hellenistic temple built on the summit of the citadel (Wace, *Mycenae* 24).

58. This might be any one of several gems described at *Myc.* 112–14.

59. Presumably, the "goblet" is similar to the vase at *Myc.* no. 349. Schliemann describes finding many of this type at *Myc.* 115f.

60. *Myc.* 105; illustrated at pl. XIX, no. 106.

61. Perhaps illustrated at *Myc.* pl. XI, no. 48.

62. Since Schliemann believed that the tombs described by Pausanias were *inside* the cyclopean walls surrounding the citadel, he rejected the view that the tholos structures outside the walls were also tombs.

63. Veli Pasha's excavation is described at *Myc.* 50.

64. For a modern discussion of the city walls see Mylonas, *MMA* 15–20.

65. *Myc.* 106f.

66. Repeated from the 7 September entry; see n. 57.

67. The first "cyclopean house" discussed is perhaps the northern part of the House of the Warrior Vase, south of the grave circle; see Wace, *Mycenae* fig. 3. The second is perhaps the southern part of the House of the Warrior Vase and part of the South House; cf. map of Grave Circle A and *Myc.* plan B.

68. *Myc.* 113, no. 174.

69. These are the seats of the Hellenistic theater; see n. 49.

70. The sentence breaks down grammatically at this point.

71. *Myc.* 115. From the reference to this inscription in the 9 September report (*Times* II) we can infer that the "9 September" report was not completed until at least 13 September.

72. *Myc.* 120f., nos. 205–209.

73. According to *Myc.* 129 the wooden fish was found close to the perimeter wall of the grave circle. The "transparent gem," an exquisite finger ring, is described at *Myc.* 131 (no. 175), where Schliemann indicates that it was found in the "cyclopean house" south of the grave circle.

74. Supply "sucking" and "udder" in the places where Schliemann left blanks. Schliemann added "pregnant" below the line as an afterthought. At *Myc.* 132 he identifies them as cows rather than pregnant hinds.

75. The recording of the find of the wooden fish is presumably a repetition of the 14 September mention. The only oyster shells mentioned in *Myc.* are reported as found in Shaft Grave V (332).

76. Again, these are the seats of the Hellenistic theater; see n. 49.

77. Plan B of *Myc.* indicates two "cyclopean cisterns" south of the grave circle, both fairly close to water conduits. These are located in buildings now known as the House of the Warrior Vase and the South House. The cistern in the House of the Warrior Vase is too far east to be the well or the five-meter-deep rectangular shaft under the west wall of the House of the Warrior Vase; see Wace, *Mycenae* 66. Wace describes no cistern-like structure in the South House.

78. *Myc.* 114, no. 187.

79. This is the famous Warrior Vase, described at *Myc.* 132–37, where the handles are said to terminate in cow heads.

80. In *Times* VI (December 14) Schliemann reports that this gem was found in the house south of the grave circle along with *Myc.* nos. 178 and 541. At *Myc.* 362f., however, where it is illustrated as no. 539, Schliemann says that he *bought* this gem from peasants, along with nos. 540 and 541, in the village of Chonika. The asterisk beside the word "bead" appears to be original rather than a later addition. Perhaps it was intended to remind Schliemann that the bead had in fact been purchased; see the Introduction to the diary.

81. The tombstone is illustrated at *Myc.* no. 24 (= Karo pl. VII, 1427); it stood over Shaft Grave V (Schl. I). The discovery of the gold-plated button appears in the 9 September report (*Times* II), from which we may infer that the report was completed on or after 19 September. Although found just below the stelae and therefore about six meters above the floor of the tomb, the gold-covered button was apparently added to the finds of Grave V. It is described at *Myc.* 325, no. 510 and Karo 684.

82. Cf. Wace, *Mycenae* 66 on the House of the Warrior Vase: "These basement rooms were floored with white clay and the walls were covered with mud plaster."

83. These are probably from the Hellenistic house built on top of the South House (cf. Wace, *Mycenae* 66).

84. *Myc.* 108, no. 163.

85. *Myc.* 132.

86. Not mentioned in *Myc.*

87. This appears to be the tripod added to the "treasure" of 25 August as described at *Myc.* 111f.; see note 36. The large tripod mentioned at *Myc.* 137 seems to be the one found on 3 October; see n. 106.

88. The vases painted with cranes and the clay figure of a horseman were found in the dromos of the Tomb of Clytemnestra; see *Myc.* 120.

89. At *Myc.* 130 Schliemann says that he found these fragments of chalk with painted murals in the grave circle but not in the houses and so supposes that they must be of comparatively late date.

90. *Myc.* no. 171, which at *Myc.* 110 is said to be made of decomposed glass.

91. *Myc.* 121, no. 154.

92. From *Myc.* 124 it appears that he means to suggest here that the double row of slabs forming the circle may have functioned as a large circular planter.

93. Exactly which tombs he means here it is difficult to say.

94. Presumably, on the site of the Ramp House. For Schliemann the term "Hellenic" embraces the Archaic, Classical, and Hellenistic periods.

95. At *Myc.* 123 Schliemann mentions having to dig through the "foundations of an Hellenic house" next to the Cyclopean house (the Granary) north of the grave circle.

96. At *Myc.* 124 Schliemann mentions the cockle shells but not the "quantities of bones and ashes of burned bodies."

97. *Myc.* 114, no. 182.

98. Since Schliemann held that the tholos tombs outside the citadel were not tombs but treasuries, he did not want to find that the material blocking the dromos was contemporary with sherds found inside the "treasury," for that would suggest that the structure was a tomb, not a treasury. At *Myc.* 120 he is more circumspect; there he merely states that some of the vases found in the dromos are later than any terra-cottas found in the shaft graves.

99. *Myc.* 119; cf. Wace, *Mycenae* 36 and fig. 51 (restoration of facade of Treasury of Atreus).

100. *Myc.* 119f. From the lack of holes in the stones, Schliemann concluded that the interior of the Tomb of Clytemnestra had not been covered with bronze plates.

101. The black jasper axe is mentioned at *Myc.* 132. The terra-cotta disks are, presumably, like those described and illustrated at *Myc.* 79; see notes 19 and 24. See note 104 for the "internal chalk coating of the ancient houses."

102. Both of these idols are discussed at *Myc.* 129f. (the second one is illustrated at no. 212).

103. The two hatchets are mentioned at *Myc.* 132. Schliemann reports obsidian knives among the finds of Shaft Grave V at *Myc.* 158 and from the slope of the rock near Shaft Grave III at *Myc.* 162, but not, apparently, in any earlier finds.

104. Schliemann persistently believed that the frescoed plaster must derive from houses of a much later period. However, we now know that it was a familiar feature of Mycenaean houses; for frescoed plaster found in the House of Tsountas see Mylonas, *MMA* 79.

105. *Myc.* 120.

106. Perhaps the crocodile-shaped handle is the other handle of the Warrior Vase; cf. entry of 20 September and note 79. At *Myc.* 137 Schliemann appears to mention the bronze tripod casserole: "two copper vessels, one of which is a tripod of very large size." The potsherds, bronze vessels, and numerous bones found here suggest that Schliemann's workmen have come across some tombs underneath the houses. Perhaps the "two large cisterns" were in fact tombs.

107. Cf. *Myc.* 33.

108. At *Myc.* 123 Schliemann mentions three bronze arrowheads, but none of iron.

109. These are further fragments of the Warrior Vase; *Myc.* 136, no. 214. "Stacheln" are prickles; "Helmbuschen" are helmet plumes. This sentence was left incomplete.

110. The slabs are tallest on the western half of the circle; see Karo p. 25.

111. *Myc.* 123.

112. This object is not reported in *Myc.* if it is different from the one found on 14 September.

113. The east wing of the Granary (map of Grave Circle A, nos. 10–12).

114. The Granary comprised at least two levels, the ground floor and the first floor. Both are of the LH III period. Wace's plan (map of Grave Circle A) shows no Hellenic or Hellenistic construction.

115. In his fifth report, dated 30 October and published in the *Times* of 13 December, Schliemann begins: "My last letter was of the 7th inst. and I have continued the excavations ever since with the utmost vigour, employing constantly 125 labourers and five horse-carts." It is accordingly with some surprise that one learns from this diary entry that Schliemann was absent from Mycenae for two weeks, 9–23 October, during which time no excavation appears to have taken place. Schliemann left Mycenae to escort Dom Pedro, emperor of Brazil, round the Troad. Schliemann could hardly have intended to deceive the readers of the *Times* in his report of 30 October, for he had sent a report of his trip to the Troad, dated "Dardanelles 17 October," to the *Times,* where it was published in the issue of 6 November. Nor does it seem likely that by 30 October he had forgotten that between 7 and 30 October there had been little more than a week of excavation. The explanation, I believe, is to be found in Schliemann's personality. It sounded better to convey the impression that the excavations had been pursued vigorously ever since the last report than to state that they had been interrupted for two weeks for an excursion to the Troad. The truth or falsity of the statement did not concern him. It is mildly surprising, however, that he did not correct the misstatement in *Myc.* (at 139), as he corrected similar falsehoods in the *Times* about Sophia, Dom Pedro's visit, and the purchased gems (see the Introduction). The rough draft of the *Times* report on his trip to the Troad now follows in the diary. It was probably written on the boat between the Dardanelles and Piraeus.

116. Comte Joseph Arthur de Gobineau, French diplomat and sociologist, is now best known for his *Essai sur l'Inégalité des Races Humaines* (Paris 1854), which inspired Richard Wagner and provided a philosophical basis for the racist views of National Socialism. He was knowledgeable about archaeology and contributed to *Revue Archéologique.* His assessment of Schliemann is remarkably perceptive, though he underestimates his intelligence. After the visit to Hissarlik and before Bunarbashi, he wrote: "Nous allons partir et monter à cheval de nouveau pour aller voir un nouvel emplacement où Troie a pu être après avoir vu hier les fouilles de l'emplacement du grand M. Schliemann qui n'est qu'un charlatan impudent, menteur et imbécile. Tout cela me gâte un peu le Troade." ["We are going to leave and get on horseback again to go and see a new site where Troy could have been, after having seen yesterday the excavations of the site of the great M. Schliemann, who is nothing but an impudent charlatan, liar, and imbecile. All of this spoils the Troad a bit for me."]

After visiting Bunarbashi, he remarked:

Du reste, nous avons fait le voyage dans un nuage de pédanterie avec le Dr. Schliemann à droite et un autre professeur allemand à gauche. Heureusement, ils s'étaient pris en horreur comme Blasius et Baldus. L'Empereur m'avait fait jurer hier matin de ne pas les contredire. J'ai tenu parole et j'ai été si fort de leur avis que je leur ai fait dire des choses inouïes, et il a ri à en être malade. Mais voyez l'ingratitude? Il m'a grondé à fond prétendant une horreur innée pur la moquerie. Ça ne m'a pas empêché d'en tant dire aujourd'hui que tout le monde a été pour moi, lui comme les autres, et les deux savants ont été abymés, ce qui était indispensable.

Moreover, we made the trip in a cloud of pedantry with Dr. Schliemann on the right and another German professor on the left. Fortunately, they had taken an intense dislike for each other, like Blasius and Baldus. The Emperor had made me swear yesterday morning not to contradict them. I kept my word and I was so strongly of their opinion that I made them say ridiculous things and he laughed himself sick over it. But how's this for ingratitude? He gave me a thorough scolding, claiming an innate horror of making fun of people. That did not stop me from saying today that everyone was on my side, including himself, and the two scholars were crushed, which was the essential thing.

See J. Buenzod, *Etudes de Lettres,* ser. 2, vol. 4 (1961) 186f.

117. A young German orientalist, Henning was also Dom Pedro's German teacher; see Buenzod (supra n. 116) 186 n. 2.

118. Initially, Schliemann wrote "H.M. perfectly agreed with me," which he later changed to "H.M. made there the just observation." Throughout the report Schliemann uses the emperor as a mouthpiece for his own views.

119. Both tumuli are on the west bank of the Scamander (Menderes) near Kum Kale; see map of Troad at the back of *Ilios.*

120. In *TroyR* 62 Schielmann makes a similar claim about his wife's knowledge of the *Iliad.* There is no reason to believe either assertion.

121. The sources of the Scamander (Menderes) are in the mountain above Eviler; see J. Cook, *The Troad* (Oxford 1973) 292f.

122. The article in question appeared in the *Times* of 5 June 1876, 12. It was by Mr. Gallenga, the *Times*'s correspondent in Constantinople. Though critical in parts, it was not polemical, but it seems to have infuriated Schliemann. Criticisms similar to Gallenga's but more vehement in tone were subsequently raised by W. Simpson in *Fraser's Magazine* of July 1877, 1–16, and by W. Borlase in *Fraser's Magazine* of February 1878, 228–39.

123. Plan 2 of *TroyR* shows that the "Scaean Gate" leads directly into a narrow passage between different sections of "Priam's Palace." The wall or pile of rubbish blocking the entrance to the passage, to which Gallenga and others referred, can be seen on pl. XIII of the same book.

124. Gallenga (supra n. 122) had described the altar as "a mere lump of earth which is rapidly crumbling to dust, and of which hardly a vestige will be found by any visitor looking for it six months hence."

125. *TroyR* 198f.

126. Though one might suspect that Kolobos is a figment of Schliemann's romantic imagination, letters from Kolobos exist in the Schliemann archive in

the Gennadius Library. Schliemann, however, may well have embroidered the truth here.

127. The Homeric passage to which Schliemann refers is *Il.* 2.791–94. Despite his later claims to the contrary, Schliemann was an adherent of the Bunarbashi theory until his meeting with Frank Calvert on 15 August, when Calvert convinced him that Hissarlik, not Bunarbashi, was the site of Troy. Accordingly, when Schliemann visited Uvecik Tepe, he agreed with the supporters of the Bunarbashi theory in identifying Uvecik Tepe as the Tomb of Aesyetes. Later, when he became a convert to the Troy-Hissarlik theory, he roundly denounced this identification. On this whole question see Traill, *Boreas* 7 (1984) 295–316.

128. Cf. *Il.* 22.147–52.

129. Excavated by Frank Calvert in 1864.

130. The identification of the acropolis on the Balli Dağ with Gergis was first made by Frank Calvert; see Schliemann, *Ithaque* 158. The inscription to which Schliemann refers is published at *TroyR* 240–44. It does not prove that the Balli Dağ is Gergis. Cook (supra n. 121) 348–50 identifies Gergis with Karincali.

131. Most of these arguments appear again and again in Schliemann's writings, e.g., at *Ilios* 18f.

132. *Il.* 1.452.

133. It will be noticed that there is no mention of what has been accomplished during Schliemann's absence. The natural inference is that the excavations were suspended while he was away.

134. This was reported in *Times* VI (14 December 1876) as found in a room at the north end of the house south of the grave circle. At *Myc.* 144, written after the discovery of the graves had shown that it was in fact a sword handle, the "door button" (i.e., doorknob) becomes associated with a bronze sword. No such sword is mentioned in the diary or in the *Times* report. The only sword mentioned in the diary up to this point is the one reported on 21 August, which was not included in the *Times* or *Myc.* report of 9 September or any subsequent report. It is reasonable to conclude therefore that the sword mentioned at *Myc.* 144 is the one found on 21 August. If so, Schliemann's association of the sword with the alabaster handle is almost certainly fraudulent. It appears from the diary entry of 5 September that it was only when his labor force suddenly increased from 50–70 men to 112 men with the arrival of the men from Cutzopodi on that day that Schliemann started to excavate south of the grave circle. If the sword is not the one discovered on 21 August, then two questions remain unanswered:

a) why did Schliemann fail to mention in the diary entry of 25 October the sword he allegedly found with the alabaster handle?

b) whatever happened to the sword discovered on 21 August?

135. See plan at *Myc.* 34, no. 22.

136. This bas-relief is one of the three sculptured stones above Shaft Grave V. It is illustrated at *Myc.* 52, no. 24 (= Karo pl. VII, 1427). Unfortunately,

no clear account of the excavation of what Schliemann took to be a tomb "just below the basrelief" is offered. It is clear, however, that on the uppermost of the two slabs lying some three feet below the tombstone Schliemann found human bones, including a jawbone; see 30 October entry and *Myc.* 151f.

137. In *Times* VI the seal ring is also described as having two female figures engraved on it. At *Myc.* 142 Schliemann identifies the two figures as one male and one female.

138. The engraved "redstone" is perhaps the one illustrated at *Myc.* no. 178. For the female idol see *Myc.* 143.

139. The "mutilated cowidol" is described at *Myc.* 142; the tripods and comb are reported at *Myc.* 143.

140. For the blue marble see *Myc.* 140, no. 215. Presumably, the "parallel[o]epipedon of terracotta" is one of the two parallelepipeds mentioned, but not described, at *Myc.* 143. The necklace beads are reported at *Myc.* 144.

141. *Myc.* 144f. This visit is also described by A. de Gobineau at Buenzod (supra n. 116) 193–95: "J'ai été ravi de revoir Mycènes. Le détestable Schliemann y fait des fouilles. Il y a trouvé des bas-reliefs qui, s'ils sont authentiques (je le juge capable de tout en fait de faussetés) sont d'un intérêt capital et changeront encore les opinions sur les origines de l'art. Nous avons fait un dîner charmant dans le tombeau d'Agamemnon sur un sol parsemé de branches de lauriers." ["I was delighted to see Mycenae again. The contemptible Schliemann is excavating there. He has found bas-reliefs, which, if genuine—I consider him capable of anything in the way of duplicity—are of capital interest and will change opinions once again on the origins of art. We had a charming dinner in the Tomb of Agamemnon, where the ground was strewn with laurel branches."]

The Nauplion newspaper *Argolis* of 23 October/4 November 1876 reports that Dom Pedro and his party had arrived at the site at 2.30 P.M. In the welcoming group were the nomarch and eparch of Argos and the mayors of Nauplion, Argos, and Mycenae. The *Argolis* reports that there was time for only a fleeting inspection of the site, whereas at *Myc.* 144 Schliemann maintains that Dom Pedro "remained for two hours in my excavation, which he attentively examined and re-examined." The visitors did not reach Mycenae till 2:30 P.M. and must have spent about an hour over the banquet in the Treasury of Atreus and another at least hour traveling to Argos, where the *Argolis* reports they arrived at 5:30 P.M. In fact, J. Murray's *Handbook for Travellers in Greece* (London 1872) 277 states: "From Mykenae to Argos is 1 hr. and 50 min." It would seem then that their inspection must have been rather cursory, lasting less than an hour.

142. Here Schliemann seems to imply that the sculptured tombstones are still in situ, whereas the following entry implies that the three over Shaft Grave V have been removed. Perhaps they were removed immediately after Dom Pedro's visit.

143. Schliemann does not include the postern gate among the parts of Mycenae visited by the emperor in either the *Times* or *Myc.* versions. In such a hurried visit it seems unlikely that they would take the time to cross and

recross the awkward terrain between the grave circle and the postern gate. If they did, it would make their visit of Schliemann's excavations even more fleeting. The *Argolis* reports that the nomarch and the eparch of Argos and the mayor of Mycenae were the hosts of the meal, but that only Dr. and Mrs. Schliemann had the honor of joining the visitors at the table. The hosts refrained from eating in order to better look after their guests. In *Times* VII and *Myc.* Schliemann makes no mention of the Greeks and the reader is left to infer that the Schliemanns were the hosts.

144. No silver ring is mentioned in *Myc.* outside of the shaft graves, but at *Myc.* 142 Schliemann reports finding two bronze rings (nos. 217 and 219) in addition to the one recorded in the 26 October entry (no 218).

145. The idols and cow artifacts are described at *Myc.* 143.

146. It appears from Schliemann's use of the past tense here that the three sculptured stones over Shaft Grave V have been removed.

147. These slabs "of calcareous stone" are probably not the flagstones covering the shaft grave; see Mylonas, *MMA* 91. Here Schliemann appears to be reporting far more of them than the three he mentions at *Myc.* 151. The presence of the skeleton on the slab and the discovery of the gold-covered button at this spot on 19 September suggests that there was at least one tomb immediately below the upright sculptured tombstones. No mention of the human bones is made in *Times* VII. At *Myc.* 152 there is a fleeting reference to a body resting on one of these slabs.

148. Apparently, Stamatakis was better informed. According to the *Argolis,* he provided breakfast for the emperor and his suite in his house in the village. De Gobineau (supra n. 141) also reports that they ate at Charvati, but does not specify where. Despite the hostility between Stamatakis and the Schliemanns, documented at Emil Ludwig, *Schliemann* (Boston 1931) 167–86, the Schliemanns were also invited. Schliemann's egocentric phrasing here is once again misleading. The reader of the diary naturally infers that the emperor was not given a meal on this occasion.

149. It is not entirely clear to what walls Schliemann is referring here and in the corresponding passage in the 30 October entry. The "large cyclopean wall in the midst of the acropolis" appears to be the wall running south from the Lion Gate on the east side of the gate. The "eastern wall" is probably the stretch of that wall between II and III on plan B in *Myc.*, about one meter east of the section running up from the gate. Wace's plan (map of Grave Circle A) confirms that only some stones of this stretch are in situ. The wall Schliemann was hoping to strike by digging alongside it in a southerly direction (see 30 October entry) would have run from III to IV on plan B of *Myc.* The water conduit Schliemann refers to is presumably the one in *Myc.* plan B that runs to the east wing of the Granary.

150. The "corridors" Schliemann mentions constitute the east wing of the Granary. By the "canal" between the double row of slabs Schliemann probably just means the space between them. At one time he thought it served as a water conduit.

151. Here again Schliemann seems to imply that there were more than three slabs below the three sculptured tombstones of Shaft Grave V.

152. The "cyclopean house" in which these fragments were found is apparently the House of the Warrior Vase. The fragments are reported at *Myc.* 93–94, no. 143 (Karo 1434–66.X) and probably Karo 1434–66.VIIa.

153. On plan D of *Myc.* Schliemann indicates that a shaft was sunk about 120 meters north of the Lion Gate.

154. This appears to be the conduit closest to the Lion Gate indicated on plan B of *Myc.*

155. The easternmost section of the Granary marked B on plan B of *Myc.*

156. Schliemann's notes here are a little imprecise. The second cistern "just S." of the first must be the narrow corridor adjacent to it. However, it is southwest of the first rather than south. The conduit running west from it is probably the drain, which in Wace (map of Grave Circle A) turns northwest to the city wall after passing through both corridors.

157. Schliemann reports "large quantities of melted lead" at *Myc.* 142. See *Myc.* 142, no. 220 for the earring.

158. Schliemann hired Lieutenant Vasilios Drosinos, an engineer, to make plans of the sites. The discovery of the Golden Treasure is attributed to his sharp eyes (*Myc.* 352). Leonardos, the chief of police at Nauplion, found himself at the center of a bizarre controversy later in November. Apparently, Dom Pedro had given him the sum of forty francs to distribute among the local police force. The mayor and other citizens of Nauplion, however, maintained that Leonardos had actually received one thousand francs but had only distributed forty and appropriated the rest. As a result, Leonardos was dismissed from his post. Schliemann championed his cause and wrote letters to the prime minister of Greece and other officials, staunchly maintaining Leonardos's innocence. He even telegraphed Dom Pedro, asking him to confirm that he had in fact given Leonardos only forty francs. This Dom Pedro did. On this episode see Ludwig (supra n. 148) 176–78. Ludwig seems to have had access to documents now lost, notably the copybook containing Schliemann's letters written in the latter part of 1876. On the back of a letter from Mrs. Drosinos dated 22 November 1876 there is the following rough draft of a telegram written (in Greek) in Schliemann's hand: "Yesterday at least 4 okes of gold. I return to Corinth Saturday. I telegraphed the Prime Minister on your behalf. Am confident you will not lose your post." Since Schliemann discovered, or believed that he had discovered, four and a half okes of gold on Thursday 23 November, the telegram was presumably dispatched on the 24th. Schliemann makes no mention in his diary of any trip to Corinth on 25 November. He has an entry describing excavations that day and workmen's receipts dated 13/25 November. No excavations, however, are recorded for either 26 or 27 November and it is possible that Schliemann went to Corinth on the 26th (or even in the evening of the 25th) and returned to Mycenae on the 27th. The purpose of the trip remains a mystery.

In view of Schliemann's expression of indebtedness in this entry of the diary, it is reasonable to suppose that he was the source of Leonardos's sudden wealth which so provoked the people of Nauplion. If so, the guarded nature of Schliemann's statement and Leonardos's apparent inability to exculpate himself by revealing how he had acquired the money suggest that his service may not have been legitimate. Various hypotheses suggest themselves; see the Introduction.

159. A description of the slab can be found at *Myc.* 121–22. Wace, *Mycenae* 53 speculated that the "deep cutting" in the center of the threshold "is a square socket presumably for the bolts to hold the doors fast."

160. There are in fact three furrows cutting across the breadth of the threshold. Two of these are irregularly shaped and are clearly ruts worn by chariots and carts. The third, at the east end, is straight and was used for drainage. At *Myc.* 122 Schliemann vehemently rejects the notion that any of these furrows were caused by wheeled traffic: "The ruts caused by the chariot-wheels of which all guide books speak, exist only in the imagination of enthusiastic travellers, but not in reality." J. Murray's *Handbook for Travellers in Greece* (London 1854) 261 observes concerning the gate that "two thirds of its height, or perhaps more, was lately buried in the ruins, but the gateway has been cleared out, and is now to be seen complete. It is 10 ft. in height; in the lintel are marks of bolts or hinges, and the pavement contains ruts caused by chariot-wheels." The 1872 edition of the guide contains the same information (276), though by then, presumably, the winter rains had washed debris down into the passageway.

161. It will be noticed that no mention is made of Sophia either here or in *Times* VII. Schliemann added her to the account at *Myc.* 145 and omitted the boy. In much the same way in *TroyR* he speaks of Sophia as participating in the excavations at Troy, when his correspondence shows clearly that she was in Athens; see Traill, *Antiquity* 57 (1983) 181–86 and *JHS* 104 (1984) 96–115.

162. For this whole account see *Myc.* 145–147. On the Mycenaean guard outpost at the summit of Mt. Profitis Ilias see Wace, *Mycenae* 47 and *MG* 17.

163. This is the only mention of Sophia in the diary; Stamatakis is mentioned twice. Her allotted task is finding workmen for Schliemann's foreman Spyros. Nowhere in the diary or the *Times* reports does Schliemann suggest that she is supervising the excavation of the treasury. The first mention of Sophia's work in the treasury occurs at *Myc.* 119: "In the Treasury, in which Mrs. Schliemann is excavating." In the corresponding *Times* (IV) report we find simply: "In the Treasury, in which I work with two engines and thirty labourers." One might be tempted to infer from this that Sophia's supervision of the excavation of the treasury was no more real than her presence at the discovery of "Priam's treasure." There is a letter, however, from Stamatakis to the Ephoria of Antiquities in Athens, dated 15/27 August, in which he describes a dispute he had with Schliemann over a wall that Stamatakis wanted preserved. Schliemann had the wall removed one morning and "then left his wife there to supervise the excavation, and went himself to the acropolis in order to avoid meeting me"; see Ludwig (supra n. 148) 167f. It is clear, then,

that on this occasion, at least, Sophia was left in charge of the excavation of the treasury. Stamatakis's letter suggests that in August this was an unusual departure and that her role was more to see that Stamatakis did not interfere with her husband's wishes than to give orders to the men. It would be taking skepticism too far, however, to argue that this was the only time Sophia was left in charge at the treasury or that her role and authority could not have expanded with time and experience. It seems likely, however, that Schliemann has exaggerated Sophia's role at Mycenae, as he did at Troy. Certainly, the biographers have inflated it beyond all recognition.

164. The first half of this entry is essentially a repeat of the 4 November entry with measurements added; cf. notes to that entry and *Myc.* 121–22.

165. A plan of the Lion Gate and the inner gateway is given at *Myc.* 34, no. 22. The "holes for the hinges" are the pivot holes in the threshold (*Myc.* 121, no. 210) and lintel. The four holes are in the doorposts (*Myc.* no. 22a).

166. E. Curtius, *Der Peloponnesos* (Gotha 1851–1852) 405: "Sockel, Schaft und Kapitell dieser Saüle haben eine von allen griechischen Bauformen abweichende Gestalt." ["Base, shaft and capital of this column are of a shape that differs from all Greek forms of construction."]

167. The passage is indicated on plan C of *Myc.* and described at *Myc.* 31f. (no. 20); there is a photograph of it at *MG* pl. 3b, where R. Hope-Simpson calls it a sally port. Tsountas denied that it was analogous to the galleries at Tiryns; see his *The Mycenaean Age* (New York 1897) 330f. If this passage was only discovered on 8 November, Schliemann could hardly have shown it to Dom Pedro on 29 October, as he reports in *Times* VII.

168. *Myc.* 325, no. 512; Karo 678b.

169. Probably the Granary.

170. On the east side of the circle the slabs rest on the solid rock; on the west side, where the ground slopes away, they are supported by a wall. The circle of slabs is discussed at *Myc.* 124.

171. *Myc.* 124: "long thin cockle shells."

172. Presumably he means the slabs about one meter below the three sculptured tombstones; see the 30 October entry and *Myc.* 151f.

173. *Myc.* 152: "small plates of gold."

174. *Myc.* 325, no. 509, or Karo 678a; *Myc.* 325, no. 510, or Karo 684; and Karo 314j(?).

175. *Myc.* 153.

176. The first button somewhat resembles *Myc.* 510 (Karo 684) of Grave V, but has in addition a central circle like *Myc.* no. 398 (Karo 337) of Grave IV. The second and fourth are variants of Karo 678, while the third is probably a poorly drawn sketch of the button at *Myc.* no. 511 (Karo 719).

177. Schliemann's description of these objects is too vague for precise identification. Possible candidates are the disks and fragments of gold bands illustrated at Karo pl. LVI; see also n. 187. The coincidence that these gold bands are associated at *Myc.* 326 with the button types first discovered lends some support to this identification. The design on the gold bands Karo 649 and 650

flanking the central sunburst is similar to that on the lowest panel of stele Karo 1429 (*Myc.* no. 141). Perhaps the stele marked the site of what appears to have been a tomb immediately below the stele rather than Shaft Grave V. In *Times* VIII and *Myc.* Schliemann suppresses the fact that these objects were found at great distances from one another. The wording of the diary leads one to wonder whether all these objects were found in the fill of Shaft Grave V, though its dimensions would certainly permit this.

178. Neither *Times* VIII nor *Myc.* mentions human bones. This suggests that Schliemann later sought to hide the fact that there were tombs *above* the shaft graves. Regarding the fill of the shaft graves in Grave Circle B Mylonas notes (*MMA* 97): "the fill of graves in which more than one person was buried contained many potsherds and broken pots; and even fragments of other articles, proving that furnishings of the earlier burials were thrown out of the grave."

179. The gold discovered at Troy was also found in "black calcinated ruins." Given Schliemann's success with this tomb, Grave V (Schl. I), it is surprising that he abandons it so suddenly. Here he offers an explanation: he cannot excavate it properly without damage to the perimeter wall, which, he thinks, it partially underlies. What led Schliemann into this false assumption is unclear, though the grave does come very close to it at its northwest corner. It is most surprising that Schliemann knows the breadth of the tomb but not its length, considering that the rock is two meters higher on the east side than on the west. Later, in *Times* VII and *Myc.*, he says that he was stopped from proceeding by heavy rain. But the rain seems not to have come until the night of 13–14 November; see the 14 November entry.

180. *Myc.* 154, no. 230.

181. This is Shaft Grave I (Schl. II); cf. *Myc.* 154.

182. When Schliemann notes that nothing has been found, he actually means nothing of value has been found; see note 52. At this stage Schliemann appears to have expected to find a tomb under each of these tombstones. These are the tombstones above Shaft Grave III; cf. *Myc.* 161.

183. *Myc.* 161f.

184. The first gold button is Karo 675a. Once again Schliemann is referring to Shaft Grave V. The identical design was found on a piece of ivory from this tomb, which Karo identifies as a spoon (Karo 824–25). The second button, with the three "parallel circles," is Karo 667.

185. A total of ten were found by 10 November. Two more on the 11th makes twelve, as Schliemann records at *Myc.* 152, not thirteen.

186. The incised bone resembling a cornucopia is illustrated at *Myc.* 152, no. 225; the other two pieces of bone are at *Myc.* 152f., no. 227.

187. On 15 November, apparently before the discovery of the second and third bodies in Shaft Grave I on that day, Schliemann wrote to Max Müller. In addition to the five diadems, five crosses, and four gold discs found on the first body, Schliemann relates that he has found "masses of gold blades with impressed circles or spiral ornaments, but nothing in situ and often separated by

3 or 6 feet" (*JHS* 82 [1962] 91). The phraseology recalls the diary entry of 10 November. What are these "masses of gold blades," some of which had been found by 10 November? Besides the twelve gold-plated buttons, Schliemann reports at *Myc.* 153 that he also found "eight long thin pieces and four large disks of thin plate" in this tomb. The four large disks are presumably four of those described at *Myc.* 318f. (no. 481 = Karo 640). The long thin pieces are the seven described in the 9 November entry plus another, and are presumably identified with those described under Karo 789.

188. Since nothing earlier in the diary or in his correspondence with Max Müller suggests that Schliemann intended to close his excavations on 13 November, his claim here that he did should be regarded as mere dramatization after the fact.

189. The description of the ornamentation on the "gold leafs," though apt for much of the gold found in the shaft graves, is not appropriate for the pieces found in Shaft Grave I. Though all have circles on them, none has the spiral, which is so common elsewhere; see Karo pl. XXXV. The leaf of "tremendous proportions" should be the diadem Karo 184. It is disquieting to recall, however, that on 10 November Schliemann found "a number of gold leafs and among them a very large one, on which were impressed a number of small circles and spiral ornaments."

190. From Karo's description of the gold leaf in Shaft Grave I it appears that all of the rays except one (185/7b) have a strengthening wire, whereas none of the diadems does.

191. These walls are indicated on the map of Grave Circle A.

192. *Myc.* 152f.

193. The two tombs referred to are presumably Graves V and I. This piece of wood is described at *Myc.* 162, no. 222.

194. There is considerable confusion in Schliemann's accounts of the stones found at different levels above Shaft Grave III. The three slabs shown here are clearly those illustrated at *Myc.* 161, no. 234. Here, these three slabs appear to have been found immediately below the two unsculptured tombstones, whereas at *Myc.* 161 two horizontal slabs were found two feet beneath the two unsculptured tombstones and the three slabs of *Myc.* no. 234 were found at a further five feet deeper.

195. Schliemann seems to have believed that "cleave" could mean "split" in the intransitive as well as the transitive sense.

196. Schliemann's second tomb is Shaft Grave I. The wall lines the inside of the shaft; cf. *Myc.* 155.

197. Both types are shown at Karo pl. CL, no. 209; cf. *Myc.* 157f.

198. This must be one of the diadems at Karo 184. The pieces in the list that follows must each comprise two rays (Karo 185/7a), which Schliemann seems to have considered broken halves of diadems. Karo reports that the rays vary in length from 28–30 and in maximum breadth from 6–6.5 centimeters. It should be noted that while the figures in the diary correspond reasonably well with those reported by Karo, Schliemann errs in *Times* VIII and at *Myc.* 155f.

in stating that the diadems are all 19.5 by 4 inches (approximately 49 by 10 centimeters). Schliemann nowhere indicates that four of his five "diadems" are broken in the middle.

199. Neither the fragments nor the eight small leaves are mentioned in *Times* VIII or in *Myc.* The only disks ("circular pieces of gold blade") from the shaft graves measuring eight centimeters in diameter are assigned to Shaft Grave V (Schl. I); see Karo 640. Some of these disks were apparently found before Schliemann turned his attention to Grave I; cf. *Myc.* 153: "four large disks of thin gold plate." The attribution of the disks to Grave V is confirmed in an unpublished letter of Stamatakis, dated 4/16 November, to the nomarch of the Argolid. (The letter is in the possession of the Greek Archaeological Society. I am indebted to G. Mylonas for kindly allowing me to see this correspondence.) There is no mention of these disks among the finds of Grave I (Schl. II) in *Times* VIII, *Myc.,* or Karo. In an unpublished section of his 15 November letter to Max Müller, Schliemann also indicates that four gold disks with the measurements given in the diary were found with the first body in Grave V (Schl. I). If the attribution here of these disks to Grave I is an innocent error, it is repeated; see note 202. The five "splendid crosses" and four "gold leafs" are illustrated at *Myc.* 156, no. 231, and Karo 188.

200. *Myc.* 141.

201. The "circular blade of gold" and the fluted column are mentioned at *Myc.* 140.

202. Given the remarkable wealth of these discoveries the tone of disappointment is surprising and almost suggests that Schliemann *knew* that much more impressive finds were still to be made. This diary report is confirmed by Schliemann's unpublished letter of 16 November 1876 to Müller in which he describes the discovery of the second and third bodies "*each* of which *precisely* with the same number of *gold* leafs, round blades and crosses as the first body." Once again, in the *Times* and *Myc.* there is no mention of the four gold disks; see n. 199. In the later reports one body is reported with only four gold crosses.

203. Perhaps the pieces of the broken bronze vessel are the "many fragments of a large silver vase with a mouth of copper" of *Myc.* 158. The "one with 4 handles" is Karo 193.

204. The disappearance of these buttons from later accounts of Grave I is suspicious. Karo does not list them among the finds of this tomb.

205. It is clear both from the use of the phrase "in the acropolis" in opposition to "in the tomb" and from the depth at which they were excavated that these fragments were *not* found in Shaft Grave I, though Schliemann makes this claim at *Myc.* 158. Elsewhere, I have argued that Schliemann reported these sherds from Shaft Grave I because he wished to show that the shaft graves were contemporary with the "Homeric" level of Troy, which he held to be Troy II; see Traill, *Boreas* 7 (1984) 312–16.

206. That is to say, he struck rock five meters east of Shaft Grave III. By the "unsculptured tombstones which are in the same line with those of the large tomb just excavated" Schliemann may mean not the original unsculp-

tured tombstones, which were removed on 13 November, but the group of three slabs which he uncovered below them; see note 194.

207. For the confusion in Schliemann's account of this tomb see notes 194 and 206. The two slabs mentioned here may be the two horizontal slabs Schliemann mentions at *Myc.* 161, though here they appear to have been found *below* the three slabs illustrated in the 13 November entry and not above them as at *Myc.* 161. The fact that the diary description of these slabs (though not the description at *Myc.* 161) corresponds exactly with the description of the slabs discovered above Grave V (*Myc.* 151f.) suggests even more confusion.

208. South of Shaft Grave I (Schl. II).

209. He has found Shaft Grave II (Schl. V).

210. These five vases are at *Myc.* 162f. As Wace points out (*Mycenae* 61 n. 5), four of these Middle Helladic vases, namely Karo 157–60, have been misleadingly included among the finds of Shaft Grave III. Karo, however, notes under the description of Karo 157 that they do not belong to Shaft Grave III proper. For the green, two-handled vase see *Myc.* no. 236 = Karo 158; the two light yellow vases are probably Karo 159 and 160; and the "particularly interesting" vase is illustrated at *Myc.* no. 237 = Karo 157.

211. For the bones and obsidian knife see *Myc.* 162. Wace concludes (*Mycenae* 61) from these skeletons that Schliemann had stumbled on some "ordinary" Middle Helladic graves on the slope of the rock.

212. For these finds see *Myc.* 158. The silver vase is Karo 213 and the two Juno idols are Karo 204 and 205. The presence of these two LH III B figurines in Shaft Grave I has caused considerable speculation. Since it is clear that at *Myc.* 158 Schliemann reports finding certain sherds in Shaft Grave I, which his diary indicates he found elsewhere (see n. 205), the most reasonable solution is to suppose that these figurines, which are closely associated with the spurious sherds at *Myc.* 158, were also found outside of Shaft Grave I. Schliemann's motive for this deception is not hard to guess. He badly wanted the shaft graves to be contemporary with Troy II. Hence, the sherds which he considered analogous to Troy II pottery were added to the tomb finds. Also, just as Troy II had its Athena *glaucopis,* so too Mycenae had to have its Hera *boôpis.* The importance that Schliemann attached to this kind of argument can be gauged from reading his 1875 note "Hera Boôpis" (reprinted at *Myc.* 19–22), from which may be quoted: "In the second stage of the development of these epithets {sc. *glaucopis* and *boôpis*} the deities were represented by idols, in which the former figurative intention was forgotten, and the epithets were materialised into a cow-face for Hera, and into an owl-face for Athena. . . . To this second stage belong all the prehistoric ruins at Hissarlik, Tiryns, and Mycenae." (*Myc.* 22). See further *Boreas* 7 (1984) 312–16.

213. The tombstone over Shaft Grave II (Schl. V).

214. Milchhoeffer describes this visit in "Erinnerungen an Heinrich Schliemann," *Deutsche Rundschau* 17 (1891) 278–89. He mentions (281) that Sophia was in bed with a fever. Of Stamatakis he says (282): "behandelte er Herrn Schliemann selber mit so unverhohlenen Misstrauen, ja fast mit Nichtachtung,

dass wir uns eines peinlichen Gefühles nicht erwehren konnten. Ich habe später Herrn Stamatakis als einen zwar etwas starren, doch überaus ehrenwerthen und lauteren Character kennen gelernt; von ihm erfuhr ich denn auch den von all zu peinlicher Gewissenhaftigkeit dictirten Grund zu seinem Verhalten." ["He treated Mr. Schliemann himself with such unconcealed distrust, almost with contempt, that we could not avoid experiencing a feeling of pain. I later got to know Mr. Stamatakis as an admittedly somewhat rigid, but extremely honorable and honest individual; I learnt from him the all too meticulously conscientious grounds for his behavior."] Regrettably, Milchhoeffer does not reveal what these grounds were.

215. When we compare this entry with the *Times* and *Myc.* reports, a fairly clear picture emerges. Between Shaft Grave I to the north and Graves II and IV to the south there was an overhanging rock (*Myc.* 163). Many figurines and other objects were to be found there, and, since Schliemann paid a bonus for every find, some workmen kept returning there despite the danger. It is, therefore, likely that there were graves there. A.D. Keramopoulos found a small cave in the rock between Shaft Graves I and IV (*ArchEph* [1918] 56f. and Mylonas, *MMA* 94). This is presumably Schliemann's overhang. Perhaps it was a chamber tomb. The presence of the numerous figurines suggests that the burials were of LH III date. In the *Times* IX version Schliemann represents himself as personally dragging the men out when the rock collapsed. If this had truly been the case, he would not have lost the opportunity of so presenting it in his diary and *Myc.*

216. *Myc.* 163, no. 238.

217. For the silver vase see *Myc.* 158 and Karo 213 (who notes it is fourteen by six centimeters); for the bronze vase see *Myc.* 158 and Karo 212.

218. Presumably, Schliemann is thinking of the type of Mycenaean cup illustrated at *Myc.* 154, no. 230, and comparing it with the Trojan cup illustrated at *TroyR* 317, no. 231.

219. On the confusion in Schliemann's accounts of the stones over Shaft Grave III, see notes 194, 206, and 207.

220. By "1" Schliemann presumably means one monument (of three slabs) rather than one slab. Several slabs were found above Grave V; see the entries for 30 October and 1 November. This is the first mention of slabs above Grave II (Schl. V); see also n. 213.

221. This is a rare instance of Schliemann writing a memo to himself in the diary.

222. By the three immense tombs Schliemann presumably means Shaft Graves II, III, and IV. The tombstone carved with two serpents marks Shaft Grave II (Schl. V). The unsculptured tombstone was removed on 16 November.

223. Shaft Grave IV; cf. *Myc.* 212.

224. From the entry of 20 November it is clear that this tombstone (along with two others) was found below the altar. There is no mention of any of these tombstones either in *Times* X or in *Myc.*

225. Presumably, by "2 unsculptured slabs below" Schliemann is referring

to the two slabs below the upright tombstones mentioned in *Times* IX and at *Myc.* 161; see also note 207.

226. *Myc.* 152, no. 225.

227. Later identified as an altar; cf. *Myc.* 120 and plan F. For an earlier drawing of the altar see M. Hood, "Schliemann's Mycenae Albums," *Archaeology* 13 (1960) 65. Schliemann apparently was not yet aware of the exact dimensions of Shaft Grave IV and assumed that the altar lay between it and Grave III.

228. No arrows are reported outside Shaft Grave IV in *Myc.* At *Myc.* 271 Schliemann reports finding in Grave IV, "in a heap together, thirty-five arrowheads of obsidian, which were probably mounted on wooden shafts and contained in a wooden quiver which has disappeared." It should be noted, however, that substantial finds of arrowheads in a single tomb are paralleled in Grave Circle B; see Mylonas, *Kyklos B* 88f.

229. Shaft Grave V.

230. Presumably Grave V (cf. *Myc.* 294), though Grave IV is similarly described at *Myc.* 213.

231. Apparently the unsculptured tombstone mentioned on 18 November and two others.

232. *Myc.* 290–92; the cup is illustrated at no. 453. By lance Schliemann means here, as often, spearhead. Sword, spearhead, and gold cup are illustrated at Karo pl. LXXII (Karo 214, 215, and 230 respectively) along with the diadem (Karo 219), which is represented by a drawing in this entry, though not specifically mentioned in the text.

233. For the green vase see *Myc.* 292 and Karo 223; for the red one see *Myc.* 293 and perhaps Karo 221.

234. Shaft Grave III; see notes 194, 206, and 207.

235. *Myc.* 162.

236. *Myc.* 164.

237. *Myc.* 164f.

238. Considerable confusion exists over these copper vessels. At this point, of course, Schliemann could not know whether they were of bronze or copper. At *Myc.* 210 Schliemann specifies "a fragmentary bronze vase, two very large copper vases with two handles, a large copper caldron with two handles, and two others with three handles"—just six in all. The National Museum inventory (which Karo followed) lists two badly damaged two-handled copper caldrons (Karo 171 and 174), two three-handled copper caldrons (Karo 172 and 173), and two copper pans (Karo 175 and 176). Karo, however, was able to identify securely only the copper pans. On pages 156–60 he describes unidentified copper vessels in the National Museum and in the Nauplion Museum. It would appear from the diary that both *Myc.* and the National Museum inventory underestimate the number of copper vessels from Grave III.

239. Originally Schliemann had written "a man and a woman."

240. Originally Schliemann had written "both."

241. For the tremendous crown see *Myc.* 184–86, no. 281, and Karo 1. The "round gold leafs" can be found at *Myc.* 165–73, nos. 239–52, and Karo 2, 4,

6, 8–14, 16, 18, 20, 21. The number of these disks varies enormously from account to account: 300 in the diary, 250 in *Times* IX, 701 in *Myc.*, and 640 in Karo. Granted that the phrase "there certainly were 300" implies a guaranteed minimum rather than a total, it is still surprising that the methodical Schliemann so seriously underestimated the number of these striking finds in both the diary and *Times* accounts. See *Myc.* 176–84, nos. 256–80, and Karo pls. XXVI and XXVII for the dress ornaments. More than one hundred of these dress ornaments are reported to have come from this tomb.

242. *Times* IX specifies that two of the gold ornaments representing an altar flanked by birds came from this tomb. In *Myc.*, however, none of these ornaments is reported from Shaft Grave III, while five are assigned to Grave IV (267f., no. 423). Karo reports two from this tomb (Karo 26) and three from Grave IV (Karo 242–44). See *Times* IX and *Myc.* 204–207, (nos. 317–22) for the "smaller and larger gold vases." Both sources specify six gold vessels. However, see note 249. For the "crystal in form of a lamp" see *Myc.* 200, no. 308, and Karo 105. For the two scepters see *Myc.* 201, nos. 309, 310, and Karo 102 and 103. Once Schliemann altered the earlier part of this entry from "a man and a woman" to "three women," the phrase "with the woman," of course, became meaningless.

243. *Myc.* 207–209, no. 323, and Karo 147–50. For a discussion of the different explanations for these copper casings and their possible use on a coffin see Åke Åkestrom, "Mycenaean Problems," *OpusAth* 12 (1978) 38–68.

244. The "necklace of beautifully incised pieces of gold" is mentioned at *Myc.* 173–76 (= Karo 33–35). For the "necklace of brown agate" see *Myc.* 201 and Karo 114.

245. From the width of the neck of the hydria in Schliemann's drawing here and from Karo's remark (p. 159) that only Karo 602 and the hydria illustrated in Karo at page 158 have wide necks, it would appear that the latter hydria is the one drawn in the diary and should be assigned to Grave III. For the smaller vase see *Myc.* 209, no. 324, and Karo 156. The phiale "with burned wood" is perhaps Karo 175.

246. An oka or oke was a weight used in Greece and Turkey at this time. It is approximately 2.8 pounds or 1.27 kilograms. Four and one half okas equals about 5.7 kilograms (12.6 pounds). Karo (pp. 166–68) estimates the weight of the gold from each tomb as follows: Grave I, ca. 500 grams; Grave II, 34.5 grams; Grave III, 3.7–4.0 kilograms; Grave IV, 6.9–7.0 kilograms; Grave V, 2.3–2.4 kilograms. It is not immediately obvious what Schliemann means by "the 2 tombs." By the evening of 23 (or 24) November, when this entry was presumably written up, Schliemann had found gold in each of the five shaft graves. Graves I, II, and III had been excavated fully and Graves IV and V partially. It seems most natural to understand "the 2 tombs" to refer to the two tombs which he had been excavating that day, namely Graves III and IV. The gold cup with dolphins was apparently the only gold object that had been found in Grave IV when Schliemann wrote up this entry, but since it is included in the Grave III finds in *Myc.* and Karo, this still leaves us with a total of 3.7–4.0 kilograms for the two tombs instead

of 5.7 kilograms (4.5 okas). However, if we suppose, as Meyer does in *Schliemann* 292, that by "the 2 tombs" Schliemann meant Graves II and III, the total is not significantly different. In his letter of 24 November to Max Müller, published at *JHS* 82 (1962) 92f., Schliemann estimates that he has found more than 5.6 kilograms from Grave III alone. Probably, then, "the 2 tombs" is simply a loose way of referring to the two sections of Grave III excavated on 23 and 24 November respectively; see note 250.

247. In *Times* X this sentence becomes transformed into a memorable picture: "Mrs. Schliemann and I—we have to do the work ourselves; the task is exceedingly difficult and painful, particularly in the present rainy weather, for we cannot dig otherwise than on our knees and cutting with our knives the earth and stones carefully away, so as not to injure or let escape any of the gold ornaments." It is noteworthy that at the corresponding passage at *Myc.* 214 the explicit reference to Sophia's participation is replaced by a vague "we"; see the Introduction.

248. Schliemann is referring to Shaft Grave IV (Schl. IV). In the 20 November entry there are three slabs below and a short column.

249. This sentence clearly states that this gold cup, which is assigned to Grave III at *Myc.* 204f., no. 317, and at Karo 73, was found in Grave IV; cf. also the letter of 24 November to Max Müller at *JHS* 82 (1962) 92f. Since the 25 November entry seems to imply that work on emptying Grave IV actually began on that day, it is easy to see how Schliemann, in looking back over his notes to write up *Myc.* could have misassigned this cup to Grave III. With the dolphin cup removed, all the gold vessels in Grave III have lids—a rather remarkable coincidence.

250. By "above work" Schliemann may mean the work above ground, i.e., measuring, as opposed to digging. However, from his letter of 24 November to Max Müller it appears that he excavated only the first two bodies of Grave III on 23 November and the third on the 24th; so probably by "above work" he means "the latter part of the work described in the preceding entry."

251. *Myc.* 291.

252. Shaft Grave V (Schl. I). For its breadth and length see *Myc.* 293f.

253. Shaft Grave II (Schl. V); *Myc.* 291.

254. Shaft Grave IV (Schl. IV); *Myc.* 213.

255. Shaft Grave III (Schl. III); *Myc.* 162.

256. The measurements of the treasury threshold, entrance passage, and door are given at *Myc.* 140.

257. The breadth of the dromos is given at *Myc.* 102. For the "large cyclopean terrace" see *Myc.* 43.

258. Excavation of Grave IV actually began on the afternoon of 24 November; see the entry for 23 November and notes 245 and 250.

259. *Myc.* 215; presumably, Schliemann means five more in addition to the four found on the 23rd or 24th, for in *Myc.* he claims to have found thirty-two copper vessels in this tomb.

260. The spiral lines and swastikas are mentioned at *Myc.* 215; the buttons are

described at *Myc.* 263–66 and Karo 312–19. The cow head (actually a bull's head) is discussed and illustrated at *Myc.* 215–18, nos. 327–28, and Karo 384.

261. For the lances and swords see *Myc.* 219. Schliemann again misuses the word "cleaves"; see note 195.

262. *Myc.* 235–39, no. 346, and Karo 412.

263. Presumably, the one hundred buttons found here are in addition to the one hundred mentioned earlier. Schliemann found more than two hundred fifty gold-plated buttons in this tomb. At *Myc.* 243 and 266 Schliemann lists nineteen silver vases, of which some eight or nine appear to be more or less complete. Karo describes eight in good condition (Karo 480, 481, 509, 511, 517, 518, 519, and 520) and many fragments of an indeterminate number of vessels. The beautiful oinochoe (flagon) can be found at *Myc.* 243, no. 353 (Karo 511).

264. For the "gold leafs" see *Myc.* 266. Schliemann, at *Myc.* 243f., no. 354, describes three gold belts (Karo 260, 261, 262). The largest of these (Karo 262) has no fastener; it cannot be the one mentioned here.

265. Mr. Phinticles was the professor of archaeology at the University of Athens and vice-president of the Greek Archaeological Society. In his letter of 27 November to Max Müller at *JHS* 82 (1962) 93, Schliemann writes: "But these immense treasures make the Greeks tremble of their shadow; thus delay after delay in the excavation; for two days they have stopped me saying that the governor of the province must be present and the governor came but said two officials from Athens must assist. But at all events I hope to continue the work tomorrow and to finish it this week."

266. Schliemann later decided that there were only five bodies in Grave IV—all men; see *Times* X and *Myc.* 213.

267. At *Myc.* 246–48 Schliemann appears to report six diadems from Grave IV but describes only four (Karo 231, 232, 235, and 234), all of which are unique, and the one he calls a "belle Hélène" (Karo 236–39). *Times* XI reports seven large diadems (including one crown) and one small one (the "belle Hélène"). Karo lists two crowns (Karo 229, 230), seven large diadems (Karo 231–35, 286, 287) including one (Karo 233) which Schliemann assigns to Grave III at *Myc.* 187f., no. 284, and the "belle Hélène."

268. For the gold comb with the bone teeth see *Myc.* 266f. and Karo 310. The bone buttons are presumably gold plated, as at *Myc.* 263–66 (Karo 312–39). The "gold leafs" are described at *Myc.* 266 and the amber necklace at *Myc.* 245, no. 355, and Karo 513. The dimensions Schliemann gives at *Times* XI for this breastplate (twenty inches by twelve inches) allow us to identify it with Karo 252. Schliemann mentions two breastplates at *Myc.* 228, but the ornamented one appears to be Karo 229, a crown.

269. The three masks are Karo 253, 254, and 259. It will be noted that when Schliemann describes these masks at the end of *Times* X, he represents them as all quite different from one another, whereas to the modern observer, Karo 253 and 254 are, apart from the distance between the ears, virtually identical. Karo even suggests (under 254) that both may have been made on

the same matrix. In Schliemann's defense it should be pointed out that when he wrote the *Times* report, he was back in Athens and did not yet have access to the masks. His vague, inaccurate descriptions reflect this. However, later, when he did have access to them, he continued to convey the impression that they are very different from one another by emphasizing small differences and avoiding any reference to their overwhelming similarity. Omission of an illustration of Karo 254 assisted, or rather made possible, the deception. Schliemann's technique here is instructive. Nothing he says about the masks is untrue, but the overall impression he conveys is quite false. Since Schliemann wanted these masks to be individual portraits of Homeric heroes, they had to be different. Whether they really were significantly different or not did not much concern him.

270. Within the next few lines, Schliemann lists six gold vessels in addition to the five found on the 25th, making a total of eleven from Grave IV, if the dolphin cup (Karo 73) found on the 24th is excluded. This total includes the oenochoe (Karo 74) ascribed to Grave III in Karo but to Grave IV in *Myc.* 232 and, presumably, the electron cup (Karo 390). *Myc.* 231–41 also lists eleven gold vessels for this grave, if we include the electron cup. Karo also has eleven, if we include both the electron cup and the oenochoe. Since these totals are so consistent, we ought to accept the evidence of the diary and assign both the oenochoe and the dolphin cup to Grave IV and not to Grave III, as they are listed in Karo. See O.T.P.K. Dickinson, *The Origins of Mycenaean Civilization, SIMA* 29 (Göteborg 1977) Ch. III, sec. 3, n. 2.

271. The three gold-plated sword handles are perhaps Karo 278 (*Myc.* 251, no. 366) and Karo 303 (*Myc.* 219). A belt is recorded for this grave in the 25 November entry; see note 264. Now Schliemann adds three more. At *Myc.* 243f. he describes only three belts (Karo 260, 261, and 262). The fourth belt is probably the armband Karo 257, which at *Myc.* 248, no. 358, Schliemann suggests might be a child's belt.

272. The "wine can" is the oenochoe Karo 74 (*Myc.* no. 341). As has been already observed (see note 270), this object should be assigned to Grave IV. The "large vase with 2 handles" is illustrated at *Myc.* 231, no. 339 (= Karo 440). For the large bracelet see *Myc.* 227f., no. 336, and Karo 263.

273. It is not clear what object is intended here.

274. For the two gold rings see *Myc.* 223–27, nos. 334, 335, and Karo 240, 241. At *Myc.* 266, Schliemann mentions not one silver vase, but "ten silver vases, which latter are all broken"; see also Karo 605–607. The "golden helmet" is actually the lion's head rhyton, which Schliemann at first considered a helmet and later a mask; cf. *Myc.* 222, no. 326, and Karo 273.

275. For the small lion see *Myc.* 251, no. 365, and Karo 275. The breastpins are illustrated at *Myc.* 249f., nos. 360–62, (= Karo 245, 246, 247). The lead vessel is described at *Myc.* 257, 260 (no. 376), and Karo 388.

276. The arrows can be found at *Myc.* 271f., no. 435, and at Karo 536–40. For the knemis see *Myc.* 230f., no. 338, and Karo 267–70. While Schliemann appears to imply that only one "garter" was found in this tomb, Karo lists four of this type. The thirteen large kettles are mentioned at *Myc.* 273f., nos. 436–39.

Appendix A
Reports in Greek Newspapers

THESE REPORTS for the most part reproduce telegrams sent to Athens by Stamatakis or Schliemann. They have been arranged according to the days whose activities they report rather than according to the date of publication. This has entailed splitting those reports which cover more than one day's excavations. Despite one or two difficulties, the sequence of excavations is clear through 1 December.[1] There seems, however, no way of distinguishing the excavations of 2, 3, and 4 December. The mummy appears not to have been removed from Grave V until the 2nd or 3rd.[2] Whether excavations were actually conducted on the 4th is also unclear. Schliemann sailed from Nauplion to Athens, an eleven-hour trip, on the night of 4–5 December.[3] His sudden closing of the excavations caused bewilderment among archaeologists in Athens.[4]

Further bibliographical details of these and other contemporary reports in the Greek and foreign press are to be found in the indispensable bibliography of G. Korres.[5] I am indebted to Professor Korres for sending me copies of some of these reports and generously facilitating my research in every possible way. I am grateful to my colleague at Davis, Professor Stylianos Spyridakis, for assistance in translating the nineteenth-century Greek; any errors, however, that remain are my own.

EXCAVATION REPORTS

25 November

1. *Ethnikon Pneuma* 15/27 November, page 1; *Ephemeris* 16/28 November, page 1
Argos 13/25 November[6]
When the rest of the tomb[7] was examined yesterday {24 November}, more gold ornaments were found with engraved designs of all kinds—more than an oke in

weight. Before noon today only a part of the other tomb[8] was examined; it is larger than the others examined hitherto. In this tomb many gold ornaments were found. Outstanding among these are five entire gold vessels and three entire silver vessels and some broken ones; the bronze head of a cow chased with silver, with gold horns, the length of each being fifteen centimeters; a gold belt; more than 180 gold buttons similar to those found earlier; many bronze swords, some of which have a gilt handle; and many bronze vessels, both entire and broken. The discoveries constitute a priceless archaeological treasure.

2. *Ethnikon Pneuma* 15/27 November, page 1
Argos 14/26 November[9]
When excavations were made in the adjoining tomb,[10] there was found a large gilt cow head with long horns made of pure gold, a huge gold belt, five gold vessels, two hundred gold buttons, nearly all very large—all very richly decorated—nine silver vessels, three of which are completely intact, countless bronze swords, ten large copper vessels, no trace of iron, many alabaster sword handles.

3. *Stoa* 14/26 November, page 2
Excavations in Mycenae: The office received further telegrams from the officials in Nauplion and Argos yesterday, announcing that yesterday afternoon a new tomb[11] had been found in Mycenae, richer than all the previous tombs in the quantity and perhaps also in the value of the ancient gold ornaments in it. It is said that sculpted heads[12] have also been found. Every day the excavations at Mycenae take on greater importance. Mr. Schliemann, we have to admit, has lucky fingers. This, at least, our archaeologists also have to admit.

26 and 27 November—Excavations Suspended

28 November

4. *Argolis*[13] 20 November/2 December, page 1f.
Within the same circle the excavations, which were resumed last Tuesday {16/28 November}, met with even more success. They found in the same shaft grave[14] of Saturday {13/25 November} half a human skeleton with a mask. The mask is gold, portraying a likeness. With it lay two other similar masks. I wonder if these masks had the purpose of immortalizing the appearance of those buried there.

Beside them there was found a gold crown. Below the face, reaching as far as the waist, was found a large gold leaf, covering the almost disintegrated skeleton; then two gold belts, of which one is very beautiful—two meters long, three inches wide and as thick as a ten lepta piece. Beside them were two gold rings of excellent workmanship and a variegated gold bracelet—a wonder to behold! The rings have engraved ornamentation on them, similar to those on the poros slabs that were found on the surface, for example, a chariot, etc. There were also found gold pins, leaves and petals of gold, and buttons, all gold—and many of them.

There were also found one sword with a gold handle, caldrons and other utensils of copper and a three-inch copper instrument, for use, no doubt, in ancient sacrifices. Very curious is a thighbone with a gold garter, like a buckle, and pin. It is very beautiful and a work of outstanding elegance. With all these was found a small lead animal, one span long, hard to describe at present—a stag or hind perhaps. All the gold weighs two to three okes approximately.

5. *Ethnikon Pneuma* 17/29 November, page 4
Argos 17/29 November[15]
When the nearby tomb was examined today, the following objects were brought to light:
2 gold diadems
2 gold masks
another gold mask with the bones of the skull and with a gold breastplate
1 bone comb with gilt top, to adorn a woman's head
perforated beads of a necklace of amber
2 spiral-shaped small gold vessels
1 small oenochoe
1 cantharos
1 gold vessel with one handle
2 broken swords with gilt handles
many gold buttons of different sizes
4 gold belts, one of which is broken in two
a skyphos
a gold vessel
1 gold bracelet weighing one hundred drams
2 gold rings with a great oval sling on which are engraved human and animal shapes
1 crushed silver vessel
1 gold crown
1 very small gold lion sitting on a base
3 gold pins, one of which has a ram
1 deer of lead
many varied buttons and other ornaments
25 stone arrowheads
2 gold greave ornaments
various small bone and crystal objects
13 copper caldrons of various shapes and sizes
many bronze swords and daggers, whole and broken.
The weight of the above gold objects exceeds four okes.

6. *Ephemeris* 18/30 November, page 1
Argos 17/29 November 9 a.m.[16]
From the same tomb in which were found the valuable pieces reported in my earlier telegrams, I brought forth yesterday a large crown and two large diadems.

29 November

7. *Argolis* 20 November/2 December, page 1f.
The excavations were continued on Wednesday {17/29 November} but they uncovered only some bronze utensils, particularly caldrons.

8. *Ethnikon Pneuma* 20 November/2 December, page 1; *Ethnophylax* 20 November/2 December, page 2; *Pnyx* 22 November/4 December, page 4
Argos 19 November/1 December[17]
When the remaining part of the tomb was explored yesterday,[18] the following objects were brought to light:
a small bronze tripod
horse equipment, namely copper φάλαρα
crescent-shaped tusks
3 clay two-handled pots without inscription.

30 November

9. *Ethnikon Pneuma* 20 November/2 December, page 1; *Ethnophylax* 20 November/2 December, page 2; *Pnyx* 22 November/4 December, page 4
Today[19] when we explored a small part of the tomb[20] on which the three well-known sculptured slabs stood and where in its fill were found some days earlier thirteen gold buttons, the following were brought to light:
the gold mask[21] of a bearded man, of life size, much finer than those found hitherto
a gold breastplate with ornaments (53 centimeters long by 37 centimeters broad)
bracelets of very fine gold with ornaments
a gold ornament
greaves
a gilt sword handle
a gold covering of a sword handle

232

10. *Ephemeris* 19 November/1 December, page 1
Argos 18/30 November, 5:30 P.M.
Beginning today the excavation of the tomb of the three sculptured tomb-stones, I found a gold breastplate and a gilt sword handle, and a gold mask,[22] and many gold leaves and gigantic bones. All the masks portray the hero whose head they cover. The excavations continue.

Schliemann.

11. *Argolis* 20 November/2 December, page 1f.
In the same circle was found on Thursday {18/30 November} a decorated gold breastplate and a gold mask likewise intact, which depicts the likeness of a young man, handsome and brave. The nose is not straight, it should be noted. He has an engraved beard four to five inches long, but no mustache.[23] In the same part was also found a gold sword handle and a large thighbone, testimony that it belonged to a man of gigantic proportions.

1 December

12. *Argolis* 20 November/2 December, page 1f.
But it was yesterday {19 November/1 December} that was to stun the excavators of Mycenae. Pursuing their researches, Messrs. Schliemann, Stamatakis, and Phinticles were searching in the same part of the soil with knives.[24] They found many gold buttons, a gold vessel, some small gold leaves, a small intact alabaster pot of the finest workmanship, on which there lay a small pot, and bronze caldrons and swords. After this, however, they found a gold mask of a young man and a great leaf of gold, like a breastplate. But what was their surprise when under the mask and breastplate they found a human skeleton intact, still preserving a human appearance, although quite pale, as if with a tan complexion. It was a kind of mummy. The jawbone still preserves all its teeth, thirty-two in number. It seems to be asleep. The chest is broad and the breastplate is still preserved on top of it as if on skin. There were found with it one fine gold belt with gold tassels, an excellent gold-handled sword far surpassing all those found hitherto; also a fine dagger, one span in length and (now for the first time) pieces of wood more or less decayed. The sight of this alone astonished everyone. No longer was it a case of ashes and bones. It was a man from an earlier age in his entirety. Amazing! They considered moving the skeleton itself. But they saw that this was absolutely impossible and that if they as much as touched it, it would break up into what it was composed of—ashes. The best idea put forward was that these remains should be preserved undisturbed, untouched, in the spot in which they were found, as a revered and priceless ornament of desolate Mycenae—that they should be covered by a large glass dome-shaped cover and that a further roof should be set above that. May this excellent proposal be accomplished with all speed!

13. *Ephemeris* 21 November/3 December, page 1; *Ethnikon Pneuma* 22 November/4 December, page 3; *Pnyx* 22 November/4 December, page 4

Argos 20 November/2 December[25]

In the same tomb of the three sculptured tombstones I found yesterday one more body covered with a heavy gold mask and a huge gold breastplate. On either side of the body were found swords and a dagger, all with gilt handles, and ruined scabbards ornamented on either side with an uninterrupted row of engraved gold buttons. In addition I found a gold sword belt and a very large gold shoulder belt. The face still has its thirty-two teeth in place, so that I hope to raise it up and transfer the upper part of the body to Athens intact. I also found wooden squares with carvings of lions and dogs, one gold vessel and six copper caldrons.

14. *Ephemeris* 21 November/3 December, page 1; *Ethnikon Pneuma* 22 November/4 December, page 3; *Pnyx* 22 November/4 December, page 4

Argos 20 November/2 December

In the last tomb there were three bodies, of which one was found without ornaments. I telegraphed to Nauplion for an artist to come here to draw the corpse which I referred to in my last telegram. This corpse very much resembles the image which my imagination formed long ago of wide-ruling Agamemnon.[26]

Schliemann

15. *Ethnikon Pneuma* 22 November/4 December, page 3

Argos 20 November/2 December[27]

Investigation of the tomb, of which a very small part remained, continued. In it the following were brought to light: nine buttons of sword handles, of which seven are of alabaster, one gold with rotten wood inside it, and one wooden divided into four; one gold shoulder belt one meter, twenty centimeters long by four centimeters broad from which a dagger hangs, on the handle of which belongs a golden button. Beside the dagger, above and below, were found many gold buttons, large and small; a very small crystal, resembling a perforated pitcher with two gold handles; another crystal, having the shape of a funnel, with four convex sides; one broken sword with a golden cover on the handle—beside it were found four gold buttons, six smaller ones, and five gold crosses, ornaments of the sword handle—another part of a sword with a part of a gold handle, of which the one part is smooth, the other decorated; a small bronze dagger; two bronze daggers, one large, one small; seven double-edged swords, whole and broken; a bronze spearhead 22 centimeters long; twenty-three gold buttons; sixty-two smaller ones; twenty-nine circular gold leaves with ornaments—broken; twenty-one pieces of various gold leaves, large and small; one gold ornament of a greave; five gold ornaments with a

234

little piece above two eagles; two gold vessels, one large, one small; a gold breastplate (thirty-six centimeters long by twenty-two broad); a gold mask (thirty-two centimeters high by thirty-two broad); a pale green clay pot, broken into many pieces; a small gold leaf resembling an officer's collar; a gold sword handle divided in two; broken silver vessels; an alabaster vessel in the shape of a pithos with a bronze rim without a lid, part of whose side is missing—in this were contained thirty-two gold buttons, small and smaller, three large ones in the shape of crosses—two small very light gold handles; one conical gold button pierced and divided in two on either side; rope-shaped gold tube; many perforated beads of sea amber; many pieces of wood of various sizes; two rectangular sides of a small wooden box, each with an engraving of a dog and a lion, the other sides of which have disappeared; four copper caldrons complete, and six broken; two broken pithos-shaped clay pots; silver tweezers and gold sword tassel.

2, 3, and 4 December[28]

16. *Ephemeris* 23 November/5 December, page 1
Argos 22 November/4 December
The pharmacist here, Spyridon Nicolaou, has undertaken to preserve the body of the corpse. I am confident that he will succeed. On the right of the corpse in question I found in addition: two hammered-gold plates, each of which portrays a cow's head and a lion pursuing a deer. In addition I found a gold cup with two rows of the symbolic sign of the sacred fire; a very large gold cup splendidly decorated; one very large gold cup splendidly decorated; one very large alabaster cup, height twenty-five centimeters; two silver cups; 128 buttons splendidly decorated; six large cross-shaped gold buttons, likewise splendidly decorated; four gilt sword handles; two gold tubings; and eleven bronze swords, of which two are entire, measuring ninety-four and seventy-four centimeters respectively. I have completed the excavations and am returning home, hoping that the tremendous treasure uncovered by me may prove the cornerstone of great riches and happiness for the illustrious Greek nation.

17. *Ethnikon Pneuma* 24 November/6 December, page 3
Argos 23 November/5 December
When the remaining section of the tomb was examined yesterday the following objects were brought to light:
—A single-handled gold vessel, thirteen centimeters high, fourteen centimeters in diameter approx. Inside two further vessels.
—Another single-handled gold vessel eleven centimeters high, fourteen centimeters in diameter. Inside it fragments of a very fine silver vase, different from the others found so far and a piece of alabaster in the shape of a disk; these are found in the vessel.
—Another single-handled gold vessel, eleven centimeters high, ten centimeters

in diameter, with an oblong bottom and three pigs running along the outside of the rim.

—Wooden sword handle half of which is covered with gold leaf.

—Another sword handle whose gold cover is preserved.

—Another small one with four fragments of wood of different sizes.

—Large gold handle covers.

—Small gold handle with varied ornamentation on either side, with which part of the bronze dagger is preserved.

—Elongated gold leaf.

—Two round covers, one of which is thirty-three centimeters long, the other twenty-six centimeters.

—Eleven large and small undecorated gold disks.

—Gold sword hilt with deer and lion engraved and a cow's head in the middle.

—Six cross-shaped gold disks, of which one is large, two are smaller, and three still smaller.

—122 gold buttons of various sizes, smaller than the immediately preceding.

—Many fragments of the wooden sword buttons.

—Three fragments of wooden handles.

—Four bases of smashed and broken silver vases.

—Two large and many small fragments of a silver vase with spiral ornaments like those on the sculptured slabs.

—Fragment of a vase with the same ornaments.

—Alabaster vase similar to a communion vase, twenty-five centimeters high and twelve centimeters in diameter, defective in the rim.

—Eleven bronze swords, nine of which are damaged, the other two intact, ninety-four and seventy-four centimeters long respectively.

A very small part of the tomb remains unexcavated because of the interruption due to the rain.

MISCELLANEOUS REPORTS

18. *Argolis* 20 November/2 December, page 3

Mr. Phinticles, professor at the university, arrived by the last steamer and went to Mycenae.[29] Since then he has been atttending and participating in the excavations. Before this the knowledgeable and excellent mayor of Mycenae, Mr. P. Nezos, had been assisting our highly esteemed ephor, P. Stamatakis, in a most praiseworthy fashion.

By the same steamer Mrs. Sophia Schliemann departed for Athens.[30] Her husband leaves tomorrow {21 November/3 December} or Monday {22 November/4 December} for Athens and from there to Paris. After this he will go to Hissarlik to pursue his Trojan researches.

A great crowd flocks every day from here and Argos to Mycenae to see the antiquities that are being uncovered. It is believed that ancient Mycenae has come back to life. Everyone has been seized by a fever of curiosity.

19. *Ethnophylax* 24 November/6 December, page 2

Mr. Heinrich Schliemann, having terminated his excavations in Mycenae, arrived yesterday and is going on to Paris on private business.

20. *Neologos Athenon* 27 November/9 December, page 3

Up till now it appears that the excavations will cease after the departure of Mr. Schliemann. But perhaps the Archaeological Society will decide to continue them. More than half of the grave circle remains untouched. Quite apart from this, the Archaeological Society ought to continue the excavations for the following reasons: public opinion, particularly among the peasantry, is very excited by the treasure that has been discovered and there is apprehension that tomb robbers may steal what is left. Mr. Stamatakis will be kept busy with the cataloguing of the antiquities, which are to be transported to Athens in a few days.

Mr. Schliemann departed from here by last Monday's steamer, as did Mr. Phinticles. On their wagon was seen a good-sized chest bearing the inscription "Archaeological Society." This chest, as I heard, contained some clay pots or sherds given to Mr. Schliemann on the instructions of the Archaeological Society, but since many people are not aware of this, it is right and proper for the office of the Archaeological Society to make an official statement, for the reassurance of the public, of what exactly that chest contained, to whom it was given and why. Mr. Schliemann is departing now for Paris.

STAMATAKIS' EXCAVATION OF GRAVE VI IN 1877

21. *Palingenesia* 24 November/6 December 1877

The excavations are continuing at Mycenae under the supervision and direction of Mr. Stamatakis and at the expense of the Archaeological Society. By 21 November {3 December} a new tomb was discovered to the north of the first, beside the entrance to the grave circle. When the new tomb was examined, the following were found in it:

a) a one-handled gold phiale
b) 2 gold greave ornaments
c) 4 gold ornaments constituting a necklace
d) 30 gold nails belonging to a shoulder belt
e) 3 bronze swords
f) 1 alabaster pommel from a sword handle
g) 11 bronze daggers, two of which have heads decorated with gilded bronze
h) 4 bronze spearheads
i) a few broken vessels
j) large numbers of broken clay vessels, one of which was brought out intact.

The tomb contained two burned corpses. Their skulls were brought out in pieces, which can be put together and restored.

NOTES

1. Sometimes the reports seem to have been written in the evening and then telegraphed the following day from Argos. Hence, terms like "yesterday" and "today" are sometimes to be understood as referring to one day earlier than the date on the telegram would appear to imply.

2. Cf. note 28 and the close of *Times* XII.

3. Cf. no. 20.

4. See, for instance, the report by a "German correspondent" in the *Athenaeum* of January 1877, 57: "the excavations were suddenly and mysteriously brought to a close by Schliemann's abrupt departure."

5. G. Korres, *Bibliographia Herrikou Sleman* (Athens 1974) 16–19 and 56–61.

6. This telegram appears to have been written by Stamatakis.

7. Grave III.

8. Grave IV.

9. Apparently, this is a telegram from Schliemann.

10. Grave IV.

11. Grave IV.

12. Presumably, a reference to the bull's head rhyton of Grave IV. The Greek word is προτομαί.

13. The reports in the Nauplion newspaper *Argolis* seem to be quite independent of the telegrams of Schliemann and Stamatakis. Presumably, the newspaper sent a reporter to the site after the exciting discoveries of 23 November.

14. Grave IV.

15. Apparently, this is a telegram from Stamatakis.

16. The use of the first person indicates that this is a telegram from Schliemann.

17. Apparently, this is a telegram from Stamatakis.

18. I assume that this telegram was written on 30 November and only dispatched from the Argos post office on 1 December; see note 1. "Yesterday" in that case will refer to 29 November.

19. This forms the continuation of no. 8; see notes 17 and 18.

20. Grave V.

21. The "Mask of Agamemnon."

22. It is noteworthy that Schliemann does not comment on the superior quality of this (the "Agamemnon") mask.

23. It is clear that, despite the error over the mustache, the "Agamemnon" mask is intended.

24. Cf. *Times* X and accompanying n. 16 and the Introduction.

25. The use of the first person shows this to be a telegram from Schliemann.

26. Cf. the similar telegram of Schliemann's cited at Ludwig, *Schliemann* (Boston 1931) 173. It is clear, if rather surprising, that Schliemann regarded the mummy and its unprepossessing mask, rather than the "Agamemnon" mask, as resembling Agamemnon.

27. Although Stamatakis makes no mention of the mummy, the reference to the mask and breastplate make it clear that it is the activities of 1 December that he is recording.

28. There is insufficient evidence to distinguish the activities of these three days. The end of *Times* XII implies that the mummy was raised only after it had been successfully treated with chemicals. Schliemann's telegram of 4 December need not be taken to imply that the treatment was still incomplete. Probably the mummy was lifted from the tomb on 2 or 3 December.

29. He apparently arrived at Mycenae on 27 or early 28 November; see the Introduction.

30. Sophia probably sailed from Nauplion on 28 November; see the Introduction. She apparently did not witness the discovery of the mummy or the "Mask of Agamemnon."

Appendix B
Reports to the *Times*

SCHLIEMANN SENT A TOTAL of fourteen periodic reports of his excavations at Mycenae to the London *Times*. These were published as follows:

I (dated 19 August) in the *Times* of 27 September 1876, p. 10.
II (dated 9 September) in the *Times* of 1 November 1876, p. 4.
III (dated 30 September) in the *Times* of 13 November 1876, p. 8.
IV (dated 7 October) in the *Times* of 13 November 1876, p. 8.
V (dated 30 October) in the *Times* of 13 December 1876, p. 3.
VI (date unknown) in the *Times* of 14 December 1876, p. 8.
VII (dated 30 October) in the *Times* of 22 December 1876, p. 4.
VIII (dated 11 November) in the *Times* of 22 December 1876, p. 4.
IX (date unknown) in the *Times* of 22 December 1876, p. 4.
X (dated 25 November) in the *Times* of 22 December 1876, p. 4.
XI (dated 28 November) in the *Times* of 27 December 1876, p. 9.
XII (dated 1 December) in the *Times* of 3 January 1877, p. 10.
XIII (undated) in the *Times* of 3 January 1877, p. 10.
XIV (undated) in the *Times* of 12 January 1877, p. 7.

These reports to the *Times* formed the basis for Schliemann's book *Mycenae*. The first five of these reports correspond fairly closely with *Mycenae* 61–141 and the fourteenth does not differ substantially from *Mycenae* 334–44. Since they are less significant, these reports are not reprinted here. Schliemann wrote the drafts of reports VII–XIV at the back of the Mycenae diary. These drafts, hitherto unpublished, rather than the final *Times* versions, from which they differ slightly, are the texts presented here. Though Schliemann designated his reports Mycenae I–XIV, they are here labeled *Times* I–XIV for convenience. Significant variations between the draft and published versions are indicated in the notes. Since the draft version of VI does not exist, that report is printed as it appears in the *Times*.

Schliemann recopied these drafts, making a few substantive and editorial changes. He sent his final versions to Max Müller, then temporarily residing in Dresden. Müller made a few more changes to improve Schliemann's sometimes Germanic English and sent the reports off to the *Times,* where they were published, perhaps with a few further editorial changes.

The date of completion of these reports can, in many cases, be shown to be later than the date given by Schliemann—sometimes much later. For instance, Schliemann's correspondence with Müller indicates that Schliemann wrote his final versions of reports V and VI between 24 and 27 November and reports VII through X between 6 and 10 December.[1]

Schliemann's account of Dom Pedro's visit to Troy (see diary note 115)— not one of Schliemann's numbered reports on Mycenae—is published in the *Times* of 6 November 1876, p. 4. Telegraphic reports, apparently based on telegrams from Schliemann, appear in the *Times* of 25, 27, and 30 November and 1 and 4 December. They add little to the longer notices in the Greek press.

TIMES VI

At a few yards from the second gate I have brought to light a very curious cyclopean water conduit, leading into one of the two long and narrow cyclopean reservoirs which I had at first thought to be corridors. There is another cyclopean water conduit and another cistern immediately south of them. Both these water conduits have doubtless brought the water from the copious fountain called "Perseia" by Pausanias, which is not, as he erroneously mentions, in the Acropolis itself, but at a distance of half a mile east of it. Its name seems to be derived from Perseus, the founder of Mycenae. In clearing out the 13–20 ft. deep masses of rubbish which obstructed the passage of the gate, I found a well-preserved bronze sealing-ring, on which are engraved two young women of marvellous beauty, which seems still to be increased by their simple and graceful hairdress. Both sit close together, but their heads are turned in opposite directions. The anatomy is well observed. There were besides found a large number of Juno-idols in cow or horned-female form, and a cow idol showing, on a light yellow dead colour, a number of dark red signs, which may be letters; also large quantities of melted lead; further, a very primitive golden earring, consisting of a quadrangular golden wire twice turned round. The same form of earrings {sic} occurs also in the first of the four prehistoric cities at Troy, with the only difference that the wire there is round. There were also found here on the virgin soil a great many fragments of hand-made vases, having either inside and outside a plain lustrous black, or red, or a light green colour with black spiral ornaments. At only six feet behind the cyclopean wall, on the east side of the passage, I have brought to light an evidently much more ancient wall of huge blocks.

The circular parallel double row of large slabs, which I have repeatedly referred to in my former letters, had originally been covered with cross slabs,

241

of which a small number are still *in situ;* they are solidly fitted in and consolidated by 1 1/2–3 1/3d inches deep, and 4-inch broad cuttings. As these latter exist on all the slabs, there can be no doubt that the whole circle was primitively covered in the same way. The slabs are from 4 ft. 2 in. to 8 ft. 2 in. long and 1 ft. 8 in. to 4 ft. broad, and the largest are in the two places where the double row descends from the rock to the wall. Inside is at first a layer of large stones 1 ft. 4 in. thick, for the purpose of holding the slabs in their position; the remaining space is filled up with pure earth mixed with long thin ⟨s⟩nails in the places where the original covering remains in its position, or with household remains, mixed with innumerable fragments of archaic pottery wherever the covering is missing. This circumstance can leave no doubt that the cross slabs were removed in a remote antiquity, and it gives at the same time some idea as to the age of the double circle of slabs.

In continuing the excavation on the north side of the large cyclopean house, I brought to light two more chambers of it, and found there, in a depth of 16 1/2 ft., three splendidly incised, perforated, round agates of a necklace, the one representing a cow-head with very long horns, the other two horses standing against each other on their hind legs and turning their heads towards the spectator, just like the two animals on the sculpture above the gate must have done.[2] Above the two horses on the agate is engraved a man with a Phrygian cap and a young woman with an uncovered head. The third agate is of a transparent red colour and represents a stag, which appears to move with great velocity, although its head is turned backwards. There were also found Juno-idols of a new form—*e.g.,* a perfectly flat cow with only one big hind-leg and two forelegs; a female idol with a very compressed bird's face, and with a Phrygian cap, instead of the usual "polos;" and, finally, a headless idol with all the characteristics of a woman, but with two long cow-horns. There was likewise found a terracotta cow-horn 3 1/2 inches long, which shows that there must have been much larger idols than those hitherto found. There were further found a number of small terracotta tripods in form of armchairs, cradles, in two instances even cradles with a child in them; all are gay-coloured and must have served as offerings; further, two perforated parallelopipeds of variegated colour 4 in. long, the use of which I cannot explain. Among the findings I may further mention a comb of bone and six perforated round, flat, transparent white pieces of stone of a necklace, a door button of alabaster, and a large fragment of a bas-relief representing a man with a line, probably a bridle, in the hand; he was no doubt represented standing on a chariot, and resembles very much the man who holds the horns of the fantastic animal in one of the bas-reliefs described in my first letter from here.

TIMES VII

My excavations have yesterday and today had the insignant {sic} honour of being visited by H.M. the Emperor Dom Pedro II of Brazil. Coming from

Corinth H.M. went directly up to the acropolis and remained for two hours in my excavations, which he attentively examined and reexamined. The immense double parallel circle of white slabs, within which are the three straight lines of tombstones, and particularly the four sculptured ones, seemed to be of paramount interest to him and he requested me to send him photographs of them to Cairo. The great gate with its curious threshhold, the large cyclopean house, the 3 cyclopean waterconduits and all the other monuments of prehistoric times, seemed also to be of very great interest to H.M, who in visiting with me the eastern part of the acropolis, discovered[3] there in its north-east triangle, a well preserved ogivelike passage, which passes under a right angle through the 16 feet 8 inches thick cyclopean wall. The ogivelike passage is perfectly like those of Tiryns, but difficult to be discovered, being hidden by the accumulation of rubbish, by a tree and by some stones;[4] it had never come under my notice, nor under that of any other traveller. H.M. went thence to the Treasury of Atreus, where dinner was served. This meal, in the midst of the mysterious nearly 40 centuries old underground building, seemed to please H.M. exceedingly. He afterwards examined with deepest interest in the village of Charvati the large collection of prehistoric Mycenaean antiquities produced by my excavations and particularly admired the enormous mass of differently shaped Juno-idols, the incisions and the sculptures. H.M. went hence to Argos & Nauplion, called here again today to see once more the Mycenaean museum and the excavations and returned hence by Corinth & Calamaki to Athens. After the departure of H.M. I ascended the very steep and 2500 feet high mount Agios Elias, which is situated immediately N. of the acropolis and crowned by an open chapel of that prophet.[5]

The summit forms a very small triangle, the eastern side of which is 35, the two other sides, which converge due west, 100 feet long. But in spite of these small dimensions the summit is surrounded by cyclopean walls which are on an average 4 feet 2 inch thick and 3 to 6 1/2 feet high; but masses of stones, which are lying alongside of them, can leave no doubt that they have once been much higher. The entrance which is on the eastern side, is followed by the short passage; in the large stone, which forms the threshhold of the door, is still visible the hole in which the lower hinge turned. At 16 to 53 feet lower are on all the three sides by which the summit is accessible 133 to 266 feet long and 5 feet thick cycl walls, which are still now on an average 10 feet high and appear to have been once much higher. Between the stones of all these walls I have been able to collect a number of fragments of handmade light green vases with black ornaments, which I consider as old as the walls of Tiryns and Mycenae, because in the former place I found them on and near the virginsoil {sic}, in the latter only on the natural rock in the recesses of the gate passage & in the tombs. I conclude from this that the fortifications on mount Agios Elias must be contemporaneous with walls of both cities and may perhaps claim even a still higher antiquity. The question now naturally arises for what purpose all these fortifications have been built? The summit being so exceedingly small and full of pointed & abrupt rocks between which it is even difficult to move, it can never have been inhabited by men, the more so as there is no water. The only explanation I venture to give of the origin of those cyclopean walls is that there must have existed on the summit a small temple of great sanctity and immense importance and probably we find in the present cultus on the summit the name of the deity which was venerated there in antiquity. There is now in the S.E. corner, in the only even place of the summit a very small, 23 feet long by 10 feet broad, open shrine dedicated to the prophet Elias and the inhabitants of the surrounding villages are in the habit of going there on pilgrimage in times of great drought to invoke the prophet to give rain. Thus it appears that the very spot has in antiquity been occupied by a sanctuary of the Sungod who has had a celebrated cultus there and who has made place to the prophet Elias with hardly any change in the name, the Sungod being originally called Ἥλιος, pronounced Eelios.

Mycenae 30 October 1876

TIMES VIII

The four sculptured tombstones having been removed to the village of Charvati in order to send to Athens, I excavated the site of them and found, to my joy, that I had been altogether mistaken regarding the nature of the soil below them, for what I had taken to be the virginsoil was the earth which had been brought there from another place. I first excavated the site of the three tombstones with the warriors and found there a 21 1/2 feet long and 10 1/2 feet broad quadrangular tomb cut out in the slope of the rock, and, at 3 1/4 feet below the removed slabs, a strange sort of a monument consisting of [of] two long and narrow slabs lying the one upon the other, and at their south end a smaller slab in an oblique position as if it were to serve as a pillow for him who would lay down on the slabs. The latter stone had a border and probably it derived from a larger monument which had occupied the place of the 3 sculptured tombstones. In digging further down I found from time to time a small quantity of blackashes and in it frequently some curious object, either a bonebutton covered with beautifully engraved gold blade or an imitation of a gazellehorn of bone with a flat side showing two holes by which the object must have been attached to something else, or other ornaments of bone or small gold leafs. I collected in this way, besides many other curious objects, 12 buttons covered with goldblades, one of them as large as a 5 franc piece; the ornaments are either spiral lines, or that curious cross with the marks of 4 nails, which so frequently occurs in Troy and which I think to be the symbol of the holy fire. All the buttons are in form of our shirtbuttons but much larger than these. The earth was intermixed with numerous fragments of lustrous[6] black red or light green pottery with black spiral lines; particularly interesting are the large lustrous black goblets with a hollow foot and horizontal flutings in the middle; further the light green or yellow ones with most fantastic black ornamentation; the larger vases of a light red dead colour with dark red circles, or

244

with two protruding female breasts surrounded by circles of black strokes;[7] the light green vases with 2 rows of protruding lumps all around.[8] Whilst in Troy nearly all vases have three feet, tripods of terracotta never occur here among the handmade pottery and nearly all the vases have flat bottoms; vases with one or two tubular holes on either side, for suspension, occur here, but they are very rare. Having dug down to a depth of [of] 10 1/2 feet, I was stopt by heavy rain, which turned the soft earth in the tomb to mud, and therefore began to take out the two unsculptured tombstones of the second line⟨;⟩ one of them is 5 the other 5 1/2 ft. long. In digging around them I found another, 11 1/2 feet broad and 21 feet long, tomb cut into the rock. It was filled with unmixed natural soil which had been brought there from another place.[9] In a depth of 15 feet I reached a layer of small stones, below which I found at a distance of 3 feet from each other, the calcined remains of three bodies, which were only separated from the rock by another layer of small stones, and had evidently been burned in the very same place, the masses of ashes of the clothes which had covered them and the wood which had consumed them; further the colour of the stones can leave no doubt in this respect. With every one of the three bodies I found 5 leafs of gold each 19 1/2 inches long, and, in the midst, 4 inches broad but terminating at both extremities in a point; I further found with every one of the bodies[10] 5 golden crosses in form of laurel leafs, each 7 1/2 inch long; the breadth of the leafs is 1 2/3 inch. I also found there many curious objects of a glazy unknown composition; the form of these objects is difficult to describe; all are perforated and have evidently served as ornaments of the dead. I further found there a number of small knifes of obsidian, many fragments of the aforedescribed handmade pottery, a rusted bronze knife, a silver cup with one handle; the upper part of a gilded silver vase; 4 perforated pieces of a necklace, 2 of stone and 2 of a composition and finally two horned Juno-idols.[11] At the bottom of the sepulcre all the 4 walls were lined by a 5 feet high and 1 ft. 8 inch thick wall of stones, which showed unmistak[e]able marks of the funeral piles. But evidently the pyre had not been large and had been merely intended to consume the flesh of the bodies because the bones and even the skulls had been preserved but the latter had suffered so much from the moisture that none of them could be taken out entire. The surface of this tomb was 32 feet below the surface.

Mycenae 11th Novbr 1876

TIMES IX

Encouraged by the success obtained in the second tomb I took out the 2 large unsculptured tombstones due south of it; one of them is 6 ft 4 inch long & 4 ft br, the other 4 ft 10 inch long and 4 ft 4 inch broad. They were extremely well fastened by square blocks, so that they could not be got out without great efforts. At some two feet below the tombstones I found two large slabs in the form of tombstones lying horizontally⟨,⟩ and in a depth of 5 feet I brought to light three slabs⟨,⟩ the one lying the other two standing. The soil consisted of black earth intermixed with fragments of handmade pottery and masses of small knifes of obsidian. Besides a small number of Junoidols, I found there a solid piece of ivory in the form of a beehive, having in the lower, flat side a tubular hole for suspension with a string; on the convex or globular side was incised a cross embellished with 5 goldpins, each of which had a small hole in the centre of the head; further a 3 inches long piece of wood with beautifully carved spiral lines, and two other pieces of wood in the form of spear-heads. In digging further down, I found that at a distance of 33 feet from the E. side of the circular double parallel row of large slabs the rock suddenly slopes, for a space of 30 feet, under an angle of 50 degrees; the perpendicular height of the slope is 16 1/2 feet; further to the W. the rock forms a 30 feet long and broad plateform {sic} with two tombs of which I shall first describe the smaller one because, at a height of 16 1/2 feet above it stood the aforesaid 2 tombstones. This tomb is cut on the E. side 7, on the S. side 3 1/3, on the W. side 2 1/3, on the N. side 5 feet deep into the rock, these different depths find their explanation in the slope of the rock, because the bottom of the tomb is of course perfectly horizontal. At about 9 feet above this I discovered[12] close to it, on the slope of the rock, at 21 feet below the surface, a number of skeletons of men, which had evidently not been burned but were so much destroyed by the moisture that none of the skulls could be taken out entire; but all I found with them were a large number of knifes of obsidian and 5 very nice handmade vases, two of which of a plain light yellow, the 3 others of light green colour with rude black ornaments. To the N. of the tomb in question I brought to light two overhanging rocks, below which in a depth of 22 ft below the surface many Junoidols were found, also a very curious sort of a bronze dagger consisting of two separate two-edged blades, which had been soldered together in the midst, so that the 4 edges are separated from each other by 1/4 inch⟨;⟩ both blades are 10 inches, the whole dagger is 13 inches long the handle has evidently been inlaid with wood or bone, which had been fastened by 3 small nails. As I considered one of the overhanging rocks particularly dangerous, I did all I could to keep my workmen aloof from it; however, two of them always returned there. But seeing that the rock had a crack which widened, I literally dragged them out by force when all at once the rock fell and we were all three knocked down by its splinters but uninjured. The 4 walls of the tomb, which now occupies us, were lined with plates of irregular size which were joined with clay and formed a 5 feet high and 3 1/2 feet broad rooflike wall. I found in this mausoleum the remains of three ladies, which, like in the former tomb, were covered with a layer of similar stones, on which the funeral piles had been dressed; this last layer of stones lay on the bottom of the tomb which was 30 feet below the surface of the mount. The three bodies were literally overwhelmed with jewels and as these are very similar and almost in equal proportions I think it superfluous to state here the objects found with each of the ladies and will give only a register of what I collected in this sepulcre:

246

12 golden crowns[13]

10 do.   diadems, in two of which is still part of the skull

1 gigantic golden crown (στέμμα) with 30 large leafs, 2 feet 1 inch long and 11 inches broad

250   round gold leafs[14]

2 large golden vases

1   do   do   goblet

3 small   do   vases

2 golden breast-ornaments in form of wreaths or garlands

2 flat pieces of gold representing houses with towers, on each of which is sitting a pigeon

6 golden butterflies for suspension

7 flat pieces of gold representing 2 lions standing on their hind legs opposite each other

11 do   do   of gold representing 2 stags standing opposite each other

2 do   do   do do   do   2 swans opposite each other

1 woman of gold holding 3 pigeons

1   do   "   "   do   1 pigeon

2 golden women with long gowns of ⟨   ⟩

4 golden lions

1   do   cross

10 do   earrings with pendants

6   do   do

1 earpendant of precious red stone on which are incised two warriors fighting together

12 plain earpendants without incisions

3 perforated quadrangular pieces of gold, which evidently derive from a necklace; the one shows Hercules killing the Nemean lion, the other represents simply a lion and the third shows 2 warriors together with lances. Though in a very archaic style, these engravings are masterly done.

1 perforated precious redstone with an incision representing a stag which turns his head

1 long necklace of amber balls

10 flat pieces of gold representing scarabees, which are however entirely different from those found in Egypt

7 small golden wheels

9 flat pieces of gold representing poppies

6 large pieces of gold almost in form of earrings, which have probably served to hold together the hairlocks or tresses

16 very curious golden pieces of a necklace, each piece being composed of a 1 inch long tube on either side of which are 3 or even 4 small disks; each of these is composed of 12 gold wires

1 enormous (πόρπη) of gold representing a woman stretching out her arms; on her head is a large crown with 3 flowers.

2 scepter(s) of silver with handles formed by a beautiful ball of rock crystal

1 silver vase

4 large kettles of bronze

and finally 4 bronze boxes, each 9 inches long and 6 1/2 inches broad and open on one of the small sides; all these boxes had been filled with wood which had become charred on[15] the funeral pile, and had been fastened in the boxes with long bronze nails, which still now exist. It is impossible to explain the existence in the tomb of these curious boxes filled with wood. Was it, perhaps, sandal-wood to perfume the tomb while the funeral pile was burning? But, if so, why put it into the boxes and fasten it with nails? There was found in this tomb some hand-made pottery, with beautiful painted ornaments. I will here only mention a can with one handle, which shows, on a light yellow dead ground, six leaves and eight circles painted with dark-red colour. It would be altogether a vain attempt on my part to try to convey to the reader only a faint idea of the splendid ornamentation of all the above jewels of gold. Nowhere can I discover a space as large as a quarter of an inch which is not ornamented. There are a thousand different sorts of spiral or circular ornamentation.

TIMES X

Encouraged by my success, I resolved upon excavating the whole remaining space within the great parallel circle of slabs, and my attention was particularly directed to the spot immediately west of the last excavated sepulchre, although the site was marked by no tombstone. But, in variance with the colour of the soil elsewhere, I found here only black earth, which—already in a depth of 15 ft.—was intermixed with nothing else than handmade pottery, which showed that the site had not been disturbed since a high antiquity, and increased my hopes of making there an interesting discovery. At a depth of 20 ft. below the former surface of the mount I struck an almost circular cyclopean masonry, with a large round opening in form of a well; it was 4 ft. high, and measured 7 ft. from north to south and 5 1/2 from east to west. I at once recognized in this curious monument a primitive altar for funeral rites, and was strengthened in this belief by two 2 ft. 9 in. long and 1 ft. 6 in. broad slabs, in the form of tombstones, and a short column, which lay in a horizontal position below the altar, and which, in my opinion, must have once been erected on the spot to mark the site of a sepulchre. Fragments of beautiful hand-made pottery and knives of obsidian continued to be the only objects of human industry I met with. At last, in a depth of 26 1/2 ft., and at a distance of only 4 ft. 7 in. from the last described tomb, I found a 24 ft. long, 18 1/2 ft. broad sepulchre, which had been cut on its west side 6 ft., on the north side 10 ft., on the south side 8 ft., and on the east side 6 1/2 ft. deep into the rock, and its bottom is 33 ft. below the former surface of the mount. It deserves particular notice that the above funeral altar marked precisely the centre of this tomb, and thus there can be no doubt that it had been erected in honour of those whose mortal remains reposed in it.

Along all the four sides of this tomb's bottom was, on a foundation of large common stones, a 7 ft. 8 in. high slanting wall of large pieces of schist, of irregular form, which had been joined with clay; this wall protruded 4 ft., and thus diminished considerably the size of the sepulchre. As in the two other tombs, the bottom was covered with a layer of pebblestones on which, in about equal distances from each other, lay the bodies of five men; three of them were lying with the head to the east and the feet to the west; the two others were lying with the head to the north and the feet to the south. The bodies had evidently been burnt on the very spot on which each rested; this was shown as well by the masses of the ashes on and around each corpse as by the marks of the fire on the pebblestones and on the wall of schist. The five bodies were literally overloaded with jewels, all of which—as in the other tombs—show unequivocal marks of the funeral piles. Here as well as in the other sepulchres I have noticed that, for a reason unknown to me, the burnt bodies with their golden ornaments had been covered with a 3 in. to 4 in. thick layer of clay, and on this rested the second layer of pebblestones. Until about 1 ft. above this upper layer of pebblestones the work of the excavation is not difficult to me, for I have merely to direct my workmen to dig here or there. But from that point—Mr. Schliemann[16] and I—we have to do the work ourselves; the task is exceedingly difficult and painful, particularly in the present rainy weather, for we cannot dig otherwise than on our knees and cutting with our knives the earth and stones away, so as not to injure or let escape any of the gold ornaments. Beginning the excavation of the lower strata of this tomb from the south side, I at once struck five large bronze vessels (λέβητες), in one of which were exactly 100 very large and smaller buttons of bone covered with blades[17] of gold, on which are engraved beautiful spiral ornaments or the symbolic sign of the holy fire; close to the same vessel I found a cowhead of bronze plated with silver and a gilded mouth, having on its front a golden sun and on its head two long golden horns. There can be no doubt that this head was intended to represent the goddess Hera, the patron deity of Mycenae. In further excavating from E. to W. I struck a heap of more than 20 bronze swords and many lances; most of the former had had wooden sheaths and handles inlaid with wood, of which [of which] plenty of remnants could be seen. Nearly all the handles showed gold ⟨casings and⟩[18] at the end of each of them was a large button of wood or alabaster.[19] On and around the swords and the wood could be seen a great deal of fine gold dust, which can leave no doubt that the handles and sheaths had been gilded. Some of the lances⟨'⟩ shafts seemed to be well conserved, but they crumbled away when we touched them. I found there, at intervals of three feet, the bodies of three men, all of whom had the head turned to the E; the bones, particularly those of the legs, were of unusually large size. One of them had the head covered with a large heavy mask. We found in this tomb two more bodies with the head turned to the N. and the heads of both of them were covered with similar golden masks. All the three masks are made with a marvellous art and one thinks to see there all the hair of the eyebrows & whimpers.[20] Each mask shows so widely different a physiog-

nomy from the other, and so altogether different from the ideal types of the statues of gods and heroes, but there cannot be the slightest doubt that every one of them faithfully represents the likeness of the deceased hero whose face it covered.[21] Were it not so, all the masks would show the very same ideal type. One of the masks shows a small mouth, a long nose, large eyes & a large head; another a very large mouth, nose, and head; the third a small head, mouth, and nose. The mask with the large mouth, nose & head is conserved with the greater part of the skull of the deceased.
Mycenae 25 November.

TIMES XI

I continue here the description of the jewels, etc., found with the 5 bodies in the 4th tomb. Among the most interesting objects of this sepulcre, I reckon the magnificently ornamented golden buttons, twelve are in form of a cross, one of them is 2 1/5 inches large and 3 long; three others are somewhat smaller, and the remaining 8 are still of a less size. Of splendidly ornamented round gold buttons were found in all 216, 2 of which have 2 inch in diameter, 7 others are of the size of 5 fr. pieces and 207 are still smaller. All those of these buttons the lower end of which consists of a bone button in form of our shirtbuttons, must have served on the clothes of the deceased, but all those which show below only a flat piece of bone or wood, have evidently served to decorate the sheaths of swords, lances, etc, to which they had been fastened. There were in all found in this tomb 25 two-edged bronze swords, 16 of which are in a perfect state of conservation; 4 of them had handles plated with gold and richly ornamented. There were also found with the swords 5 large handle-buttons, 4 of which of alabaster and 1 of wood; all are ornamented with golden nails. Further, 2 golden *telamons* or sword-girdles, which were worn on the shoulder across the breast; they are 4 ft. long & 1 3/5 in. broad. There were further found 2 large golden belts ornamented with circles and flowers; one of them consists of 2 pieces; there was also found part of a similar belt and a golden child's girdle belt only 1 ft. 4 inch long, and 2 1/5 inch broad. Further a splendidly ornamented large golden handle, probably of a sceptre; it terminates in a dragon's head whose scales seem to have been imitated by square pieces of crystal which are inlaid like mosaic; this is an object of marvellous beauty, or, as father[22] would call it: a wonder to look upon (θαῦμα ἰδέσθαι). There were also found 7 large and 1 small diadems, one of the former is ornamented with golden leafs; all show splendid ornaments of circles and spiral lines. Further 4 golden ornaments of the knimides {greaves} almost in form of a bracelet; 1 comb of bone in a large handle or casing of gold in the usual form as ladies wear it; 1 enormous most magnificently ornamented massive bracelet weighing 360 grammes; on the centre of the ornamentation of this bracelet was soldered a separate piece of gold representing the sun with his rays; the size of this bracelet is so enormous that the person who has worn it must have had

250

gigantic arms; I would therefore suggest that it may have been worn on the legs. Quite in opposition to the size of the bracelet are 2 massive golden sealrings, the opening of which is so small that they would only suit for a child of 10 years. I suppose therefore that they have been only used as seals. One of the seals represents two warriors on a twowheel chariot with 2 horses who seem to run at full gallop; one of the warriors holds a bow in his hand and has just shot an arrow on a stag who is wounded and in anguish turns his head round. The other sealring represents a warrior who has just vanquished his 3 enemies; he is just in the act of giving with his uplifted sword a last blow to one of them who is already wounded and lies before him on one knee; he tries to parry the blow with his uplifted hands and with a lance which he holds in his right and seems to throw at his opponent. Another appears to have been mortally wounded, for he lies on the ground leaning on both his hands. The third, who alone of all the four warriors has a helmet with a crest, is flying, under the cover of an enormous shield which reaches from his neck to his heels, but turns his head towards his opponent and is in the act of throwing a lance at him. The anatomy of all the men is so well observed⟨,⟩ their posture is so faithful to nature and every thing is executed with so much art that when I brought to light these rings I full of admiration involuntarily exclaimed: "The author of the Iliad & the Odyssey can only have been born and educated in a civilization which could produce such wonders; only a poet who had such objects of art like these continually before his eyes could compose those divine poems.⟨"⟩

At the head of one of the bodies was found a large and heavy golden helmet;[23] but it had been much rumpled and had become nearly flat by the ponderous weight which lay upon it and in its present state it is difficult to describe it; on its forepart the openings for the eyes and mouth, as also a protuberance ornamented with stars are distinctly visible as also, on the top of the helmet, the tube (λόφος) for the crest; the back part is beautifully ornamented with an imitation of hairs.

The face of the same body was covered with one of the masks mentioned in my last letter and its breast and sides by a 1 ft. 8 inch long, and 1 ft. broad, thick plate of gold, which was no doubt intended to represent the coat of mail.

There were further found 100 leafs of gold, either of circular or of crosslike form, with impressed ornaments, consisting either of spiral lines or of circles; further three very heavy golden breastpins, of which the one is 5 1/4, the other 5, and the third is 4 1/2 inch long. The latter is crowned with a ram, the two others with an ornament in shape of helmets and the heads of all are perforated, probably to put in a flower. There were further found two masterly ornamented objects of massive gold in the form of crosses. Also a large golden vase weighing 1 7/8 kilogr; it has two handles, a large foot and is ornamented with 3 upper and 2 lower parallel lines, between which is a row of 14 stars; further a large golden vase with 1 handle and ornamented with 7 beautiful flowers. Another golden vase with 2 handles, further a splendid little golden oenochoe or vinevessel {sic} with spiral ornaments; further, 6 golden drinking

cups, one of which an amphikypellon with 2 handles, on each of which is a pigeon; each of the two handles are joined to the foot by two separate golden blades. This goblet reminds us of Nestor's goblet described by Homer (Ilias XI, 632–635). One of the other goblets is ornamented with parallel flutings. There were further found two small golden vessels; also 8 silver vases, 3 of which are well conserved; one of the other 5 has the bottom and the mouth of bronze; below its bottom were found 100 of the aforesaid golden buttons. I further found in this tomb 13 large bronze vessels (λεβητες). This kind of vessel was in high esteem in the heroic age and we see them continually mentioned by Homer as prizes in the games & Gastgeschenke. I suppose that to each hero were given in the grave the goblets and other objects which were dear to him in his lifetime, having been won by him in the games, or having been given to him by his host as a pledge of hospitality and friendship. There was also found a large quantity of perforated small amber balls of necklaces and a bronze fork with 3 teeth, which has probably served on the funeral pyres. Further 35 arrowheads of obsidian. Nothing could give a better idea of the great antiquity of these tombs than the presence of these stone arrowheads, for in the Ilias only arrowheads of bronze are known (see e.g. ⟨   ⟩).[24] Probably there have also been deposited bows and Köcher with arrows in the tomb but they had been of wood, and rotten {sic} away. To my greatest regret among the thousands of gold ornaments there is not even a single sign resembling writing, and it appears therefore certain that the sepulcres belong to an epoch previous to the introduction of the Phoenician alphabet, because had the latter been known, the Mycenaean goldsmiths, whose continual efforts appear to be directed to the invention of new ornaments, would have been very ambitious to show the novelty of the alphabet. A second proof of the immense antiquity of these tombs is the entire absence of any vestige of either iron or glass, or of any pottery made on the potter's wheel. But the hand made pottery had reached a high degree of perfection, such as has never been attained here in later times by the pottery made on the wheel.
Mycenae 28 Novbr 1876

Garrison[25]

Already, whilst engaged in the excavation of the large 4th tomb the results of which I have described in my two last letters, I excavated the fifth and last sepulcre, which is immediately to the N.W. of it and which had been marked by the large slab with 2 serpents in bas-relief and by an unsculptured tombstone, both of which were 11 2/3 ft. below the surface of the [a]mount so as it was when I began the excavations. In a depth of 10 feet below the two tombstones or of 21 2/3 below the former surface I found 2 evidently much older unsculptured tombstones and only 3 ft 4 inch below these I found an 11 1/2 ft long 9 ft 8 inch broad tomb, which had been cut out in the rock to a depth of only 2 ft, so that its bottom is 27 ft below the former surface. There was no inner wall,[26] the bottom of which was strewn with pebble stones. On this latter I found the mortal remains of only one person, who, like all the other bodies, had been burned on the precise spot w⟨h⟩ere it lay. This was proved as well by calcined pebbles below and around the corpse as by the undisturbed masses of ashes with which it was covered and finally by the marks of the funeral fires on the rock. Around the skull of the body, which was unfortunately too fragile to be safed {sic}, was a golden diadem with impressed ornaments, representing in the midst two suns; the remaining space being filled up with spiral ornaments. At the right side of the body I found a lancehead with a ring on either side, further 2 small bronze swords and 2 long knifes of the same metal; on its left was found a golden drinking cup with one handle, the ornamentation of which represents two horizontal rows of fishspines and one row of arrows. With the swords were found several small rags of beautifully woven linen, which probably derive from the sheaths of these weapons. In the same tomb was found a 6 1/2 inches high, handmade, light green vase, ornamented with two series each of three protruding humps; further a light red vase ornamented with black spiral lines, further with two female breasts surrounded by circles of black strokes.

The mud in the first sepulchre, whose site had been marked by 3 sculptured tombstones, with bas-reliefs (see my letter of the 11th Novbr) having dried up in the present fine weather, I continued the excavation there and struck at last the bottom of the sepulcre, which is on the N. side 17 1/2 ft., on the S. side 17 ft. deep cut out in the rock;[27] as afore stated, it is at the top 21 ft 6 inch long and 10 ft 6 inch broad. But the W. and E. walls being a little overhanging the breadth of the tomb at the bottom is 12 ft. The 4 inner sides were lined with a 3 ft high and 2 ft. broad Cyclopean wall, and this latter had been superseded by a slanting wall of schist plates which reached to a height of 6 1/2 ft. and protruded on all sides by 3 ft. on the bottom of the tomb. In variance with the other sepulcres, the bottom of this tomb was not covered with the usual layer of pebble stones; the three bodies which the sepulchre contained lay at a distance of 3 feet from each other and had been burned in the very same place where I found them. This was evident as well by the marks of the fire on the rock below and around the corpses and to the right and left on the walls as by the manner in which the remains of the two men to the N. and S. clung to the rock and finally by the undisturbed state of the ashes with them. Only with the body which lay in the midst the case was different; the ashes had evidently been disturbed; the clay with which the two other men & their ornaments were covered and the layer of pebble stones which covered the clay, had on this body been removed and as besides it was found almost without any gold ornaments it is evident that it had been rifled; this my opinion is also confirmed by the 12 golden buttons, the small golden blades, and the numerous small objects of bone, which had been found, together with small quantities of black ashes, at different depths below the 3 sculptured tombstones which adorned this sepulchre. It is further confirmed by the fragments of the usual Mycenaean pottery of later times, which in this tomb were mixed up with the very ancient handmade vases. Most likely somebody has sunk here a shaft to examine the tomb, has struck on the body in question, has [w]recklessly plundered it, and, from fear of being discovered, has carried off his booty in such a hurry that he only thought of saving the large massive gold ornaments such as the mask, the large breastcover, the diadems, and the bronze swords and dropped in mounting to the surface many of the smaller objects such as the 12 golden buttons etc. which I found at intervals in digging down. There can be no doubt that this larceny occurred already *before* the capture of Mycenae by the Argians in 468, for if it had taken place when the posterior Greek city was built on the top of the prehistoric ruins, I would also have found fragments of Greek pottery in the tomb, but of these I saw no vestige.

The 3 bodies of this tomb lay with the head to the E. and the feet to the W.; all three were of gigantic proportions and appeared to have been squeezed with force into the small space of only 6 ft 6 inch which was left for them between the afore described walls; the bones of the legs, which are nearly uninjured, are really of enormous size; although the head of the first man was covered with a large massive golden mask[28] and immense golden breastplate, his skull crumbled away on being exposed to the air and but a few bones could be saved besides those of the legs and the same was the case with the 2d body which had been plundered in antiquity. But of the 3d body, which lay at the N. extremity, the round face with all its flesh had been wonderfully preserved under its ponderous golden mask;[29] there was no vestige of hair, but both eyes were perfectly visible, also the mouth which by the enormous weight that had been pressing upon it, was wide open and showed 32 beautiful teeth; by these all the physicians who came to see the body were led to believe that the man must have been at the age of 35. The nose had entirely gone. The body having been too long for the space between the 2 inner walls of the tomb, the head had been pressed in such a way on the breast that the upper part of the shoulders were {sic} nearly equal with the vertex of the head. In spite of the large breastplate so little had been conserved of the flesh of the breast that the innerside of the spine was visible in many places. In its squeezed and mutilated state the body measured only 2 ft. 4 1/2 inch from the top of the head to the beginning of the loins; the breadth of the shoulders did not exceed 1 ft. 1 1/4 inch and the breadth of the stomach 1 ft 3 inch and the pressure of the rubbish and stones [and rubbish] had been such that the body had been reduced to a thickness of 1–1 1/2 inch but the 1 ft 8 inch long thighbones could leave no doubt regarding the real proportions of the body. The colour of the corps {sic} resembled very much that of an Egyptian mummy. The front of the man was ornamented with a plain round leaf of gold and a still larger one was lying on the right eye; I further observed a large & a small gold leaf on the breast below the large gold cover. The news, that the tolerably well preserved body of a man of the mythic heroic age had been found, spread like a rolling fire through

the Argolid, and people came by thousands from Argos and Nauplium to see the wonder, but nobody being able to give advise {sic} how to conserve the body, I sent for a painter to get at least an oil painting made, for I feared every moment that the body would fall to pieces. But to my great joy it held out for 2 days when a droguist {sic} from Argos, Spiridon Nicolaou by name, consolidated it by moistening it with spirit in which he had dissolved sandarac. Thus I have now strong hopes that it can be saved the more so as it can be lifted with an iron plate there being no pebble stone below it.
Mycenae 1 Decbr 1876.

TIMES XIII

The now nearly mummified body was decorated with a 4 ft. long 1 3/4 inch broad telamon (shoulder belt), which by some cause or another was not any more in its place, for it now lay across the loins of the body and extended in a straight line far to the right of it; in its midst is suspended and fast attached a small bronze sword, on which is soldered a beautifully polished perforated object of crystal in form of a jar (πίθος) with two silver handles; it is pierced in its whole length by a headless silver pin; together with it was found a small object of crystal, in form of a funnel, with 4 concave sides. To the right and left of the body lay long bronze swords, to the left was besides a long bronze knife, all of them had probably been suspended to a belt of embroidered silk, which had disappeared; the sheaths of the swords had been of wood, many *debris* of which remained, all the sheaths had been gilded, and had in their entire length been adorned with round blades of gold, which showed many different sorts of magnificently engraved spiral lines. The handles of the swords were plated with gold and every one of them was decorated with splendid engravings. Instead of the usual large wood or alabaster buttons of the handles, the sword handles of this body seem to have had at their extremity richly ornamented golden plates, 10 of which were found close to the body, each of them is 3 4/5 inches long and 1 3/5 broad, and every one of them represents a large cowhead with long horns and immense eyes; further a lion pursuing a stag with such velocity that his four legs are in the same horizontal line with the body; the stag, though still running at full speed, feels that he is lost *full of anguish turns his head at his merciless pursuer and looks at him.* To the reverse side of these wonderful plates still sticks a good deal of a blackish matter, perhaps a sort of lime, which may have served, I do not know how, to fasten them to the handles. Two plates must necessarily have been required for each handle. To the sword on the right of the body was attached a 9 3/5 in. long golden tassel.

The massive golden mask which covered the head of this body and which I mentioned in my last letter, is 12 2/3 inch long and 12 1/3 inch broad; it shows a large round face with large eyes and a large mouth, much resembling the features of the body when first uncovered, and I feel now still more than ever heretofore convinced that all the masks faithfully represent the features which

255

they cover. In fact, one has only to look on these splendidly made masks to convince oneself that they are real portraits and not ideal types. The breast-cover of this body, which I likewise mentioned in my last letter, is 14 2/5 inches long and 8 4/5 inch broad. At a distance of hardly more than 1 foot to the right of the body I found 11 bronze swords, of which 9 had more or less suffered from moisture; but the other two were well preserved; one of them had the enormous length of 3 ft. 1 3/5 inch; the other 2 ft. 5 3/5 inch. Together with the swords I found 4 swordhandles with richly ornamented golden plates, several golden tubes with remnants of wood, 124 large, beautifully engraved, round golden buttons, two of which were of enormous size, also 4 which had only the size of a frank; further 6 large most splendidly ornamented gold buttons in form of crosses, 3 of which are 3 inches long and 2 1/4 in. broad. These buttons consist either of flat pieces of bone covered with a golden blade, and in this case they have invariably been pasted as embellishments on sword sheaths or other objects, or they consist of real bone buttons resembling our present shirt buttons, and covered with gold blades which must have been used on clothes. The indescribably magnificent engraved ornaments of both these kinds of buttons can leave no doubt as to the importance attached to them. I may add that not only all the buttons in cross form, but also all the large round gold buttons have on their lower side a flat piece of bone.

There was further found to the right of the body a very large golden drinking cup with one handle having not less than 6 inches in diameter and 5 inch in height; it has two parallel horizontal rows of ornamentation, of which the lower one represents fish-spines, the upper one windows; further a very large one handled golden goblet having 5 3/5 inch in diameter; it is decorated with 2 parallel horizontal lines of beautiful spiral lines, in which occur a large number of ⟨the⟩ curious cross (svastica) which is so frequent on the Trojan whorls (see my Troy and its Remains, P. xxiv, 348); there was found a third one handled golden goblet ornamented with three lions running with great velocity. There were also found 2 silvern drinking cups and fragments of various silvern vases, some of which [have] show spiral ornaments; further a large drinking cup of alabaster 10 1/4 inch high and 4 4/5 inch in diameter.

With the body which lay in the midst of the tomb were only found some round golden leafs with impressed ornaments and the remnants of a wooden comb. As mentioned in my last letter, the head of the body at the S. end of the tomb was likewise covered with a golden mask and its breast with a massive golden cover, both are exactly of the same size as those which covered the body at the N. extremity of the sepulcre. I found besides with the body at the S. end 15 two edged bronze swords; 10 of which lay at his feet. 8 of them are of very large size; about one half of all the swords are in a good state of preservation; also the upper part of a bronze sword with a handle ornamented with golden nails; 1 small sword and 2 long bronze knifes, one of which with a very long handle, which consists of the same piece as the knife. I found with the body further 27 engraved large round golden buttons one of which measuring 2 1/4 inch, the others 1 3/4 to 2 inch in diameter and 68 round golden buttons of smaller size; in none of the former has remained the bonebutton on which the golden blade was fastened; most of the buttons have doubtless served as ornaments of the wooden swordsheaths of which many remnants could be seen. Together with the swords at the feet of the body I picked up 2 golden sword handles, one of which [is] consists of 2 pieces; in the other is visible a piece of wood; both are richly ornamented; further 7 large swordhandle buttons of alabaster and one of wood; all are ornamented with golden nails; a piece of gold in the shape of a watchkey, and a *bronze lancehead 1 ft 8 3/4 inch long;* its tube (αὐλός), in which the lance is fastened is 8 4/5 inch long. There was further found with the body; 37 round gold leafs of various size with impressed ornaments; 21 fragments of gold leafs, a golden ornament of the greaves (knemides); 5 golden plates representing in bas relief 2 eagles; a golden plate without ornament; a richly ornamented smaller one on which seem to be represented 2 hair-tresses; 1 gold ornament for the neck, much resembling our present military decoration; as this object has all around small holes, it may also have been sown {sic} upon and used as ornament of some rich cloth. I found there further 2 much damaged silvern vases, a pair of silvern tongs, and a large vase of alabaster in form of a jar (πίθος), the border of the orifice is of bronze; in this vase were found 32 richly ornamented small and 3 large golden buttons as well as 2 large golden buttons in the shape of crosses each with 2 very small handles, further a large golden button of conical form and a wedgeshaped golden tube. I further found there a bronze battleaxe perfectly resembling the Trojan battleaxes (see "Troy and its Remains," p. 330), but more svelt & elegant. In variance with our present axes, the Trojan battleaxes have no hole in which the wooden handle might be fixed and thus they have evidently been fastened in the handle instead of the handle being fastened in them; there were also found 10 large bronze kettles or casseroles (λέβητες), 1 of which has 3 ft. in diameter and 2 handmade terracotta vases, further masses of small perforated balls of amber which were undoubtedly used as necklaces. Perhaps still more interesting than all the jewels found in this tomb was a small quadrangular wooden box (νάρθηξ), of which I picked up two sides, on each of which is sculptured a dog and a lion. Small as these sculptures are, they are nevertheless of capital interest to science, because they prove to us that the art of [of] sculpturing on wood was flourishing already in the mythic heroic age. A whole basket full of wood, deriving from sword sheaths or domestic utensils, was collected in this tomb and I have strong hopes that the remainder of the box may still be found. All the wood is moist and soft like a sponge when taken out, but I hope that with proper care it can be preserved.

NOTES

1. In his letter to Müller of 27 November Schliemann writes: "I beg him {the editor of the *Times*} meanwhile to publish the two enclosed letters, which

will be followed by a short third one, after which I shall exclusively treat of the tombs and the treasures." The three reports referred to are clearly V, VI, and VII; see *JHS* 82 (1962) 93. In his letter of 6 December Schliemann promises "on the 10 inst. I shall be able to send you 2 or 3 more short articles for the *Times*"; see Meyer's edition of the letter at *JHS* 82 (1962) 93. In the postscript to that letter, dated 10 December, he adds: "I send you today 4 articles for the Times." Meyer omits this latter section from his edition.

2. At *Myc.* 362–64 Schliemann notes that two of these three gems were purchased from villagers in Chonika. For further discussion see the Introduction.

3. For "discovered" the *Times* has "examined." It was in fact Drosinos who discovered the passage; see the diary entry of 8 November.

4. After "stones" the *Times* has "it was discovered by my engineer, Mr Drosinos, in making the plan of the Acropolis." At *Mycenae* 145 Schliemann refrains from including the visit to the "ogivelike passage" in Dom Pedro's itinerary, having noticed, no doubt, that it had not been discovered until 8 November, i.e., ten days after Dom Pedro's visit.

5. At *Mycenae* 145 Schliemann claims that Sophia accompanied him. There is no mention of her in any earlier version.

6. Before "lustrous" the *Times* adds "handmade."

7. After "strokes" the *Times* follows immediately with: "Having dug down to a depth of 10 1/2 ft., I was stopt by heavy rain, which turned the soft earth in the tomb to mud, and therefore began to take out the two unsculptured tombstones of the second line." The intervening observations on the rarity of the pottery which Schliemann considered analogous to what he had found in Troy II—tripods and vases with tubular holes for suspension—are omitted. It is noteworthy that in the *Times* version, though not in the draft, Schliemann specifically reports finding fragments of a vase with two tubular holes for suspension in Grave I (Schl. II). See note 11 below and *Boreas* 7 (1984) 312–16.

8. Before "Whilst . . ." Schliemann had originally written and then deleted: "As all this handmade pottery only occurs in the tombs and as I never found a trace of it even in the deepest recesses at the foot of the cyclopean circuit walls of the acropolis I think it probable that it is more ancient than the walls."

9. Schliemann had written and then deleted "and not even a fragment of pottery was found before I reached a . . . "

10. Schliemann originally had "every one," which he then scored out and wrote in "two." Then he deleted "two" and restored "every one."

11. The *Times* has "two horned Juno-idols; and finally, many fragments of beautiful handmade pottery, among which was part of a vase with two tubular holes on either side for suspension with a string. There are also fragments of terra-cotta tripods, which are of rare occurrence here, nearly all the vases having a flat bottom." It is fairly clear that Schliemann has added to the finds of Grave I (Schl. II) fragments of pottery which he had found elsewhere and which he considered analogous to the pottery found in Troy II; see note 7. The

observations in the draft version that tend to underscore the differences between Trojan and Mycenaean pottery have been rephrased in the *Times* to suggest similarities.

12. At this point Schliemann had written and then deleted "on the eastern s."

13. Between this item and the following one Schliemann had written and then deleted, "14 golden diadems each composed of 2 pieces."

14. There are at least three hundred in the diary entry of 23 November and 701 at *Mycenae* 165.

15. At this point a leaf is missing from the diary. The remainder of *Times* IX and the first half of *Times* X are taken from the published versions.

16. Sophia is not mentioned at the corresponding passage at *Mycenae* 214f. It seems likely that Sophia left Mycenae before much of Grave IV was excavated, and it is questionable if she got down on her hands and knees in the mud in the excavation of *any* tomb (cf. her dress on plates V and VII of *Mycenae*); see the Introduction for further discussion.

17. The lacuna in the diary ends with the word "blades." From here to the end the text is again that of the draft in the diary.

18. "Casings and" has been supplied to suit the sense. The words in the draft are illegible.

19. Instead of this sentence the published version reads: "All along and in the heap of swords I found a large quantity of splendidly ornamented round blades of gold, with remnants of flat round pieces of bone, which had once, in uninterrupted series, adorned both sides of the swordsheath; the largest blade was at the broad end of the sheath; the smallest at the opposite extremity, the wooden handles of the swords had likewise been ornamented with richly engraved large round blades; the remaining space had been studded with gold pins, and large gold nails can be seen in the large alabaster or wooden handle buttons of the swords."

20. Someone, presumably Max Müller, corrected this to "whiskers" for the *Times* version. But Schliemann really meant "eyelashes" (German: Wimpern).

21. See the discussion of this passage at diary note 269.

22. The published version has "of which Homer would have said."

23. This is the lion rhyton (*Mycenae* no 326, Karo 273).

24. The reference, which is omitted in the draft, is given in the *Times:* "*Il.* 13.650, 662."

25. The word "Garrison" was added as an afterthought. In the published version Schliemann expanded this word into a paragraph:

For the first time since its capture by the Argives, in 468 B.C., and thus for the first time since 2,344 years, the acropolis of Mycenae has got a garrison, whose watchfires by night-time can be seen throughout the whole plain of Argos. But this time the object of the occupation by soldiery is of a more peaceful character, for it is merely intended to inspire awe among the country people, and to prevent them from mak-

259

ing clandestine excavations in the tombs, or to approach the latter while I am working in them.

26. Schliemann originally began this sentence as follows: "On all four inner sides of the tomb was a 3 1/2 ft high slanting wall of schist plates joined with clay, which protruded by 2 feet in the tomb." After deleting this and substituting "There was no inner wall," he failed to adjust the second half of the sentence to suit. In erroneously attributing lining walls to Grave II (Schl. V) Schliemann had probably been thinking of Grave V (Schl. I).

27. Instead of this sentence and the next one, the published version reads:

But from these points the slope is so abrupt that, although the upper breadth of the sepulchre does not exceed 10 ft. 6 in., yet the greater part of its west side needed only to be cut 11 ft. deep into the rock to make a level bottom. Besides, this west side of the tomb is close to the Cyclopean wall, which bears the parallel double row of large calcareous slabs and rises vertically over the sepulchre. For all these reasons it appeared to me, in first excavating this tomb, that the wall passed through its north-west angle, and I wrote this on the 15th of November to a venerated friend, who published my letter in *The Times*. But by propping with planks and beams the earth and stones which cling to the wall and overhang the north-west corner of the tomb, I have cleared the latter now in its entire length, and visitors will perceive that the wall does not pass through the tomb, and merely touches its brink in the north-west corner. The length of the tomb is 21 ft. 6 in.; its breadth at the bottom is 12 ft., and thus 18 in. more than at the top.

28. It is surprising that Schliemann does not comment on the superior quality of this mask, as do Stamatakis and the *Argolis* reporter (see Greek newspaper reports nos. 9 and 11), but cf. Greek newspaper report no. 10.

29. This is the less attractive mask from Grave V, *Myc.* no 473 and Karo 623.

Bibliography of Recent Work
on Schliemann

Note: With few exceptions only those books and articles that have been published since 1972 have been listed. For earlier works, see bibliographies in Deuel, *Memoirs,* and Meyer's biography and, above all, the excellent Schliemann bibliography by G. Korres.

Arndt, K.J.R. "Schliemann's Excavation of Troy and American Politics, or Why the Smithsonian Institution Lost Schliemann's Great Troy Collection to Berlin." *Yearbook of German-American Studies* 16 (1981) 1–8. (Contains new letters by Schliemann.)

Arnott, W.G. "Schliemann's Epitaph." *Liverpool Classical Monthly* 3 (1978) 93.

Calder, W.M., III. "Schliemann on Schliemann: A Study in the Use of Sources." *GRBS* 13 (1972) 335–53.

———. "Heinrich Schliemann: An Unpublished Latin *Vita.*" *CW* 67 (1973–1974) 271–82.

———. "Nonnulla Schliemanniana." *CW* 69 (1975–1976) 117–18.

———. "Wilamowitz on Schliemann." *Philologus* 124 (1980) 146–51.

———. *Studies in the Modern History of Classical Scholarship.* Antiqua 27. Naples 1984. (Contains all of Calder's articles on Schliemann with addenda and corrigenda.)

Deuel, Leo. *Memoirs of Heinrich Schliemann.* New York 1977. (German edition, *Heinrich Schliemann: Eine Biographie mit Selbstzeugnissen und Dokumenten.* Munich/Vienna 1979.)

Dickinson, O.T.P.K. "Schliemann and the Shaft Graves." *G&R* 23 (1976) 159–68.

Döhl, Hartmut. *Heinrich Schliemann: Mythos und Ärgernis.* Munich 1981. (Reviews: *CR* 33 [1982] 286f. [Easton]; *Gnomon* 55 [1983] 149–52 [Traill]; *German Studies Review* 6 [1983] 602f. [Calder]; *Deutsche Literaturzeitung* 104 [October 1983] 898–901 [Schindler]).

Easton, D.F. "Schliemann's Discovery of 'Priam's Treasure': Two Enigmas." *Antiquity* 55 (1981) 179–83.

———. "The Schliemann Papers." *ABSA* 77 (1982) 93–110.

———. "Schliemann's Mendacity—A False Trail?" *Antiquity* 58 (1984) 197–204.

———. " 'Priam's Treasure.' " *AnatSt* 34 (1984) 141–69.

Ehrhardt, C. "Vultus Fortunae Schliemannianae." *CW* 73 (1980) 301–302.

Finley, M.I. "Schliemann's Troy—One Hundred Years After." *ProcBritAc* 60 (1974) 393–412. Reprinted in his *The World of Odysseus²*. Harmondsworth 1979.

Herrmann, Joachim. *Heinrich Schliemann: Wegbereiter einer neuen Wissenschaft.* E. Berlin 1974.

———. "Heinrich Schliemann and Rudolf Virchow: Their contributions towards developing historical archaeology." *Towards a History of Archaeology.* Edited by Glyn Daniel. London 1981.

———. "Heinrich Schliemann und Troja." *Troja und Thrakien: Katalog zur Ausstellung.* E. Berlin 1981.

Iakovidis, S. "A Hundred Years of Mycenaean Archaeology." *AntJ* 58 (1978) 13–30.

Irmscher, Johannes. "Über Heinrich Schliemanns erstes Trojaerlebnis." *EAZ* 21 (1980) 659–66.

Isserlin, B.S.J. "Schliemann at Motya." *Antiquity* 42 (1968) 144–48.

———. and du Plat Taylor, Joan. *Motya: A Phoenician and Carthaginian City in Sicily.* Leiden 1974. (Contains text of Schliemann's 1875 diary dealing with Motya.)

Korres, Georgios S. *Bibliographia Herrikou Sleman.* Athens 1974.

———. "Epigraphai ex Attikes eis Katochen Herrikou Sleman." *Athena* 75 (1974–1975) 54–67 and 492 (French résumé).

———. "Les Inscriptions d'Iliou Mélathron." *Euphrosyne* n.s. 7 (1975–1976) 153–67.

———. "Epistole Herrikou Sleman pros Erneston Curtion." *Platon* 28 (1976) 32–36.

———. "Hai Epigraphai tou Germanikou Archaiologikou Institoutou ton Athenon." *Platon* 28 (1976) 252–64.

———. "To 'Iliou Melathron' hos ekphrasis tes prosopikotetos kai tou ergou tou Herrikou Sleman." In G. Korres, *Anadromai eis ton Neoklassikismon.* Athens 1977.

———. "He Sylloge Nomismaton tou Herrikou Sleman kai ho Katalogos auton ho syntachtheis hypo tou Achilleos Postolaka." *Deltion* 29 (1977) 245–69.

———. "He Prosphora tou Sleman dia ten Anadeixin tou Historikou Parelthontos tes Hellados kai he Opheile enanti autou dia to ergon tou." *Platon* 31 (1979) 231–47.

———. "Das Mausoleum Heinrich Schliemanns auf dem Zentralfriedhof von Athen." *Boreas* 4 (1981) 133–73.

———. "Neues zum Mausoleum Heinrich Schliemanns in Athen." *Boreas* 7 (1984) 317–25.

Krenkel, W.A. "Schliemannianum: The couplet of the Green Gate." *CW* 71 (1977) 125–36.

Luce, J.V. "Five New Schliemann Letters in Belfast." *Hermathena* no. 132 (1982) 8–14.

Maddoli, G. "Appunti sulla formazione culturale di Eduard Meyer: La *Geschichte von Troas* e gli anni di Schliemann." *Revista Storica Italiana* 43 (1981) 809–20.

Marinatos, S., and Mylonas, G. "Peri tes Prosopikotetos kai tou Ergou tou Herrikou Sleman." *PrakAkAth* 47 (1972) 212–38. (Contains new letter by Schliemann.)

Meyer, Ernst. *Heinrich Schliemann: Kaufmann und Forscher.* Göttingen 1969.

Richter, Wolfgang. "*Ithaque, le Péloponnèse et Troie* und das Promotionsverfahren Heinrich Schliemanns." *EAZ* 21 (1980) 667–78.

———. "Ein unveröffentlichter Brief Heinrich Schliemanns aus dem Jahre 1869," *Wissenschaftliche Zeitschrift der Universität Rostock Gesellschafts u. sprachwissenschaftliche Reihe* 29 (1980) 55–64.

———. "Die 'altgriechisch geschriebene Dissertation' Heinrich Schliemanns und die Darstellung seiner Promotion im biographischen Schrifttum." *Antikerezeption, Antikeverhältnis, Antikebegegnung in Vergangenheit und Gegenwart = Festschrift für J. Irmscher zum 60. Geburtstag.* Edited by J. Dummer and M. Kunze. Schriften der Winckelmann-Gesellschaft 6. Stendal 1982.

Schindler, Wolfgang. "Heinrich Schliemann: Leben und Werk im Spiegel der neuen biographischen Forschungen." *Philologus* 120 (1976) 271–89.

———. "Schliemanns Selbstporträt: Die Inszenierung eines Selfmade-man." *EAZ* 21 (1980) 655–58.

Traill, D.A. "Schliemann's Mendacity: Fire and Fever in California." *CJ* 74 (1979) 348–55.

———. "Schliemann's American Citizenship and Divorce." *CJ* 77 (1982) 336–42.

————. "Schliemann's 'Discovery' of 'Priam's Treasure.' " *Antiquity* 57 (1983) 181–86.

————. "Further Evidence of Fraudulent Reporting in Schliemann's Archaeological Works." *Boreas* 7 (1984) 295–316.

————. "Schliemann's Discovery of Priam's Treasure: A Re-examination of the Evidence." *JHS* 104 (1984) 96–115.

————. "Schliemann's 'Dream of Troy': The Making of a Legend." *CJ* 81 (1985) 13–24.

————. "Schliemann's Mendacity: A Question of Methodology," *AnatSt* (forthcoming).

Wood, Michael. *In Search of the Trojan War.* London 1985.

Zimmermann, K. "Heinrich Schliemann—ein Leben zwischen Traum und Wirklichkeit." *Klio* 64 (1982) 513–32.

Indexes

Note: This index is divided into two sections. The first section covers Part One, pages 17–140, and the second covers the Schliemann diary and Appendixes.

PART ONE

264

PART TWO AND APPENDIXES

William M. Calder III is Professor of Classics at the University of Colorado, Boulder. He received his M.A. from Harvard University and his Ph.D. degree from the University of Chicago. In 1964–65 he was a Guggenheim fellow and a Fulbright resident scholar in Germany. Professor Calder has previously taught at the University of Rostock, University of Copenhagen, Boston University, Columbia University, and at the American School of Classical Studies, Athens, of which he also serves as a member of the managing committee. In addition to several hundred articles, Professor Calder has published the book-length works *Ulrich von Wilamowitz-Moellendorff: Selected Correspondence 1869–1931* (1983) and *Studies in the Modern History of Classical Scholarship* (1984). He also edited *Wilamowitz nach 50 Jahren* (1985).

David A. Traill is Professor of Classics at the University of California, Davis. He was educated at the University of St. Andrews, Scotland (M.A., 1964) and the University of California, Berkeley (Ph.D., 1971). He has also taught at McGill University, Montreal. Professor Traill has published several articles and the book *Walahfrid Strabo's Visio Wettini: Text, Translation, and Commentary.*

Contributors Wolfgang Schindler and Hartmut Döhl are scholars and archaeologists of international repute. Professor Schindler is Ordinarius for Classical Archaeology and Art History at the Humboldt University, Berlin, German Democratic Republic. An authority on Greek vase painting, Roman portraiture, and the archaeology of Eastern Europe, he has written many articles on these subjects and on Schliemann. His book *The Roman Emperors* will appear in 1986. Professor Döhl, former professor of Archaeology at the University of Göttingen, Federal Republic of Germany, is a professional archaeologist and was an excavator on the German team at Tiryns. He is the author of studies on Mycenaean culture, Hellenistic art, and Pompeii. He also recently published a defense of Schliemann entitled *Heinrich Schliemann: Mythos und Ärgernis* (1982).

The manuscript was edited by Anne M. G. Adamus. The book was designed by Jim Billingsley. The typeface for the text and display is Times Roman. The book is printed on Warren's Olde Style Wove and is bound in book cloth from Holliston Mills. Manufactured in the United States of America.